A PLURALISTIC APPROACH TO LEADERSHIP

This thought-provoking book adopts a pluralistic framework to examine leadership and raises important questions about how leadership studies scholars see and do their work.

This book begins with an interdisciplinary discussion of what a pluralistic mindset is – a distinct framework for acknowledging and managing a diversity of opinions while retaining an abiding faith in the merits of rigorous investigation. Nathan W. Harter argues that pluralism is an important consideration for leadership scholars, and threads this throughout a series of chapters that explore such topics as the proper duration of leadership episodes, the benefits of dedifferentiation in leadership, the importance of grievance as a motive, the prevalence of noise in decision-making, and the evolving utility of OODA loops. It concludes with a phenomenological experience in the spirit of Michel Serres that considers the role of leadership amid a welter of multiplicities. Throughout, readers are introduced to a number of scholars whose work is not often cited in leadership literature, including Julia Kristeva, Richard McKeon, Pierre Hadot, Eric Voegelin, and John Boyd.

Bringing together important lessons and themes from literature, philosophy, and social science, this book offers a novel approach to leadership studies for advanced students and scholars.

Nathan W. Harter is completing 14 years as Professor of Leadership Studies at Christopher Newport University in Virginia, USA, after devoting 22 years to Purdue University in Indiana, USA. This is his eighth book about leadership.

Leadership: Research and Practice Series

In Memoriam
Georgia Sorenson (1947–2020), Founding Editor

Series Editor

Ronald E. Riggio, Henry R. Kravis Professor of Leadership and Organizational Psychology and former Director of the Kravis Leadership Institute at Claremont McKenna College.

Leadership on a Blockchain
What Asia Can Teach Us About Networked Leadership
Frederique Covington Corbett

Navigating Leadership
Evidence-Based Strategies for Leadership Development
Susanne Braun, Tiffany Keller Hansbrough, Gregory A. Ruark, Rosalie J. Hall, Robert G. Lord, and Olga Epitropaki

Snapshots of Great Leadership, Third Edition
Jon P. Howell, Isaac Wanasika and Maria J. Mendez

Heroic Leadership, Second Edition
An Influence Taxonomy of 100 Exceptional Individuals
Scott T. Allison and George R. Goethals

A Pluralistic Approach to Leadership
Interdisciplinary Perspectives
Nathan W. Harter

For more information about this series, please visit: www.routledge.com/ Leadership-Research-and-Practice/book-series/leadership

A PLURALISTIC APPROACH TO LEADERSHIP

Interdisciplinary Perspectives

Nathan W. Harter

Routledge
Taylor & Francis Group

NEW YORK AND LONDON

Cover Image: Philipp Tur via Getty Images

First published 2025
by Routledge
605 Third Avenue, New York, NY 10158

and by Routledge
4 Park Square, Milton Park, Abingdon, Oxon, OX14 4RN

Routledge is an imprint of the Taylor & Francis Group, an informa business

© 2025 Nathan W. Harter

ISBN: 978-1-032-88957-3 (hbk)
ISBN: 978-1-032-88947-4 (pbk)
ISBN: 978-1-003-54052-6 (ebk)

DOI: 10.4324/9781003540526

Typeset in Sabon
by codeMantra

To everyone who doubted me
(you know who you are)

CONTENTS

ACKNOWLEDGMENTS

At critical phases, I was able to draw from the opinions of a number of colleagues, only some of whom I can name here: Ted Baartmans, Willy Donaldson, Elizabeth Fleury, Abby Haney, John Hyland, Michelle Kund-mueller, Jenna McElhannon, Ben Redekop, Oliver Thomas, Thomas Williams, as well as Scott Allen, the late Bob Brown, Bradley Buszard, Charlotte Cartwright, Joanna Ciulla, Edward Elgar, Mike Menefee, Linda Naimi, Lynn Shollen, and JoDell Steuver. Rachel Wagner, a gifted young scholar, honors me with a foreword. The many professionals at Routledge have shepherded this project through to completion, with special thanks to Zoe Thomson-Kemp, Maddie Gray, Hannah Rich, and Saranya Megavan-nan and her team at Codemantra. As has been my practice since coming to Christopher Newport University in Newport News, Virginia, I have shared many of the topics found in these pages with my Private Study Group, a gathering of selected undergraduates whose practice of dialogue is the professional highlight of my week. To be sure, the faults in this book are mine alone.

To God be all the glory. And to Karin, who always believed in me, my gladness.

FOREWORD

Rachel Wagner

The following text is neither simply nor primarily a book, but rather an invitation. Reading it demands something of you – both a form of participation and a willingness to follow the author into what might appear unfruitful fields. Rest assured, however, that soil long left uncultivated contains the conditions necessary for further life.

In the fall of 2016, during my second year of undergraduate study at Christopher Newport University, a familiar face approached me after a presentation hosted by the President's Leadership Program. While we had not yet spoken, I recognized this man from other campus events – for if there was a conversation about leadership studies, he was there. After introducing himself as Professor Nathan Harter, he asked me, "So, what books have you been drawn to lately?"

This question marked the start of both a long-lasting intellectual mentorship and the red thread that has tied together 8 years of conversations. After reading the pages that follow, you will grasp the significance of Harter asking about *books*, in the plural, and also recognize that he was referring to those texts that echo within the reader's mind. I strongly suspect that this is Harter's favorite question – for one's answer may reveal a great deal about their inner life and willingness to participate in the kind of dialogue that he has captured in the present text.

His eighth book on leadership studies, this is perhaps Harter's most revealing work as he blurs the lines between academic prose and personal confession (if these three parts are separate at all). And while Harter has addressed the importance of dialogue for leadership studies before, here dialogue represents not the text's subject but rather its mode. Acting as a conductor, Harter steps forward to lead an orchestra of seemingly dissonant methodologies or approaches toward the study of leadership. The authors that serve as his primary interlocutors will likely surprise readers, sending them along forgotten and untrodden paths. Perhaps even more importantly, in this work, Harter invites his readers into a dialogue both with the text and within themselves, while capturing in words something he has long achieved in deed through his "Private Study Group."

Describing PSG – as it is affectionately called by its participants – proves a daunting task. Part of the trouble lies in defining the 'study' that brought the group together. Our group's members hailed from almost every academic department in the university – from computer science, neuroscience, and physics to American studies, philosophy, political science, English, linguistics, and business. Most of us met Professor Harter in the context of a leadership studies course, but we otherwise lacked shared intellectual fodder at first glance. We also diverged sharply in temperament, political affiliation, religion, and upbringing. Each week, we gathered at the Harter residence, carrying our own unique personal history and curiosities into his cozy, book-filled living room. As it lacked any explicit subject matter, agenda, or structure beyond Harter's diligent time-keeping and a mandatory dessert break, PSG could hardly be considered a "study" group in the typical sense.

You never knew what might come up during our meetings. Within two hours, we might oscillate between the notion of chaos theory and artificial intelligence, or ponder a particular moment during an ancient war. We might mull over an event we all struggled to understand or be led toward a puzzle haunting one of our members. From the outside looking in, it might appear that Harter aimed to cultivate conversational chaos, for just as we seemingly reached consensus or common ground (and could therefore assure ourselves that we were quite clever), Harter would scratch his head, turn directly to the person silently observing our discussion, and prompt them to pull the rug from under our feet once again. Whatever it was, the "study" in PSG always remained unfinished, and the longer one participated, the more they confronted the epistemic limitations revealed by truly interdisciplinary dialogue.

While our formal education often assured us that we did indeed "know" something – a knowledge surely proven by success on exams, papers, and a laundry list of academic accomplishments – PSG seemed to confirm the nagging suspicion that so much of reality slipped through our fingers unnoticed. To remain open-minded, one must bear a great deal of uncertainty. But Harter never provided wormwood without honey (and I'm not referring to the desserts, which were made by his wife and daughter). The tensions, dissonance, and clash between our ideas would echo throughout that living room, and in so doing reveal to us that there were not merely differences in opinion or thought but different ways of thinking. The structure of thought itself hung in the air, and assumptions we each took for granted became glaringly obvious through our attempt to understand the world, and each other, together. Such an experience can be both painful and delightful, uncomfortable and beautiful.

Among Harter's most impressive (and, in my view, most perplexing) achievements as a teacher, scholar, and leader was ascertaining a set of conditions that carefully balanced the opportunity for conversation and reflexivity, while requiring neither indoctrination nor relativism. The pluralistic approach of PSG only necessitated that participants take seriously the possibilities that many things could be true at once, that there could be multiple paths toward truth, and that those around us might have grasped something that we had not yet seen. Although some participants rejected the notion of objective reality, while others sought wisdom in divine revelation, artistic expression, or scientific inquiry, our meetings were nevertheless a space for both child-like wonder and a serious endeavor toward truth. By accepting Harter's invitation to participate in this unique form of study, we learned to play with, rather than merely interrogate ideas, staying curious in ways often neglected by the disciplinary confines of the ivory tower. For many of the young people he mentored, this seemingly aimless group, study without a subject, and dialogue without direction helped cultivate the capacity to genuinely declare Harter's Socratic rephrasing of the Delphic Oracle: "I had no idea!"

I had no idea during my time in PSG that when we often circled back to the topics of dialogue, the task of capturing an idea in words, and the differences between our disciplinary lenses, we were discussing methodology. We occasionally joked that our time together was therapeutic, but I now recognize that these considerations of method, in particular, had a way of revealing tensions within our own souls.

The two-fold work of the group's *study* served, therefore, as the bridge between *private* reflection and *group* dialogue. We first aimed to learn from and with one another, and then turned to the dialogue within our own minds, often uncovering fallow fields within ourselves. What had been beneath our feet now held the possibility for further growth.

After wading through the text at hand, it strikes me that Harter was both studying what happened within PSG and honing the particular type of leadership that he implicitly urges his audience to take up. As scholars of leadership, by following Harter's example, we too may become the conductors of an intellectual orchestra, bringing together seemingly dissonant views of the same mysterious world. What better challenge could we rise to, and what better gap could we fill? In this text, Harter emerges as a leader for our arguably still nascent field in the same way that he stood before and among those of us who had the opportunity to attend PSG.

For these reasons, I once again declare that what you are about to read cannot be properly described as simply or primarily a book, academic study, or theoretical exploration of methodology in the field of leadership studies. This text is an invitation to participate in a different type of study altogether, one which leads us to wonder about what it means to study in the first place.

While the demands upon you will be high, the writing perhaps unconventional, and the path at times uncertain, the fallow fields Nathan Harter shall urge you to cultivate promise to be quite fruitful indeed.

Rachel Wagner
Summer, 2024

SERIES FOREWORD

This is Nathan Harter's third book in the Leadership: Research and Practice series. In this book, as in Harter's other works, the reader is challenged. Challenged to expand beyond traditional, disciplinary-guided perspectives on studying leadership. These disciplinary-based approaches seem to offer "depth" in the study of leadership but at the expense of "breadth." Harter argues for a true integration of disciplines to reach a better and fuller understanding of leadership (or any complex subject matter). Throughout, Harter challenges you to question your own understanding of leadership, and to look at it from different perspectives. The goal is to expand the reader's personal understanding, but the second goal is to impact the approach that is used to study leadership. Importantly, the lessons and insights gained are not limited to leaders and leadership, but there are critical insights about followers and followership.

This is also Harter's most "personal" book. We gain insights into his approach to studying leadership, his methods, and his thoughts (sometimes in an almost stream-of-consciousness format – see the Appendix). Students of leadership will definitely benefit from this book, but I think academics – those scholars who study leaders and leadership – will benefit even more.

Ronald E. Riggio, Ph.D.
Kravis Leadership Institute
Claremont McKenna College

INTRODUCTION TO THE BOOK

Opening remarks

This is my eighth book about leadership. Each one of them taught me new things. In these pages, my goal was to reflect on the methods we use to make sense of leadership. Since 1989, I have encountered different ways of writing about leadership and tried a few myself. Each method arrives with its own theoretical justification, even if the author is not consciously aware of what that might be. (I am certainly guilty of doing this.) Happily, though, these gaps in my understanding from one book have given me more to write about the next time. Hence, eight different books! By now, I suspect it might be a bottomless pit. It might be the case that no matter how often I probe beneath the surface of an argument, there is more for me to investigate. Beyond a certain point, one has to decide when to stop digging.

Let me take a giant step back for a moment. The field of Leadership Studies is relatively new and still inescapably interdisciplinary. It grows like a weed in every direction. Periodically, however, scholars must pause in order to reorient themselves and start over from fresh perspectives. The preliminary goal should not be to branch off endlessly, becoming scattered and isolated from one another, but instead to return to basics and begin again, in search of some newfound coherence, not unlike transitioning from a geocentric model of the solar system that no longer works toward a heliocentric one. Scholars often do this; they progress from a familiar linear model ($A \to B \to C$) to a new one, presumably a better one ($A_1 \to B_1 \to C_1$). But that strategy's not good enough. Not anymore. This book argues with

DOI: 10.4324/9781003540526-1

Michel Serres (2017) that instead of creating yet another linear model in this way, hoping to replace one with another, we must operate with multiple complementary models *simultaneously*, for such an approach respects both the reality we experience and the literature on leadership as we find it.

In 1993, Walter Watson remarked that the sheer diversity of opinions about any one thing might require a **pluralistic mindset**, which is a mindset altogether different from relativism and from a post-modern rejection of anything to be characterized as truth. Pluralism is a distinct framework for acknowledging and managing a diversity of opinions while retaining an abiding faith in the merits of rigorous investigation. We can (and should) employ multiple models for the same reality. Much of what appears in these pages will develop this theme. This book explains pluralism and why it promises to assist those of us who conduct research into leadership. Thereafter, the example of pluralism will have become a kind of ribbon through subsequent chapters – chapters about leadership in time, about social change and group decision-making.

Along the way, the reader will become introduced to a number of scholars whose work is not often cited in the literature on leadership – scholars such as Richard McKeon, Pierre Hadot, Eric Voegelin, Michel Serres, and John Boyd. By importing lessons from history, biology, systems thinking, military strategy, and philosophy, the reader will see a striking topology emerge. It will be my contention ultimately that leadership is the name we give to processes of folding and unfolding the surfaces of social change. But we have to get to that conclusion in stages.

Several chapters take up these topics in a conventional way, and I hope that you find them useful, but toward the end of this book, an extended appendix adopts a highly unconventional tone. I should probably say a few words here in the introduction about its provenance. A while ago, after suffering from COVID, I was emerging with scattered thoughts after months and months of reading English translations of the work of a French philosopher named Michel Serres. What should I do with it all? It was too much to contemplate and hopelessly disjointed in my brain. So I decided to set aside two weeks in June to write down my reactions, without all of the familiar infrastructure that academics use – things such as footnotes, quotations, a bibliography, an index. I just sat down every day and started to write, as surprised as anybody else to discover what I would say. After two weeks, I stopped.

The result of my little experiment will be hard to classify. I won't even try to do that here. But I will say that in my excitement, I shared a copy with many of my peers, two of whom wrote back to say that they refused to read it – it is that strange. To be fair, a few brave folks did respond with thoughtful, even heartfelt remarks. I can probably disclose this much before you turn to those pages: my little experiment relied on a completely different way of knowing, a more spontaneous and personal response, partly a plea, partly a rant, during which I trusted my mind to create something out of all that intellectual ferment. In many ways, therefore, it is actually more honest than the tidy prose I have stayed up late composing for reviewers out there to judge. The appendix is more authentic as a transcription of what I think, anyway. Let me add that the exercise was highly therapeutic. I'd recommend it.

Here though let me indicate some of the theoretical groundwork for the chapters that follow.

McKeon's lectures on knowing

Richard McKeon was a philosopher involved in creating UNESCO and the Universal Declaration of Human Rights.[1] He taught for many years at the University of Chicago, where he helped to found its core curriculum. While serving as dean, McKeon taught a class at the University of Chicago on methods. What survives from that experience are his lecture notes and a number of audiotapes. In 2016, the University of Chicago Press published these lectures as they pertain to the social sciences. The following pages derive from his lectures.[2]

McKeon started out by explaining that the process by which a social scientist arrives at a conclusion that is either true or probable is one's **method**. A scholar must prove or show in some way that it is true or probable. He wrote, "Method is the means by which one discovers or establishes knowledge about something [or] the sequence of steps leading to a conclusion.... Method answers the question, How did you achieve this result in fact or in argument (2016, p. 5f)?" What McKeon wanted to do was show how one conducts an investigation into topics in the social sciences, which presumably would include leadership.

McKeon then schematized four distinct methods in the social sciences as a place to begin. He named them the dialectical method, the operational method, the logistic method, and the problematic method (2016,

---

1 Background on McKeon and his lectures appears in a foreword written by David Owen and Joanne Olson (2016). Overviews of his work appear in Garver and Buchanan (2000), Watson (1993) and Plochmann (1990).
2 Equivalent books reproduce his lectures on the natural sciences (1994) and the humanities (forthcoming).

pp. 10–12).[3] Let us take a look at them one at a time, so we can recognize the differences.

- **Dialectic** posits two or more positions placed together in order to arrive at a superior, shared position. The conventional mode for doing this will be known as dialogue. Is it possible that both of us are correct? Can we somehow combine or – better yet – transcend our differences? The ideal end result will be some kind of comprehending system.
- The **operational** method also posits two (or more) positions placed together, but in this method, the two are contrasted, set into conflict, by means of debate, so that one might think in terms of sorting: which position is acceptable? And which is not? Then, going forward, we will all agree to adopt the acceptable position or positions and ignore the rest. In other words, operational methods set out to declare winners and losers.
- The **logistic** model builds from simple premises, step-by-step, toward more complex structures. You agree on something that is simple and clear, then figure out what follows logically from this. The ideal end result of this method will be a proof.
- The **problematic** method, as you might have guessed by its name, originates with some real-world conundrum, a difficulty or frustration that requires us to think things through toward an acceptable resolution. The method calls for hypotheses to be tested, which is to say that the solution must ultimately accord with reality. Either it works well enough, or it doesn't. The conventional mode for doing this will be known as experimentation.

The following book on leadership looks more closely at methods of investigation. And it relies primarily on what McKeon called the dialectical methods. We will begin with multiple positions, different possibilities, and instead of having them compete with one another, we will try to find out whether there is a way to integrate them, to encompass them within a comprehending system. In this way, nobody has to feel attacked. The dialectic begins by giving every position its due. The objective is to hear them out, one at a time, and even generate a few new ones, if need be, so that we find ourselves with an array of possibilities. Then, instead of deciding which ones we prefer, we go in search together, you and I, toward the possibility that they might all be true or useful (to one degree or another), but that makes sense only if we allow for the wider aperture. Is there a

---

3 Walter Watson elaborated on these same four methods as well (1993, ch. IV).

way to incorporate them all? McKeon wrote about "higher truths which synthesize the apparent disagreement (2016, p. 229)."

George Kimball Plochmann (1990) wrote that McKeon "allowed, indeed demanded, a width of meanings of terms, interpretations of propositions, and construing of arguments that forced his readers to conclude that no one analysis was final, uniquely true, and ultimately verifiable by 'the facts' (p. xiv)." He added that McKeon replaced earlier beliefs "not by refuting or otherwise shoving the older views out of the way but by finding means for locating a unique place for them in something ... much broader (1990, p. 25)." His method was to accept nearly all methods and allow other truths to be true (1990, p. 28).

It seems important at this juncture to point out that plenty of philosophers pick alternate methods. Some rush in, with sword and shield, to combat adversaries (operational). Some prefer to seek agreement on first principles and on core facts, then work outward in a linear fashion from there (logistic).[4] Some want to ask, from the outset, what practical difference we are trying to make (problematic)? These last, the problem solvers, are frequently the critics who ask, So what? Contrary to all of these possibilities, the post-modern turn will challenge the search for truth (and even for probability) as a game, if not a fiction, maybe even an exercise in delusion, whereas we supposedly have no reason to believe that paramount reality will ultimately make sense. Some say that maybe the quest for truth and probability is misguided. This book takes the opposite position, which is to say that dialectic begins with the assumption that paramount reality is intelligible, even if we are limited in our ability to understand it (McKeon, 2016, p. 20).

There is no reason to believe that once you choose a method, you must never use another. Methods are complementary. Each has its place in the broader project to understand leadership. Nevertheless, it helps to be clear which method is being used at the time one is using it. Otherwise, folks might start talking past one another, trying to do entirely different things with the same information. The dialectical method puts a premium on clarifying what is meant, so that we can recognize how the various positions are related. Think, for example, how Socrates interrogated his interlocutors. He often drove the conversation toward defining key terms, because until we understand one another, we won't understand the underlying

---

4 It is important to recognize that the logistic method proceeds in a linear fashion, like walking a labyrinth from point A to point B. It is a path. The objective is to arrive at one, incontrovertible conclusion. By way of contrast, dialectic keeps drawing larger and larger circles around the various possibilities. Rather than being linear, we might say that it is recursive.

phenomenon we say that we want to understand. The purpose is not to show that the other person is mistaken so much as it is to help one another recognize and avoid mistakes. The former purpose seems hostile. The latter seems wholesome. I prefer the latter.

I said that this book relies primarily on the dialectical method, a method that fosters the practice of dialogue. So, how is a book such as this one fostering dialogue? A book is univocal in the sense that only one person is speaking. It is not really a dialogue. It is not a dialogue unless it is, like the Platonic dialogues, an account of other people having a conversation, such as a theater piece. And yet I would contend that even within the mind of a single person, there can be dialogue. Hubert Hermans called it the dialogical self (see Hermans & Kempen, 1993; Hermans, Kempen, & van Loon, 1992). The mind is a composite, a multiplicity. (Neuroscience is coming to the same conclusion.) And therefore one can entertain seemingly incompatible thoughts. Even though this book is in one sense univocal, in the sense that I am the sole author, I aspire to share with the reader some sense of the interior dialogue that will have been taking place in my own mind. Furthermore, to compensate for my limitations, I will import thoughts and ideas from other sources, so that we have an array to work with. Not to make too much of this claim, but my goal is to model the dialectic, so that the reader can follow along with the process. But let's not stop there, because my ultimate aspiration, my hope, is that the reader will engage in the same questions and lend his or her voice to the conversation. What I am writing is by no means the final word. On the contrary. My goal is to provoke the reader to conduct further conversations, over and over, in what might seem to be an interminable activity.

Because it is.

The never-ending search for principles

Both dialectical and operational methods begin with the same task. The first step is to gather up and start making distinctions. What one does with those distinctions is step two, and this is where the two methods part ways. Nevertheless, neither can proceed until we accumulate various perspectives and approaches and then discriminate among these (McKeon, 2016, p. 96). We assemble, in a manner of speaking, and then we disassemble. We dump my grandmother's tin of assorted buttons onto the table. The mental activity of differentiation prepares us to do something with them.

What differentiates the two methods (dialectical and operational) is the role of one's underlying principles. The operational approach attempts to take that "array" of multiple possibilities and judge according to some preexisting principle, which McKeon labels holoscopic – as it pertains to the whole (2016, pp. 57f & 81f). The investigator already possesses the standard by which to judge. With this method, we ask ourselves: which of these positions is **logical**, which of these accords with the **facts**, which of these fits everything else that we believe, so that our view of the universe is **coherent** (Plochmann, 1990, p. 49)? Dialectical methods, on the other hand, do not begin with a preexisting principle; instead, they *go in search of* a holoscopic principle. They suspend judgment in order to discover what the underlying principle ought to be. They presuppose that the universe is ultimately intelligible; it is just that as human beings, we have not yet reached a sufficient level of understanding. Dialectical and operational methods are decidedly different ways of proceeding, of course, yet they both accept that holoscopic principles exist, somewhere out there (McKeon, 2016, p. 66). Not every method of investigation accepts that there are such principles, but these two do. Again, one of them *begins* with these principles (operational), whereas the other goes in search (dialectical).

In his lectures on the natural sciences, McKeon (1994) had schematized the sequence in this way (p. 67). First, we notice something about which we are puzzled or curious. This step involves a single term. ("Why did Congress fail to pass that legislation?") Second, we interpret what we experience. This involves two terms, i.e. the original term and the term we introduce to explain it. ("Maybe Congress failed to pass that legislation because the President said he would veto it.") Third, we compare what we think with what others think about the same thing. This involves at least three terms, namely (a) the original, (b) our interpretation, and now (c) the interpretation of somebody else. ("It may also be the case that Congress failed to pass that legislation because the voting public disapproves.") Fourth, we try to find out together whether our experiences can be explained by some shared principle. This last step aspires to include all examples out there, so that the set of terms is *n*. In this notation, the letter "n" represents an unknown number of instances that belong to the same set. ("So maybe Congress failed to pass that legislation for the same reason that the President threatened to veto it, namely that as elected officials they must constantly be mindful of what the voters think.") In this way, we progress toward broader or holoscopic principles that account for the various interpretations that are floating around out there.

In the chapters that follow, the primary method will be dialectical, which accords with my own temperament, as well as with the example of writers I have come to admire a great deal, such as Heraclitus, Plato, Augustine, Bergson, and Whitehead (McKeon, 2016, p. 373). On his deathbed, my intellectual hero, Eric Voegelin, was still writing, and the title chosen for his uncompleted last work was *In Search of Order* (1987). The so-called search for these holoscopic principles requires collaboration – collaboration vertically, i.e. across time, and collaboration horizontally, i.e. in community. And the mechanism for conducting this collaboration is dialogue, a process about which I have written elsewhere (e.g. Harter, 2020, ch. 8).[5] None of which is to say that humankind will ever complete the process and arrive at overarching principles that are forever and indisputably true. I am not committed to that possibility. Previously, Voegelin had written that "the mystery of this stream of being is impenetrable (2000, p. 24)." Rather, I will become highly suspicious of anyone who believes otherwise. I share this suspicion with one of my favorite authors, Michel Serres, whom you will meet in these pages. It seems important at this juncture to acknowledge that Voegelin and Serres are two of the most important influences on my own philosophical journey to date.

Consider this book a part of that ongoing search for the principles that help to make the universe more intelligible.

Before going forward, though, I would like to add that McKeon also subscribed to a version of this posture about the academic life as a never-ending search for principles. Most scholars regard themselves as subject matter experts, complete with doctorates and a list of publications validated by double-blind referees. They are in the business of pursuing a thing called truth. In the twentieth century, of course, a large number of scholars argued that there is no such thing as truth. (Maybe you are one of these.) Looking at these two alternatives, caricatured as dogma and relativism, McKeon wanted us to question the little word "thing." Is there such a "thing" as truth? He suggested that the pursuit of truth is a process, an activity, and not a thing at all. So much of what academics do originates in the assumption that there is a reality, on the one hand, and an investigator of some sort, on the other. The common image is binary. A chemist and a specimen. Scholars see themselves as beholders of reality, in a position to observe and judge, like a biologist peering into a microscope. For McKeon, however, scholars are participants in a flux, no less a part of the reality they wish to understand (Buchanan, 2000, pp. 148 & 154). Once scholarship "supposes it can find a final and comprehensive solution, it ceases to be inquiry and becomes either apologetics or propaganda (Buchanan, 2000,

---

5 McKeon had argued that certain fundamental or basic ideas are in constant opposition, yet that does not mean that we must choose. These oppositions, he said, "are productive of discussion, inquiry, and progress (1994, p. 7)." See generally, McKeon (1990a) where he defined dialogue as when "two or more speakers or two or more positions are brought into relations in which it becomes apparent that each position is incomplete and inconclusive unless assimilated to a higher truth (1990a, p. 28; see p. 45)." Dialogue synthesizes contraries and assimilates divergent views (pp. 38 & 41). And yet, it would be implausible to believe that dialogue ever results in complete agreement (p. 44).

p. 153, quoting John Dewey, 1938)."[6] Instead, inquiry of the sort we will be attempting in this book begins in a state or condition of perplexity, whereby scholars do not so much arrive at answers as they convert something indeterminate into a problem (Buchanan, 2000, p. 151).

[The appendix to this book exhibits my own raw perplexity.]

Richard Buchanan apparently heard the complaint repeatedly that McKeon never took a position. Even the experts were annoyed (2000, p. 148). "Make up your mind!" But how could he do so in good conscience when there are multiple positions? Wayne Booth noted this.

> [W]hen you probe [McKeon's] writings in a search for the final, ultimately correct, version of the range of philosophical possibilities, hoping for a single philosophy of everything, you are doomed; studied carefully, his final schema will yield far more than just 16 x 16 squares but thousands of legitimate possibilities.... He was an ontological monist, while laboring as a philosophical pluralist.
>
> *(2000, p. 218f; see also p. 225)*

If anything resembling the truth is out there, scholars must appreciate the alternatives and put them into dialogue with one another. Such is my ambition.

Implications for the study of leadership in history

Leadership takes place in a context. It is an event within the flow of human history. In order to understand leadership in context, therefore, one must possess an understanding of that flow. As you might imagine, Richard McKeon categorizes four different understandings of history, depending on the method one is using (2016, lecture 11). And since this book relies most on a dialectical method, its understanding of history will conform most with one of these four understandings. As always, McKeon observed that each understanding has its merits; these are complementary understandings and not competing. Nevertheless, the book will find itself drawn toward what McKeon called an epochal understanding of history. What does this phrase mean? And what are its implications for the study of leadership?

Let us begin by reviewing the four understandings and how they pertain to Leadership Studies (see Plochmann, 1990, p. 134f). A dialectical method

---

6 McKeon had made the point that "it can be shown that ideological agreement on one philosophy by all mankind is neither possible nor, if it were possible, desirable (1994, p. 8)."

tends to conform to an epochal history. The other three understandings McKeon called exemplary history, causal history, and disciplinary history.

An **epochal** history tends to imagine history as a series of epochs or "chunks," frequently labeled as an age or era, such as the Renaissance or Enlightenment, each of which aspired to reach a coherent whole. People living in the same place and time will tend to think in similar ways, and even though everybody's involvement in these periods is uneven, there will have been a distinctive approach to understanding the world – shared laterally, more or less, which is to say simultaneously, but distinct from what had been understood before. In other words, the people at that time (or at least their thought leaders) searched together for some underlying (or holoscopic) principles. They had reached a more or less coherent worldview, getting closer and closer to an understanding of the universe and their place in it. History records the coming together of these worldviews (unity) and the subsequent disintegration (multiplicity), repeatedly. Humanity moves from one epoch to another, in stages or phases.[7] Culture folds in upon itself and then unfolds. Leadership, therefore, superintends this dynamic, both the coming together and the falling apart, the folding and the unfolding. Leadership is the individual's role in these endless fluctuations.

Exemplary history, by way of contrast, relies on the method that McKeon had referred to as operational. Remember what this means: the investigator starts out with a set of principles and goes about studying leadership by identifying those historical figures who champion these principles. These historical figures are the protagonists in a drama whom we are being urged to emulate. They are literally exemplary. From this method, one holds up those who advanced the principles of particular value to the investigator. Consequently, the investigator will have identified heroes, role models, and patterns of perfection. In Leadership Studies, this approach often accords with what is known as the Great Man Theory, by which we identify those figures who are in some sense great, and so we expect their stories to inspire the rest of us. In the classroom, therefore, students are urged to become like them.

Causal history strips away the whole idea of underlying principles. It simply examines the ebb and flow of events, looking for what was responsible for what happened. It might not be a singular character. It might be economics or geography or technology. Or even luck. But when it comes to identifying individual human beings, these persons are not to be judged as

---

7 Walter Watson gives a lucid example of his approach in his 1993 book *The Architectonics of Meaning.*

good or bad, blameworthy or praiseworthy. The sole question is this: what impact did their actions have on the world around them? What behavior can be said to have caused subsequent events? That's it. That's causal history, as its name implies. The person who actually made a difference may have been an assassin, a madman, or a fluke. Or a complete fiction.

Disciplinary history is similar to causal history in its rejection of underlying principles. But instead of looking at the ebb and flow of events, out in the external world, it looks within, at the historians and the participants, at the ones who experience and then interpret what has been occurring. It puts a focus on the phenomenon of duration and its significance for any sense of life's meaning. What must it have been like to undergo that terrible plague or that war? How did people understand themselves? For this approach, history is always an account from a particular point of view. So the critical task is to interpret the historical record through the lens of those who lived and wrote about it. There is really no way to know what happened except through the experience of it. Leadership then is a gloss, a word used by those in the midst of the events and afterward to explain to themselves and to one another about what happened on that day and why. Leadership is a story that reduces a complex occurrence to something manageable. It is in the truest sense a myth, a heuristic, and often a falsification intended to render a troubling world explicable.

The following book will prefer an epochal sense of history, largely as it scrutinizes how leaders superintend the fluctuation between unity and multiplicity. People come together to do a lot of things. Their consolidated efforts might even harden into institutions that outlive the founders. Frequently, that was the purpose of coming together in the first place, i.e. to build something intended to last. By the same token, leaders also sometimes resist unity, sometimes holding back and often actively breaking apart an existing unity – perhaps for the sake of a different unity (such as a subunit or a rival), but also sometimes for the sake of freedom itself, without any ambition to create unity at all. These leaders might be characterized as rebels, heretics, insurgents, subversives, or traitors. But because we are studying leadership through the dialectical lens, none of these epithets matter nearly so much as the role these persons play in the ongoing search for order. If we can judge with hindsight how to fold together the two competing sides, both the guardians of the status quo and the revolutionaries, even though they are shouting at one another across the barricades – if we can judge them as participants in a common quest, then we can understand our own times and the people around us as participants in the exact same quest, even when we disagree. Even when we imprison, assault, deprecate, and ostracize one another. We are all just trying to make sense of our situation. We are all part of this shared epoch. Seen from a distance, we are all on the same "side" of history. What we need are the voices of other people to help us along the way.

Different objects require different methods

It was Eric Voegelin who taught me that different objects require different methods (2000). There is not only one legitimate method. When you say that a particular method determines what is true, then you have flipped the script. Methods are handmaidens, tools, subordinate to the aims of science generally. Voegelin insisted that putting method first perverts science. One cannot walk around with a solitary method, no matter what it is, using it to determine the truth of everything around you. Instead, one selects from among multiple, different methods, depending on the object to be investigated and on one's purpose.

One of the implications of Voegelin's argument is that we begin with a pre-scientific understanding of reality. Nobody in the social sciences is a blank slate. Not only does the person doing the investigation possess a prescientific understanding of whatever it is, but he or she will discover a plentiful array of prescientific understandings handed down to them from the past. There will already be books about it and cultural expectations and educators offering their two cents. The trick, as Voegelin put it, was to begin with these prescientific understandings and move toward increasing clarity. In other words, one doesn't start from a stop position. The same is true in leadership studies. All sorts of folks write about leadership, and they have been doing so for centuries.

It may not be possible to bring to the surface every relevant belief tucked within a person's tacit understanding, for that is what it means to be tacit (Polanyi, 2009). Having said that, however, it would certainly help the avid investigator to become aware of his or her implicit leadership theory ... or theories, plural (Schyns & Meindl, 2005).[8] I am trying in these pages to make my own approach explicit, even if it would be impossible to exhaust everything I take for granted as I write them. The investigator is always limited, with only a dim awareness of certain aspects of his or her thinking – even assuming they can be stated clearly. Each of us brings a raft full of bias to our investigations. I certainly have mine. I take it as an operational assumption that this is true for each of us. This is one of the reasons we need dialogue, if only to hear ourselves say things aloud. Yet this paragraph is addressing tacit understanding, is it not? This book

---

8 This book adopts as its purpose the goal of tolerating, generating, and using multiple theories for the same reality.

overall examines the gaps, the fallow fields, the things that are not in any sense tacit, precisely because *we never thought about them before*. That is a different problem. We work at dialogue in part so that we are able to say to somebody, "I had no idea." Because maybe now, thanks to listening to other people, we do have at least some idea about whatever it is we were talking about.

Modern readers sometimes disdain practices epitomized by Aristotle, because that was so long ago and far away. Surely we have outgrown the ancients. Except that we haven't. Besides which, the ancients make up a substantial part of that prescientific understanding I was just writing about. Before we can go making pronouncements about leadership, we should probably consult our predecessors, even if we reject them ultimately. The same can be said about their methods. Aristotle (1952) looked around at what other people had already said on a topic before he presumed to begin his own investigations. We can learn a thing or two from Aristotle. I say this not to cite him as any kind of authority to be obeyed, although that would not be such a bad idea; instead, he shows us a method that has had its uses, and to the extent that I concur, I should probably acknowledge his precedence.

Any pre-scientific understanding of leadership must acknowledge as an empirical fact that different people have different opinions (Garver & Buchanan, 2000, p. x; Watson, 1993, pp. 1–5). Some opinions are more useful than others. A few are probably mistaken. But it is unnecessary to believe that an understanding of reality requires a single point of view. The goal is not to drive toward uniformity of thought. Alternatives can coexist. Walter Watson credits McKeon with the premise that "truth has no single expression (2000, p. 10)." What McKeon concluded after a lifetime of scholarship is a position referred to as pluralism. That means that not only are there many ways of knowing, but for the sake of thoroughness, there really *ought to be*. All too often, confusions originate in the fact that two persons have adopted complementary – not incompatible – perspectives, yet they seem not to appreciate that fact about one another. In many scholarly disputes, the two sides are talking past one another; they are talking about completely different things, or about the same thing in completely different ways, yet they seem not to recognize that this is happening.

Inter-disciplinarity in leadership studies as opposed to multi-disciplinarity

Writing in 1941, Michael Polanyi insisted that one of the hallmarks of a free society is the distribution of scientific work into autonomous circles, where the experts are not constrained by popular or political boundaries.

He said, "Truth is so complex, and each particle of it hangs together directly with so many others, that it can be revealed only by a continuous series of independent individual initiatives (p. 448)." For this reason, specialists must separate themselves, one from another, in order to develop their unique understanding. Nephrologists must confer with one another; hepatologists must confer with one another. None of which is to say that only one specialization is the correct one. Polanyi wrote about "aspects of the truth," a multitude of ways of knowing the same reality. And it helps to maintain these distinctions. To that extent, he spoke in favor of multidisciplinarity.

By way of contrast, *inter*-disciplinarity is the process by which these "particles" become reattached to one another, integrated. And Polanyi embodied interdisciplinarity in his own work, having studied medicine, chemistry, engineering, economics, and a host of other fields. He conferred routinely with experts in other disciplines. In fact, he had a name for this process: conviviality (see Wigner & Hodgkin, 1977). What he ultimately recommended was a rhythm of withdrawal and engagement, isolation and conversation, protecting the process by which specialists work together, to be sure, and respecting each of their unique missions, but not allowing them to splinter indefinitely and refuse opportunities to collaborate across the disciplines. A classic both/and. In the same way that the individual learns by a process of subsidiary-focal integration (see Meek, 2014), paying attention to one thing while figuring out how that one thing fits everything else, so also the field of science must be intentional about both its focal awareness (its disciplinary specialty) and the gradual accumulation of knowledge into an encompassing whole.

Interdisciplinarity then is not in any sense a combat among competing visions, like a debate after which we declare winners and losers. It is more of a dialogue in which each participant gives an account and listens to what others have to say, thereby working toward shared understandings (see Plato, *Theaetetus* 167e). At its best, dialogue has no destination. It is a never-ending process whereby differing perspectives and opinions are gathered together and everybody works together to establish some overarching framework or schema so that nobody has to be wrong (Watson, 1993, p. 88). Not only is it possible that the participants can "fit" their respective specialties into a coherent whole, but it may be that they can learn from one another and recognize when the same principles are operating in their respective activities. A prime example of this is systems thinking, which emerges in so many different areas of study. Dialogue provides participants with an opportunity to capitalize on what others are doing, to assimilate, to mimic. "Maybe we could do something like that."

I have had to say this before, but interdisciplinarity does not mean being *anti*-disciplinary. The goal is not the eradication of our separate pursuits. It is not a defiance of expertise and accumulated knowledge. Participants must respect one another's integrity. The academic boundaries exist for a reason. And to be honest, it can help sometimes to revisit where those boundaries lie. But like farmers, we can chat across the fence and occasionally climb over when being neighborly. "What you do is awfully similar to what I do. Can I come see how you do it? Furthermore, what you do impacts what I do. Maybe we should get our heads together to talk about that."

For leaders especially, one must be able to crosswalk, which means being able to engage people from different places and with different interests. A leader must occupy the space where differences meet, like an intersection, primarily in order to facilitate cooperation. Separate departments, each with its distinctive purpose, must coordinate what they are doing for the greater good. Leaders bring together a variety of members with independent thoughts, ideas, and knowledge, so that the firm or organization can put all of this intellectual capital to use. I guess what I am saying is that scholars in Leadership Studies as a field of study need such leadership themselves.

The ideal of dialogue has its limits, of course. In addition to the obvious limit that specialists must spend most of their time and energy concentrating on their specialties, there will be times that the group decides that a subunit is misguided, misaligned, or wrongheaded, adding little or nothing to the encompassing mission and possibly even detracting from the shared goal. Interdisciplinarity as a process must cleanse itself and make some tough decisions about who can join and what they can bring to the proverbial table. At some point, for example, scientists must declare that phrenology or astrology or alchemy be excluded. Or, when a legitimate participant steps out of line, encroaching on somebody else's territory, let us say, the group might need to mediate as to where exactly to put the boundary fence. The group must police itself. But notice that the remedy is not to send everybody to their separate corners and shut down their interactions, such that they become further ensiled. On the contrary. We cannot afford what Watson called idiocentric perspectives (1993, p. 16). If anything, the remedy is to bring folks together and *intensify* their interactions in search of some mutual accommodation.

Polanyi was not against somebody serving as the gatekeeper. After all, somebody has to moderate these exchanges. What he opposed was gatekeeping from outside of the community that had been so patiently built, outsiders such as politicians with little or no training, with little or no vested interest in the long-term success of the group. The strange thing is that each subunit can make the same assertion about interference from "outsiders." It starts to look like an infinite regression. If group A (such as scientists) can reject interference from group B (such as politicians), then why can't group A_1 (such as chemists) resist interference from group A_2 (such as physicists)? By that logic, we subdivide and split and increasingly splinter, muttering that "nobody tells me what to do." Polanyi even defines academic freedom in terms of individual autonomy (1998, p. 41). But this objection overlooks the extent to which people can intellectually separate what they are doing as specialists and what they are doing as part of the larger whole. People can govern themselves at each magnitude, knowing what is within their purview and what is shared. So yes, scientists can confer with politicians. In fact, they ultimately must do so. We must continuously coordinate our efforts with one another (1998, p. 43; see also p. 49). Even so, scientists also need to be cautious against untutored interference. Polanyi even differentiates: "The function of public authorities is not to plan research, but only to provide opportunities for its pursuit (1998, p. 111)."

Interdisciplinarity therefore is a constant negotiation among various interests, making distinctions where it is needful, but cooperating where it is helpful, again and again. Yet the image of units and subunits and their interrelation neglects the situation where Leadership Studies finds itself. We who study leadership are not a unit with its own subunits such as psychology and sociology and anthropology. It is not as though we are the master who is governing its servants, the big circle within which these little circles move. As a field of study, we have crept laterally through existing academic disciplines, like a ribbon, discovering a common interest, to be sure, but not presuming to tell anybody what to do. We exist precisely to invite scholars from completely different disciplines to have these conversations and explore how we can complement one another. Our gatekeepers do not judge so much what is worthwhile as psychology, sociology, or anthropology, for instance. That is not their job. Instead, they judge as to what contributes to our shared purpose. And to do that, they (these gatekeepers) must become conversant with a range of disciplines. Can we include design thinking, ethics, business practices, military science, literary theory, and so forth? If so, can we discern what exactly they each contribute? In order to judge correctly, of course, we have to engage in this thing we are calling interdisciplinarity, whereby the social scientist examines an article on the epic of Gilgamesh and the management guru contemplates the works of Shakespeare.

Using the metaphor of how different academic disciplines might "fit" together presupposes that they occupy distinct intellectual spaces, like jigsaw puzzle pieces we are hoping to assemble. Often, yes, that is the case, as we devise some kind of division of labor. The kidney is not the liver. The problem is that in many cases what we are trying to integrate are alternative visions of the same reality. Watson wrote that "philosophies do not differ from each other because each has a part of the whole, but because they have different ways of appropriating the whole (1993, p. 72)." That is something altogether different and probably more challenging for us to accept.[9] What we are compelled to consider is what Watson called reciprocal priority: how each worldview accounts for every other worldview (1993, p. 10). Worldview A must account for worldviews B and C, whereas B must account for both A and C, and C must account for A and B. These worldviews are incompatible, he said, only to the extent that a scholar must use them one at a time and not mix them together indiscriminately (paraphrasing Watson, 1993, p. 10).

It all begins with how we imagine what leadership is. Leadership is a performance, a practice, a phenomenon, a problem, a puzzle – and that's just words that begin with the letter "P"! My plea throughout this book is that those of us interested in investigating leadership – whatever it is, however we conceive it to be – learn to step outside of our comfort zones and ask one another questions, with tact and due respect, out of a spirit of mutuality. Rigorously, I might add, because we should all want to get it right. We have a shared problem, you see, and it is this: so much being written and taught about leadership (especially in the popular literature) is unhelpful and even incorrect.

A concluding remark about America in 2024

One of the following chapters considers the extent to which leadership might be fueled by a spirit of resentment. Resentment, you see, is a response, a reaction to something else. It is metaphorically the echo of some reverberating noise. In the time when I am writing these words in the United States, the cacophony of conflicting echoes has made public discourse nearly impossible. For instance, many scholars and pundits hope to explain the phenomenon of Donald Trump as a politician, and they adopt some version of resentment on the part of a large sector of society. They have concluded that as a politician he stokes, he exploits, he represents their grievances. But what disturbs me in the midst of their condescension is the complete lack of interest in what it is that these benighted voters

---

9 Polanyi made a similar claim when he wrote that "even in the scientific handling of inanimate systems different approaches are possible, which are mutually exclusive (1998, p. 24)."

resent. Assuming that they are correct, the question has to be asked: why exactly are they resentful? What might have happened to make them this way? Is it conceivable that they have been mistreated, scorned, or ignored by society's elite? Have they been subjected to contempt? In full disclosure, I can despise Trump as both a person and a leader, and I can be disappointed in his supporters; but as a scholar, I have to probe beneath the banal excuses that make that very same opinionated elite – overwhelmingly represented among leadership scholars – feel better about themselves as deservingly better, even superior, somehow immune from the pathologies they deplore, when in fact their driving professional animus is so obviously steeped *in their own resentment*.

It seemed important to say as much here, in the introduction, given the times in which we live. Furthermore, as my dedication makes plain, I walk around with my own set of grievances, accumulated over the years, and I believe it is important as a scholar to own that about myself and then struggle to transcend those grievances where I am able.

References

Aristotle. (1952). *The works of Aristotle* (vol. 1). Encyclopedia Britannica. Reprinted for Great books of the Western world from W.D. Ross (ed.). *The works of Aristotle*, by arrangement with Oxford University Press.

Buchanan, R. "The ecology of culture: Pluralism and circumstantial metaphysics." In Garver, E. & R. Buchanan (eds.) (2000). *Pluralism in theory and practice: Richard McKeon and American philosophy* (pp. 135–162). Vanderbilt University Press.

Garver, E., & Buchanan, R. (eds.) (2000). *Pluralism in theory and practice: Richard McKeon and American philosophy*. Vanderbilt University Press.

Harter, N. (2020). *Leadership across boundaries: Passage to Aporia*. Routledge.

Hermans, H.J.M., & Kempen, H.J.G. (1993). *The dialogical self: Meaning as movement*. Academic Press.

Hermans, H.J.M., Kempen, H.J.G., & Van Loon, R.J. (1992). "The dialogical self: Beyond individualism and rationalism." *American Psychologist*. 47(1): 23–33. https://doi.org/10.1037/0003-066X.47.1.23.

McKeon, R. (2016). *On knowing: The social sciences*. University of Chicago Press.

McKeon, R. (1994). *On knowing: The natural sciences*. University of Chicago Press.

McKeon, R. "Dialogue and controversy in philosophy." In Maranhão, T. (ed.) (1990). *The interpretation of dialogue* (ch. 1). University of Chicago Press.

Meek, E.L. (2014). *A little manual for knowing*. Cascade Books.

Owen, D., & Olson, J. "Foreword." In McKeon, R. (ed.) (2016). *On knowing: The social sciences* (pp. xiii–xxi). University of Chicago Press.

Plochmann, G.K. (1990). *Richard McKeon: A study*. University of Chicago Press.

Polanyi, M. (2009). *The tacit dimension*. University of Chicago press.

Polanyi, M. (1998). *The logic of liberty: Reflections and rejoinders*. Liberty Fund.

Polanyi, M. (1941). "The growth of thought in society." *Economica*. 8(32): 428–456.

Schyns, B., & Meindl, J.R. (eds.) (2005). *Implicit leadership theories: Essays and explorations*. Information Age Publishing.

Serres, M. (2017). *Geometry: The third book of foundations* (R. Burks, trans.). Bloomsbury Academic.

Voegelin, E. (2000). *Collected works* (vol. 5) (M. Henningsen, ed.). University of Missouri Press.

Voegelin, E. (1987). *In search of order*. Louisiana State University Press.

Watson, W. "McKeon: The unity of his thought." In Garver, E. & R. Buchanan (eds.) (2000). *Pluralism in theory and practice: Richard McKeon and American philosophy* (pp. 10–28). Vanderbilt University Press.

Watson, W. (1993). *The architectonics of meaning: Foundations of the new pluralism*. University of Chicago Press.

Wigner, E.P., & Hodgkin, R.A. (1977). "Michael Polanyi 1891–1976." *Biographical Memoirs of Fellows of the Royal Society*. 23: 413–448.

1

METHODOLOGICAL PLURALISM FOR THEORY WORK

Incessantly swinging around on a pivot

Introduction to this chapter

Scholars must periodically attend to the theories they are using to conduct their studies. It is a contention of this chapter that theory work is among the legitimate types of scholarship. The particular theory of interest in these pages is known as methodological pluralism, which is a way of approaching one's investigation by bringing disparate voices together into dialogue. How are they going to fit so that we all learn from one another about the complexity of the phenomenon we refer to as leadership?

Standing in the way of dialogue is what Michel Serres referred to as umbilical thinking, by which one person insists not only on the rightness of one's conclusions but also on the principle by which those conclusions were obtained. In contrast, methodological pluralism seeks not to disprove any conclusions, nor even to reject the underlying principles; instead, it disputes the insistence that there is only one way to conduct these investigations. This is as much to say that there is more than one way to slice the watermelon. The practice of phenomenology offers a construct known as "bracketing" that allows an investigator to proceed, knowing that there is always more to reality than it is ever possible to include – which is one reason why scholars need one another. What each of us "brackets" and sets aside can be investigated profitably by somebody else, but only so long as we periodically confer with one another.

DOI: 10.4324/9781003540526-2

Theory work in leadership studies

Scholarship comes in many shapes and sizes. Different scholars adopt different methods, depending in part on whatever it is they are studying. One scholar might adopt quantitative methods. Another might prefer qualitative methods. Yet another might use historical methods. There is no single, universal method for doing research. Among these various methods is the work of theory. This is to say that scholarship can be about theory itself. Scholars certainly use theory. They rely on theory. Like a pane of glass, scholars can be said to "see through" theory in order to understand the world. But every now and then, somebody has to look at the pane of glass itself (Heidegger, 2018, pp. 107–120).

The sociologist Don Levine once set forth a taxonomy of theory work, to show the range of possibilities (2015, p. xxviii, figure P1). He mentioned, for instance, recovering seminal works from the past, cataloguing interpretations of that seminal work, building new conceptual models, reflecting on the ethical implications of scholarship, and examining the philosophical preconditions for what constitutes knowledge in a particular field of study. One of the specific examples that Levine mentioned refers to syntheses with other disciplines and perspectives. He called this genre: "heuristic work external to a given discipline" (2015, part III). The sociologist consults the literature from economics, for example, or the philosopher confers with biologists. It is at such a nexus that one finds true interdisciplinarity – not multi-disciplinarity, in which two separate academic disciplines stand side-by-side, but inter-disciplinarity, where two separate academic disciplines engage one another directly.

In another book, Levine (2018) continued his consideration of this type of work, namely this "heuristic work external to a given discipline." When combining two different disciplines or perspectives, it is possible that they are mutually irrelevant, perhaps because they are addressing wholly different problems. But it may be that they are trying to address the same problem in different ways. One must discern whether these disciplines or perspectives are **competing** against one another or **complementary**. If they are complementary, the question becomes the following: are they complementary because they are addressing different parts of the same problem, on the same level (horizontally), or is it because they are addressing the same problem at different levels in some kind of hierarchy (vertically)?

An example of complementary perspectives on the same level might be two physicians who specialize in kidney function and liver function, respectively: Nephrologists and Hepatologists. Each specialization is looking at a part of a larger whole, so they are separate from one another in one sense, yes, and at the same level of analysis. Each specializes in a different bodily organ. An example of complementary perspectives at *different* levels might be physicians who specialize in kidney or liver functions, on the one hand, and the integrated concern for patient health as a whole, on the other hand, oftentimes entrusted to primary care physicians. One of the functions of theory work is gaining clarity about the overall structure within which scholars do their work (Levine, 2018, ch. 15).

Leadership Studies have been confronted from the very beginning with this kind of interdisciplinary work, inasmuch as we are descended from management, military science, sociology, psychology, political science, ethics, anthropology, and so forth (see Harvey & Riggio, 2012; Goethals & Sorenson, 2007). Lots of different studies were conducted in lots of different ways. Levine offered a typology of responses available to scholars when confronted with an array of disciplines and perspectives such as this (2018, ch. 15). One possibility is to have them fight it out for supremacy. He called this the **polemicist** response. Either I will win, or you will win, so let's clash and find out. Often, the method for doing this work among scholars is for them to debate one another. (In the introduction, we saw that Richard McKeon called this an operational approach.) Another possibility is to clarify our language, over and over, until we come to some kind of agreement on what our terms mean. He called this the **semanticist** response, whereby we can both end up winning, assuming that we are careful and patient with our words. In Leadership Studies, many authors try to convince their readers that their definition of the term is the best. A third possibility tries to identify the one right answer and to insist that only this can be correct. There is no alternative. He called this the **monist** response, and it simply ignores every other voice. Yet another possibility questions whether there will ever be an answer. It challenges the idea that any statement about leadership can be said to be true. Levine called this the **skepticist** response. If there are multiple possibilities about what is true, this approach tends to reject them all. A fifth possibility keeps an open mind and welcomes every alternative as equally true. It sees no reason to quarrel. Throw the doors wide and let them all come in. Levine called this the **eclecticist** response. From this point of view, truth is whatever you say that it is and that's cool. Levine himself adopted a sixth possibility. He called it **methodological pluralism**.[1] Some claims are true, he wrote. Others

---

1 William James (1909) observed that we begin life as pluralists. We experience the world pluralistically; he called it "phenomenal diversity" (p. 47). We live each day as though it were true. The alternative viewpoint, he claimed, is improbable (p. 111), even though

are false. We need to know the difference. Saying that something is true has to mean something. Often, what appear to be incompatible truth claims X and Y can be reconciled – if, that is, we sort through them properly. But to get to that conclusion, one must put the existing alternatives into dialogue. We can list the possibilities as follows:

- Polemicist   A versus B
- Semanticist   A and B are really the same thing
- Monist   A. There is no B.
- Skepticist   Neither A nor B
- Eclecticist   Both A and B
- Methodological pluralism   A ← ? → B

What does it mean to put alternatives A and B into dialogue? Perhaps it might help to offer a concrete example where dialogue would have served the interests of science.

The evolution of scientific knowledge toward dialogue

Several of the possible responses listed by Levine will seem at first glance to intend that as a result of scholarship, scientists should arrive at some conclusion, declare it to be true, and move on to other matters. The so-called pursuit of knowledge would have as its purpose reliable answers (Rauch, 2021), in much the same way that astronomers kept approximating the model of our solar system as heliocentric in which the earth moves in two ways: rotating on an axis and orbiting around the sun. It certainly took a long time for scientists to get there, and the reason for many of these delays was that scientific knowledge does not expand in a linear progression, from one point to the next. It evolves, and that is a very different process.

Arthur Koestler told this story beautifully in *The Sleepwalkers* (1959). It is no accident that, as Koestler lamented, time and time again the titans of science failed to confer with one another. They quarreled and spurned and abused one another. Toward what end? If they had simply talked openly, sharing their knowledge and opinions, they would have made swift progress, without so many blind alleys and loose ends. Instead, they let

---

it does console the mind to believe in some unifying absolute. Congruent with Levine's emphasis on dialogue, James remarked, "Compromise and mediation are inseparable from the pluralistic philosophy (p. 313)."

The term pluralism has other meanings as well as plenty of other champions, such as Isaiah Berlin (see Kocis, 2022, introduction).

language, politics, religion, and personality get in the way.[2] Furthermore, they also tended to avoid consulting the reality they were trying to understand. They held on to prejudices and traditions that turned out to be completely at odds with observable facts, as for example, insisting that when heavenly bodies orbit one another, they must travel in circles. They do not do so, as it happens, but for the longest time, scholars refused to believe it. In other words, not only should these men have practiced dialogue with one another, he wrote, but they should also have been on speaking terms with the universe.

At one point, Koestler stated that the mind can split, believing two or more incompatible things. This is not so unusual. A scientist can operate as though the heliocentric model is somehow true, while also adhering to church teachings that would indicate otherwise.[3] Science and theology can diverge, even in the same individual person's mind. Once they diverge, each can (in his words) "develop autonomously by inbreeding, cut off from the balancing influence of [the other] (1959, p. 106)."[4] For Koestler, individuals as well as humanity writ large must periodically examine these divergences and see if they can be integrated somehow. This was the genius of Pythagoras, Koestler thought, whose quest for a unifying vision concentrated less on the pieces of the puzzle and more on the interrelationships among them (1959, p. 27ff).[5]

Part of what prevented greater collaboration among the learned men who studied the sky after Ptolemy was that they often missed what was truly revolutionary in what the other was saying. Kepler and Galileo understood that Copernicus was moving toward a heliocentric model of the solar system (which had been proposed hundreds of years before, among the Greeks), but they regrettably neglected what made his model so revolutionary. Not only did his model expand the map of the universe

---

2 Koestler acknowledged the commendable counterexample of the Royal Society hoping to make sense of Isaac Newton's research (1959, p. 510). Here was a group of experts willing and able to make sense together of Newton's breakthroughs.

3 A more concrete example comes from Michel Serres (2018), who pointed out that scientists must conduct their research using the metric system, yet in many of their cultures, they must then use "miles, gallons, and ounces" when they stop at the grocery store on the way home from work (p. 218).

4 The same is true among academic disciplines, by the way, ensiled into departments with their own separate journals, their own conferences, their own textbooks, their own intellectual heroes, their own laboratories. Each one creates a kind of echo chamber and closes itself off from everything else.

5 Koestler wrote that a diseased state "is characterized by a weakening of the integrative controls, and the tendency of its parts to behave in an independent and self-assertive manner, ignoring the superior interest of the whole, or trying to impose their own laws on it (1959, p. 527)." The imagery of a cancer comes to mind.

toward infinity, wrote Koestler, but it also decentralized it radically (1959, p. 221). He had opened the way to a vast new space – a limitless theater of phenomena – that has no center whatsoever anywhere. Kepler and Galileo were not prepared for that news. They apparently had enough trouble with the heliocentric model itself.

Yet Koestler suspected that the primary culprit in keeping great minds apart was a very old nemesis and quite mundane: Ego. He wrote that resistance to innovations in science comes *not* from the untutored masses who fail to comprehend what is being said. Instead, the problem lies *with other experts* who should know better, representatives of the status quo, gatekeepers, those who are the ones who feel threatened by the implication that they are somehow mistaken (1959, p. 433). Nobody who went to graduate school, published articles in peer-reviewed journals, and taught hundreds of students with institutional legitimacy wants to accept that they might be wrong.[6] And yet the possibility of being wrong lies at the heart of the scientific process. It even has a name: Fallibilism (see Reed, 2022; Peirce, 1955).[7]

Just to cite one recent example from the *Journal of Organizational Behavior*, Kelemen et al. in February of 2023 identified three core dimensions of something they refer to as **humble leadership**. These core dimensions are (1) a willingness to view oneself accurately, (2) a displayed appreciation of others' strengths and contributions, and (3) teachability. The authors were not saying that followers fail to demonstrate the same three dimensions. Both leaders and followers can be humble. Furthermore, they were not saying that all leaders are humble. By no means is that the case – not by a long shot. In the real world, even those identified as humble might lapse every once in a while, so that even the humblest leader can stumble. Nevertheless, to the extent that a leader is willing to view oneself accurately, displays appreciation for others, and proves to be teachable, then we can say that we are in the presence of humble leadership. What then

---

6 Richard McKeon wrote that dialogue occurs when "two or more speakers or two or more positions are brought into relations in which it becomes apparent that each position is incomplete and inconclusive unless assimilated to a higher truth (1990b, p. 106)." He explained, "There have been philosophers…who argue that…plausible arguments can be found to support the contradictory of any proposition or doctrine; dialogue explores the plurality of positions, and it is transformed into controversy by dogmatisms which must therefore be refuted (1990b, p. 104)." Later in the same essay, McKeon wrote, "Dialogue is interrupted in controversy only by dogmatisms which refuse to submit opinions about ultimate reality or the compelling evidence of experience or thought to the test of other opinions and hypotheses (1990b, p. 121)."

7 Ilana Redstone (2022) calls the alternative the Certainty Trap, defined as "a resolute unwillingness to consider the possibility that we might not be right or might not be right in the way that we think we are (p. 92)."

did Kelemen et al. subsequently show about this construct? A literature search shows that for the most part the effects of humble leadership are positive. (Note the qualifying language of "for the most part.") With due reticence, then, they subsequently catalogued some of the limitations in this body of research and recommended future directions to explain more fully what the phrase even means, how it works, and what it is likely to do for organizations. In other words, they scrupulously avoided making dogmatic claims, drawing a bright line, and then associating humble leadership exclusively with certain dimensions. They humbly suggested that with sufficient care the distinction might ultimately yield useful results. Such humility reflects well on these scholars and also models fallibilism.

For many reasons, scholarship has not progressed in a linear fashion, relentlessly upward. Instead, it evolved. Progress and evolution are two different ideas. Evolution has proven to be a sloppy process, without any apparent direction. Koestler wrote that "'evolution' is known to be a wasteful, fumbling process characterized by sudden mutations of unknown cause, by the slow grinding of selection, and by the dead-ends of over-specialization and rigid inadaptability (1959, p. 525)." Best if those of us who study the same phenomenon, such as leadership, actually talked with one another regularly, helping one another to add knowledge, clarify language, and avoid vehemence. The evolution of our understanding does not have to be so blind and chaotic.[8]

By the same token, there is a risk when experts collaborate. As a group, they increasingly resist criticism from the outside. They form themselves around dogma. They draw a boundary. They close in upon themselves in what Koestler referred to as intellectual in-breeding. In the same way that individuals close themselves off from conflict, becoming oblivious, hardening their beliefs, a group can become isolated from fresh ideas, contrary evidence, and the discouraging word. We call this phenomenon **Group-think**. Because of this tendency, after a period of time somebody will have to blow the whole thing up. Koestler wrote about the recurring need for somebody to enter the lists ready to challenge the status quo, even the sacred cows, and instead consider alternative frameworks. He wrote:

This operation of removing a problem from its traditional context and placing it into a new one, looking at it through glasses of a different colour as it were, has always seemed to me of the very essence of the

---

8 Christopher Watkin (2020) wrote, vis-à-vis evolution: "The sort of changes to the species that previously required many thousands of years and the costly process of natural selection can now be consciously engineered and accomplished in decades or even months… (p. 364, citing Michel Serres's *Hominescence*; see also Serres, 2018)."

creative process. It leads not only to a revaluation of the problem itself, but often to a synthesis of much wider consequences, brought about by a fusion of the two previously unrelated frames of reference.

(1959, p. 341)

Dialogue can create cohesiveness among participants, yes, which can morph into groupthink, if we are not careful.

Challenges to umbilical thinking

Another theorist who recognized the risk of groupthink among scholars was Michel Serres. He dedicated his career to fighting what he called umbilical thinking. **Umbilical thinking** imagines that there exists some fundamental, unifying principle or discourse out of which all other human understanding derives (Watkin, 2020, p. 39). That fundamental, unifying principle or discourse – whatever it is -- links humanity with reality by a single cord, hence the metaphor.[9] One might predict that Serres had made it his mission to refute those who operate with umbilical thinking, proving that they are mistaken. Often, academic squabbles consist of such competitions, whereby scholars contend that we should swap out somebody else's umbilical thinking for one of their own. Serres was not interested in polemics of this sort. He used a different method. He demonstrated that there are other pathways to the same outcome, different viable possibilities. You do not have to be wrong for me to be right. We can get where we are going by alternate routes. So it is unnecessary to judge another person's "umbilical." What you are judging is the need to insist that there is only one. Serres once wrote, "No solution constitutes the only solution: neither a particular religion, nor a particular politics, nor a particular science (Watkin, 2020, p. 89, quoting *The Troubadour of Knowledge*)."[10]

---

9 David Foster Wallace made a similar point in his famous commencement address at Kenyon College in 2005 titled "This is Water" (2009), where he said, "[T]he exact same experience can mean two totally different things to two different people, given those people's two different belief templates and two different ways of constructing meaning from experience. Because we prize tolerance and diversity of belief, nowhere in our liberal arts analysis do we want to claim that one guy's interpretation is true and the other guy's is false or bad...." And yet the problem lies more so in "blind certainty, a close-mindedness that amounts to an imprisonment so total that the prisoner doesn't even know he's locked up." Having different opinions can be fine. Insisting too strenuously on your own, however, might be going too far.

10 Methodological pluralism, as I am describing it here with regard to Serres's opposition to umbilical thinking, will resemble enumerative combinatorics in mathematics and certain methods of construct validation in psychology by which alternatives can be judged to be equivalent (Peterson & Lindsay, 2023).

It is interesting how Serres does this. He takes two seemingly unrelated things and reveals an interrelationship between them (Watkin, 2020, p. 47). Despite appearances, they are actually alike somehow. Or they rely on the same precept (e.g. water and air both exhibit similar turbulent dynamics). Or one is a dilation, at one magnitude of the other at a different magnitude (the solar system resembles the structure of an atom). One doesn't *deny* the umbilical claim; one *multiplies* the possible paradigms that can be used to explain it (2020, p. 57). Instead of saying "you are wrong," one can say, "Here's another way to look at things." It is not, as Watkin calls it, an opposition by negation but an opposition by generalization (2020, p. 72). Systems thinking calls this **equifinality**, which means that there can be more than one way to achieve the same result. Rather than puncturing another person's balloon, therefore, I simply add more balloons to the bouquet.

There is only one reality. Serres would not deny it. Yet that reality is a web of symbiosis, multiple interdependent parts going this way and that. He often used the word "**multiplicity**" – reality is a multiplicity comprised of multiplicities. Any unity that we as humans recognize is constructed by the mind to explain how anything moves around among the multiplicities. A **unity** is a human convenience, a heuristic. Any unity, such as a body, a planet, or a house, can be treated as a form or pattern that helps us manage our understanding of a complex world. That is, *we think* in terms of unities. And most of the time, we should.

From the outset, for example, scholars in our field of study originally regarded the leader as a unity, a whole. We studied them as though they were specimens. We read their biographies. We gazed at their portraits. We tried to identify their traits and behaviors. Leadership Studies began as a **leader-centric** activity. Only with time did we acknowledge that no leader exists in a vacuum. A leader is a leader only because of a relationship with followers. In this way, we pushed outward from the individual person to relationships, groups, organizations, and society, which is to say toward larger unities. That was a wholesome development, expanding the investigations outward.

We also pushed inward, recognizing that the leader is a composite of many things – of hopes and fears, knowledge and wishes, thoughts and feelings. A leader is fundamentally a multiplicity, often riddled with contradictions (see Serres, 2018, pp. 39–85). The fact that leadership as a process explains unities out there in social reality is a testimonial to the power of the human imagination to "see" the world in new ways. The unity we in Leadership Studies want to be able to explain – whatever it is, a new hospital or a basketball team or an orchestra – is a temporary structure built first in the minds of participants. It is the emergence of a unity comprised of countless multiplicities. How remarkable is it that radically segmented beings in a radically segmented world can gather to bring about a unity! Leadership studies exists to discover how that happens at the interpersonal level.

One remarkable application of this idea that leadership results from more of a multiplicity comes from the collective decision-making research of Iain Couzin, 2022 recipient of the Leibniz Prize, who relies on studying biological systems such as flocks, herds, swarms, and schools of fish – not only animal behavior, but then also immersive virtual reality and machine learning. He tracks collective behavior to discern what he refers to as a geometry of decision-making (see e.g. Couzin et al., 2005; see also Dyer et al., 2009). Derek and Laura Cabrera (2015) use the example of many fish swimming together that resemble a much larger fish in order to deter aggression -- a multiplicity assembled to constitute a unity.

In summary, according to Koestler, breakthroughs in science depend on routinely seeing reality in new ways. According to Serres, then, there is in principle an infinity of ways to see reality. None is umbilical, but many are useful. The fault lies in limiting yourself to only one. Except....

You can't say everything about anything: A phenomenological tactic

Except that, of course, one must limit oneself temporarily, provisionally, for limited purposes (Plochmann, 1990, p. 83f). Nobody can comprehend reality in all its fullness simultaneously. Like whiteness, you could discern nothing when you try to see it all in every conceivable way, without any shadows. White is white. As Watkin put it, "Not only can no discourse say everything about everything, no discourse can say everything about anything (2020, p. 120)." To adopt one of Serres's metaphors, white is not a color; neither is it the absence of color. It is the combination of all of the colors (2020, p. 86). Serres acknowledged the whiteness. The human mind needs at least some chiaroscuro to make sense of reality. It requires both the shadow and the light. How is this done?

In order to begin making sense of any multiplicity – especially one so unruly as the processes of social change – a scholar must draw **distinctions**. THIS is not THAT. The underlying reality of course is entire, interconnected, blurring incessantly. So the scholar must start from a stop position and make some distinctions (see Collinson, 2014). Systems thinking, to cite one example, sets apart the system from its environment (Cabrera & Cabrera, 2015). The physician examines the patient out of his or her context, removed from the conditions where the patient lives. The artist paints the landscape without depicting the crisscrossing electrical wires one can plainly see with the naked eye. By paying attention to one thing, a person must ignore everything else. Temporarily, you have to forget about the rest. Philosophers call this procedure "bracketing," setting aside what you know to be out there, in order to focus on one thing at a time (see Beyer, 2022; see Serres, 2018, p. 33). One might think of this as a limitation of the human mind, or what Herbert Simon (2000) referred to as **bounded rationality**. Neuroscience is slowly validating this insight, disproving for instance the fiction known as multitasking.

There is even a symbol in logic to denote the process of making distinctions. It looks like this: System $\neg$ Environment. The symbol "$\neg$" indicates which part of reality is about to be considered (system) and everything else that will have been suspended, held tacitly (environment) (see Luhmann, 2013). The item on the left will be the focus of this study. The item on the right will be held in abeyance. The symbol suggests that the focus now will be on the near side of the boundary, on the system (2013, p. 47). As a practice, then, "we must always indicate to which side of the distinction we are referring (2013, p. 146)." To make a distinction of any kind is to identify a plurality, an inside and an outside, a this-but-not-that, such that what appears on the left hand side of the symbol will occupy our attention for the time being. We might say that we are temporarily bracketing everything to the right. We recognize that something is over there, outside the system, and it is certainly important, but we must get back to it later. Right now, we pay attention to whatever appears on the left of that symbol, i.e. the system. As Luhmann stated, "When handling a distinction, you always have a blind spot or something invisible behind your back (2013, p. 104)." Dirk Baecker (2015) put it this way: "observe the mark 'a' [on the left] in the context of its distinction from something indeterminate, basically from all that is 'not a' (p. 2)." When mapping systems, the portion on the right is represented by a cloud.

If I am interested in learning to play the piano, I might represent it in this way: piano $\neg$ music. I cannot truly master the piano and ignore the broader topic of music, such as compositional notation and genres, but in order to acquire a rudimentary awareness, I must do so in steps. Creating the distinction is a way of managing one's energy. Yes, I *could be* studying composition, and I probably *should* do so at some point, but I'm not doing that yet. Right now, I am concentrating on the gross mechanics of striking a keyboard with my fingers.

By definition, specialization means making and adhering to certain distinctions. The nephrologists and hepatologists among us concentrate on different, though related, bodily functions. They have to. It requires years of training just to master one specialty. And so, by a division of labor, we expect most people to specialize. After all, we did the same thing in school, turning our attention to grammar for an hour, then arithmetic for an hour, then civics for an hour, as though these were distinct topics … because they are distinct topics. The sequencing of such topics is artificial, but we need such an approach to accommodate our limited capabilities (pace John Dewey). Specialization is simply a more elaborate and sustained attempt to direct one's powers onto one and only one thing at a time.

If you will indulge me in this recollection: my mother had a little tin where she tossed hundreds of buttons of various kinds in anticipation of future sewing projects. If you were to dump the buttons out onto a table, as I sometimes did, you would see a mixed-up pile of varied objects. Going forward, you could sort by color, size, or shape. It is the same pile of buttons, mind you, but it can be sorted in different ways. For instance, suppose you are looking for a red button. Red buttons ⌐ Non-red buttons. Suppose you are looking for round buttons. Round buttons ⌐ Non-round buttons. In effect, you can draw your distinctions in a variety of ways, depending on your purpose. One reality from multiple points of view.

Think of a deck of playing cards. They can be sorted by color (red or black) or suit (spades, clubs, diamonds, and hearts) or number (Ace, 2, 3, 4…). They can be arrayed in rank order, or you can set aside only face cards (king, queen, jack). Maybe the game you are playing has trump. It pays to notice the trump card! And this is not to ignore the distinction between the front and back of the cards. One reality, multiple ways to make distinctions.

As a community of scholars, we engage in such pivots, swinging that symbol " ⌐ " incessantly, like so many lenses.

The necessity of using analogies

Philippe Descola wrote a wonderful treatise on anthropology, translated into English in 2013. In its pages, Descola schematizes four distinct worldviews possessed by various peoples throughout the world. Each of these four worldviews has implications for practice. It is not surprising that people with one worldview cannot always understand people from another worldview. This does not prevent them from interacting periodically for limited purposes. But part of Descola's message was that anthropologists specifically must become aware of all four and conduct their investigations accordingly. None of the worldviews is necessarily correct in some abstract sense. They are simply different. As he wrote, only in our eyes as human beings are they differentiated (2013, p. 77). The structure by which we understand the world does not inhere in reality itself (2013, p. 98). There are multiple ways to taxonomize reality (2013, p. 240). Nevertheless, here are Descola's four worldviews.

- **Animism**, which holds that unities in reality have dissimilar physicalities (bodies, appearances) yet similar interiorities (2013, ch. 6).
- **Totemism**, which holds that unities in reality have similar physicalities and similar interiorities (2013, ch. 7).
- **Naturalism**, which holds that unities have dissimilar interiorities and similar physicalities (2013, ch. 8).
- **Analogism**, which holds that unities have dissimilar physicalities and dissimilar interiorities (2013, ch. 9).

Chapter 7 in my book will examine analogism more closely, but we can look at it briefly here. Descola argued that analogism dominated the European Renaissance (2013, p. 300).[11] According to analogism, the world is constructed of a range of beings, separable in discernible ways. Even within categories, such as humanity, no two persons are alike. Descola wrote that anyone who subscribes to this worldview "divides up the whole collection of existing beings into a multiplicity of essences, forms, and substances separated by small distinctions and sometimes arranged on a graduated scale... (2013, p. 201)." The best one can hope for when dealing with the world is to make analogies, which holds that to some extent two things are similar. Not identical, but similar. We cannot function unless we find resemblances. Descola wrote, "A world saturated with singularities is almost inconceivable and is in any case extremely inhospitable (2013, p. 235)."[12] For instance, according to some Renaissance thinkers, a person's soul can share traits with certain chemicals, animals, or weather. Resemblance, yes, but no identity. "The only thing that really counts in an analogical collective...is to integrate within an apparently homogeneous whole a host of singularities that are inclined to fragment spontaneously (2013, p. 401)."[13] It is still the case that according to analogism no two

---

11 Watkin points out that Serres borrowed this worldview directly from Descola (2020, pp. 106–108).
12 Friedrich Nietzsche once remarked that proceeding in this fashion is unhelpful. He wrote, "He who wants to mediate between two resolute thinkers shows that he is mediocre: he has no eye for the unique; seeing things as similar and making things the same is the sign of weak eyes (2001, no. 228)." But this is precisely what Serres hoped to avoid. He said there are no identities, yet there are similarities that on occasion reflect some shared principle at work.
13 Serres objected to the usage of "identity" as a social construct for precisely this reason. Identity means that two things – especially two persons – are literally the same, identical. They aren't in reality, however, and never can be. For purposes of social organization,

things are ever identical. The challenge lies in bringing and keeping them together somehow regardless, which is of course a leadership function.

Descola presented a tidy schema of four worldviews and then complicated his book's lesson by reinforcing the idea that one can adopt multiple paradigms in the investigation of a single reality when he wrote that not only can a researcher subdivide his or her subject matter in anthropology by tribe or worldview, but also a researcher can subdivide the experience of any single tribe or worldview *across time* (2013, ch. 15). One of his examples is the process of domesticating wild animals (2013, pp. 377–386). At one time, a people did not have pets. Then they did. Historical analysis would be a different framework, because we know that whatever one discovers about a community at a given point in time, it wasn't always thus. In conclusion, Descola showed that none of these paradigms (by tribe, by worldview, by historical era) is necessarily wrong, mistaken, obsolete, or lame. They are simply different.

It is a fact that scholars in Leadership Studies operate from competing paradigms or worldviews (Goethals & Sorenson, 2007). One scholar investigates a leader's traits. Another investigates Leader-Follower relations. Yet another scrutinizes the impact of urgency on leadership tactics. In principle there is probably an infinity of ways to slice the watermelon, i.e. to make distinctions and then investigate one facet of the complex whole – not pretending that the rest does not exist, but stowing it for the time being, leaving it off to one side. One scholar writes about women in leadership, while another one conducts historical research regarding colonial Ecuador. Each of them draws the line differently, depending on his or her interests. It makes absolutely no sense for me to tell one of them they are mistaken in making the distinction where they did, that only my distinction is the correct distinction. We are all merely investigating different questions.

Watkin wrote this: "The problem is that we have accepted the premise that we need to draw a line anywhere… (2020, p. 256)." But then of course we do, for the time being, for the duration of our study, long enough to grasp the lesson. Line drawing is only a problem if we insist that the line is real, persist in using it, and otherwise stop thinking about it. Let us call this process the poor man's *epoché*.

---

he preferred to speak in terms of belongingness (2018, pp. 71–85). My race, ethnicity, religion, age, and so forth might form my "identity," but I *belong to* a race, an ethnicity, a religion, and age group. I am not identical with everybody in these groupings. Not all white folks are alike, just as not all Lutherans are alike. One can belong without being identical.

One of the most articulate champions of the approach I am describing was Michael Polanyi (2009), who wrote about the relationship between that which is tacit (kept in the background temporarily, subsidiary) and that which is focal (where one pays attention). Let me illustrate how this works. (I mentioned how this works briefly in the introduction to this book.) When shining a flashlight around a dark room, the beam falls on the focal, going this way and that; but what had been seen moments before can and must be integrated in one's mind to construct an internal map, as it were, of the whole room. Looking at what the flashlight reveals is the point of using the flashlight, though it accomplishes very little if you cannot fit what you see with everything else you know about the room. The purpose is to keep moving the flashlight. Esther Lightcap Meek has since given a name to this epistemic process – a name for it that I have embraced: **Subsidiary-Focal Integration** (SFI) (2014).

This incessant swivel can make a person dizzy. And to be fair, without that integration step, Leadership Studies can look pretty scattered, random: first this, then that, then some other fool thing over there. Toward what end? It is my contention that scholars are meant to pivot, again and again and again.[14] What I am urging onto my peers in these pages is that intermediate, liminal phase between normal science and the proverbial paradigm shift, when a scholar steps back from the disciplined scrutiny of some phenomenon, which will have been necessary, to be sure, and suddenly sees the world holistically, wondering how it all fits together. Heidegger (2018) called it **inceptual thinking,** paying attention to the originating reality on which everything is based. Such a moment is radical in the etymological sense of the word: it is the root of all else. As Heidegger wrote, the seed is in the sprouting and the flower is in the blooming. Can we as scholars of leadership attain such a simple vision? Jacques Derrida (1966) suggested a version of this move as **freeplay,** in which the structure's foundation can be questioned, leaving none in its place. It is the space between one structure and conceiving its successor. We might say that momentarily our minds are de-differentiated. Then do the same thing all over again with a different frame.

---

14 I would contend that this is what Eric Voegelin and Michel Foucault did at critical points in their career. They did not have to disavow what they had previously written; they simply decided to pivot away toward a different framework for thinking. It would not be difficult to name others who have done the same thing.

The dangers of abstractive dichotomies

A common tactic in Leadership Studies is to make a distinction and then explain how the two things are different.

- "A leader is not a follower, and here's why…."
- "A transactional leader is not a transformational leader, and here's why…."
- "An ethical leader is not an unethical leader, and here's why…."

But the reality is such that sometimes the leader is a follower and vice versa. Sometimes, a transactional leader is a transformational leader. Sometimes, an ethical leader is unethical. The distinction is conceptual and not actual.

Examples of such distinctions abound in the literature pertinent to leadership. One person contends that leadership is good, then somebody else points out when leadership is bad. One person contends that transformational leadership is effective, then somebody points out when it is not. Such counterexamples reduce the impact of the original assertion; they do not nullify what the original author was trying to say, not completely. But they challenge the idea that what supposedly differentiates one thing from another requires clarification or is not always true. After decades of challenging one another's distinctions, we fall back to the far more defensible posture that one thing is *more likely* than another. These assertions about leadership in our published articles are really about probability, because exceptions do abound. Nevertheless, we can do more to problematize any proposed dichotomy than simply cite counterexamples.

What does this mean? For instance, after differentiating A from B, did we omit something? It becomes relatively easy to ask this question in the presence of two extreme, polar positions in society such as rich and poor; this dichotomy overlooks the entire middle class! So of course, a binary distinction might omit intermediate layers between the two. One can often find the gray area between black and white. That is another way to challenge a given distinction. Maybe it is not a distinction at all; maybe it is a **dimension**.

Yet another way to challenge a distinction is to look at some particular bipolar model and ask whether we may have forgotten *a third pole* (Watkin, 2020, p. 308, citing *The Parasite*; see also Watkin, 2020, pp. 384–387; see Plochmann, 1990, p. 64). Between Leaders and Followers, for instance, have we failed to acknowledge some relevant third party, such as a witness, journalist, or historian (Harter, 2012)? Not everything can be reduced to two and only two alternatives.

I would add a word of caution about making all of these distinctions, even those that tell us something useful. Beyond a certain point, as scholars we will subdivide our labors and just stop talking to one another. In much the same way that voters retreat into competing camps, we have a tendency to cluster and forego dialogue outside our chosen circle. Christian scholars, feminist scholars, woke scholars, military scholars – it is not just that we gravitate into academic disciplines; it makes sense that individuals with a shared interest will seek one another out and create panels, if not entire conferences, around their commonalities. And the rest of us who are not conversant with the nuances and the literature probably stay away and opt for other outlets. These clusters obviously exist. They inform the mission of certain journals and associations. Not only do these various clusters gradually harden, becoming increasingly remote from one another, but the process of subdividing continues into smaller and more specialized factions so that the entire field of study splinters into marginal sects.

Aside from the understandable motivation to cluster with like-minded others who understand and reinforce one another, I have noticed that hiring committees and tenure committees expect each candidate to articulate a coherent narrative about his or her research. There seems to be an assumption that scholars need to stick with their tribe. Perhaps it is because we just need to know how to label one another. Oh, we say brightly, you are the I/O expert, the DEI expert, the historian. Or perhaps those of us on these important committees assume that you can't be very impactful *unless* you specialize. Many years ago when I came up through the ranks, however, I could not integrate the various topics that animated me. My oeuvre was all over the place, because I just kept swinging on that pivot, from topic to topic, so that now I belong to no tribe, no community, no alliance – spinning in empty air.

Every now and then, scholars in Leadership Studies ought to commit to open-ended dialogue in a spirit of methodological pluralism, not to find out who is doing things wrong and certainly not to win converts to our dogma, but to help one another see the phenomenon whole, to the extent that we can, and maybe in the interstices discover ways to collaborate. None of which is to suggest that there is no such thing as reality as the rock-solid arbiter, for that must be part of methodological pluralism. One cannot belong to Leadership Studies and at the same time speak of "my truth" and "your truth." In fact, it is my position that dialogue pays greater respect to a very big, very complex reality that we are each trying to comprehend as best we can, from our many points of view.

The word "theory" derives from the same word for "theater" – a way of seeing, a perspective. And we in Leadership Studies have so many of these viewpoints now! My contention is that it constitutes theory work to bring them together somehow. And that, I am insisting, is a legitimate type of scholarship.

References

Baecker, D. (2015 June 14). "Working the form: George Spencer-Brown and the mark of distinction." *Mousse Magazine*. Retrieved 6 February 2023 from https://ssrn.com/abstract=2618146.

Beyer, C. "Edmund Husserl." In Zalta, E. & U. Nodelman (eds.) (2022, Winter). *The Stanford encyclopedia of philosophy*. Retrieved 30 May 2023 from https://plato.stanford.edu/archives/win2022/entries/husserl/.

Cabrera, D., & Cabrera, L. (2015). *Systems thinking made simple: New hope for solving wicked problems*. Plectica Publishing.

Collinson, D. (2014). "Dichotomies, dialectics and dilemmas: New directions for critical leadership studies?" *Leadership*. 10(1): 36–55.

Couzin, I.D., Krause, J., Franks, N.R., & Levin, S.A. (2005). "Effective leadership and decision-making in animal groups on the move." *Nature*. 433(7025): 513–516.

Derrida, J. (1966). *Writing and difference* (A. Bass, trans.) (pp. 278–294). Routledge.

Descola, P. (2013). *Beyond nature and culture* (J. Lloyd, trans.). University of Chicago Press.

Dyer, J.R.G., Johansson, A., Helbing, D., Couzin, I.D., & Krause, J. (2009). "Leadership, consensus decision making and collective behaviour in human crowds." *Philosophical Transactions of the Royal Society of London, Series B.* 364(1518): 781–778.

Goethals, G.R., & Sorenson, G.J. (eds.) (2007). *The quest for a general theory of leadership*. Edward Elgar Publishing.

Harter, N. (2012, Summer). "Point of view: Leadership studies from different perspectives." *Journal of Leadership Education*. 11(2): 158–174.

Harvey, M., & Riggio, R. (eds.) (2012). *Leadership studies: The dialogue of disciplines*. Edward Elgar.

Heidegger, M. (2018). *Heraclitus* (J.G. Assaiante & S.M. Ewegen, trans.). Bloomsbury Academic.

James, W. (1909). *A pluralistic universe: Hilbert lectures at Manchester College*. University of Nebraska Press.

Kelemen, T., Matthews, S., Matthews, M., & Henry, S. (2023, February). "Humble leadership: A review and synthesis of leader expressed humility." *Journal of Organizational Behavior*. 44(2): 202–224.

Kocis, R. (2022). *Isaiah Berlin: A Kantian and post-idealist thinker*. University of Wales Press.

Koestler, A. (1959). *The sleepwalkers: A history of man's changing vision of the universe*. Penguin.

Levine, D. (2018). *Dialogical social theory* (H. Schneiderman, ed.). Routledge.

Levine, D. (2015). *Social theory as a vocation: Genres of theory work in sociology*. Transaction Publishers.

Luhmann, N. (2013). *Introduction to systems theory* (P. Gilgen, trans.). Polity.

McKeon, R. (1990b). *Freedom and history and other essays*. University of Chicago Press.

Meek, E.L. (2014). *A little manual for knowing*. Cascade Books.

Nietzsche, F. (2001). *The gay science* (J. Nauckhoff, trans.). Cambridge University Press.

Peirce, C.S. (1955). *Philosophical writings of Peirce* (J. Buchler, ed.) (ch. 3). Dover.

Peterson, J., & Lindsay, J. (2023). "Marxism, religion & everything in between." *Daily Wire*. Retrieved on 9 July 2023 from https://www.youtube.com/watch?v=bnrdyphape4.

Plochmann, G.K. (1990). *Richard McKeon: A study*. University of Chicago Press.

Polanyi, M. (2009). *The tacit dimension*. University of Chicago Press.

Rauch, J. (2021). *The constitution of knowledge: A defense of truth*. Brookings Institution Press.

Redstone, I. (2022, Summer). "Breaking out of the certainty trap." *Sapir*. 6: 90–99.

Reed, B. "Certainty." In E. Zalta (ed.) (2022). *The Stanford encyclopedia of philosophy*. Retrieved 16 May 2023 from https://plato.stanford.edu/archives/spr2022/entries/certainty/.

Serres, M. (2018). *The incandescent* (R. Burks, trans.). Bloomsbury Academic.

Simon, H.A. (2000). "Bounded rationality in social science: Today and tomorrow." *Mind & Society*. 1(1): 25–39.

Wallace, D.F. (2009). *This is water: Some thoughts, delivered on a significant occasion, about living a compassionate life*. Hachette UK.

Watkin, C. (2020). *Michel Serres: Figures of thought*. Edinburgh University Press.

2

LIMITS OF TIME IN THE INVESTIGATION OF LEADERSHIP

The present moment and the *longue durée*

Caesar at the Rubicon

A man stands gazing down at a stream. He is accompanied by close advisors, though nobody speaks. Behind them, stretching for miles, columns of soldiers have come to a standstill. Amid the vexilla rippling in the breeze, the flags and banners of a Roman Legion on the march, golden Aquila, the Eagle itself, catches the morning sunlight. What happens next would have enormous consequences for Julius Caesar, for the Republic, and for Western history, and this man knows it. Every man in his company knows it.

The Rubicon was a relatively insignificant watercourse separating Rome from the territory of Gaul. It was a symbolic boundary, easy to cross. The law of the time provided that a military commander returning home must lay down the imperium and command before entering. Otherwise, to lead troops into the homeland was a capital offense – not only for the commander but also for any soldier who accompanied him. Crossing at the head of an army in this fashion precipitated civil war. Caesar hesitated to break the law, being greatly troubled by the implications; yet eventually on a date in January 49 BCE he said aloud to his men, "The die is cast (ālea iacta est)." And with that, he took the river.

Now, let us pause for a moment as Caesar stands there on the far side of the border, uncertain whether to advance. He was struggling in his own mind, without speaking to anyone. We can presume that the rest of them were waiting silently, expectantly, with a fair degree of anxiety. They had reached the hinge of history. Nothing would be the same. The republic would likely plunge into chaos, Caesar himself would be assassinated for

DOI: 10.4324/9781003540526-3

his brazen act, and the conflict would finally resolve itself for hundreds of years as an empire that encompassed most of Europe, as well as northern Africa and the Near East.

In that silent tableau, when nobody but fidgeting horses moved, while the water babbled and the breezes blew, clearly something implicating leadership was afoot. Nevertheless, no scholar could say that, empirically, for the duration of such a caesura, leadership was taking place. Leadership is widely regarded as a process that requires the passage of time; it has a temporal dimension. It strains credulity to say that such a pause, like the freezeframe in a film, gives evidence of leadership. Yet something of real significance, beyond observing, is indeed happening. All that the conscientious historian can do with such a scene is wait, like the restless subordinates on horseback, waiting for the die to be cast and Caesar leaps ahead.

For purposes of gaining perspective, let us now take a giant step back, finding ourselves at a vantage point from which we can observe the Big Bang and all of the subsequent tumult that brought us to the present day, not unlike a time-lapse film that makes the action seem much faster. From this vantage point, almost a God-like perspective, we are witness to creation. Balls of fire burst in every direction like projectiles, as the boundaries of creation expand. Many of them swirl together into clusters we know as galaxies. Planets, meteors, and comets careen into the darkness. If we could compress all of time into a 30 minute drama, so that the universe reaches its present configuration – all of time, that is, in half an hour – nobody would notice the occurrence of leadership. The time scale is simply too fast and too vast for the exertions of anybody on little earth to register. Even the greatest episode of leadership in human history would escape detection. Here at the outer extremes of time, involving the sum total of every discrete moment since the very beginning, a leadership scholar has nothing perceptible to work with. The only proper response is to stand mute. Leadership is just so microscopically brief and puny by comparison.

The renowned historian Arnold Toynbee once made the following comment:

> Our modern Western physical science tells us that the human race has been in existence on this planet for at least 600,000 or perhaps a million years, life for at least 500 million and perhaps 800 million years, and the planet itself for possibly 2000 million years. On this time scale [Toynbee continued] the last five or six thousand years that have seen the births of civilizations, and the last three or four thousand years that have seen the births of higher religions are periods of such infinitesimal brevity that it would be impossible to show them, drawn to scale, on any chart of the whole history of this planet up to date.
>
> *(1948, p. 36f)*

Leadership occurs within a range of time, beyond which even to speak of leadership seems to be a mistake. Leadership has a distinct duration – neither too abrupt nor too gradual. Too abrupt, and the occurrence cannot be said to have fulfilled the definition. The attempt hasn't played out. Too gradual, though, and so many other influences intrude like crosswinds, confusing what in fact the leader can be credited with accomplishing. The causal thread becomes just too attenuated. One likely term for this unit of analysis, between too short and too long, is an "episode." Leadership consists of episodes. Our powers to understand leadership diminish the further one gets outside the range of an episode. Leaders stand between two boundaries. And at the limits of our power to investigate are these horizons, the isolated moment on the one hand (with Caesar at the Rubicon) and the entirety of history on the other (that 30 minute drama of cosmic creation).

Operating within a range that is less than everything

Of course, scientists have had to operate within a certain "range" for centuries. Our eyes, for example, can see only the visible spectrum, and neither infrared nor ultraviolet (see Dawkins, 1991). In time, human beings could develop tools such as telescopes and microscopes to see what was otherwise invisible to the naked eye. Maurice Merleau-Ponty once said that "there are no intrinsic limits to the process of observation: we could always envisage that it might be more thorough or more exact than it is at any given moment (1948/2004, p. 44)." Nevertheless, this passage accepts that no matter how sophisticated our science becomes, in principle there is always more to see, more to hear, more to access. The scientist operates within a range, even if that range can be made to expand.

To illustrate, consider the sense of hearing. The ears of an ordinary person can hear only so many sounds before they fall outside the range of pitch; some noises are simply too high or too low. Apparently, "[h]umans can generally sense sounds at frequencies between 20 and 20,000 cycles per second, or hertz (Hz)." As Sarah Williams explained in *Science* (2014), sounds you can't hear can still hurt your ears. Our range of perception is narrower than reality, and things that human beings are unable to sense might have an impact on us anyway. On either side of the continuum, beyond the limits of our power, reality extends and might work mischief, catching us unawares. Nevertheless, science must operate within its given compass, hoping with time and ingenuity to expand its powers and otherwise make inferences about what lies elsewhere. That is to say, human beings find themselves within perceptual horizons.

During his lectures to introduce systems thinking, Niklas Luhmann explained that the human brain is structurally coupled with its environment, which is to say it is attuned to what's going on. Human survival depends on this. However, in order to perceive the world with sufficient acuity, it must operate within "a very narrow bandwidth of sensibilities that reduces what can be seen, limits the spectrum of colors, and equally reduces what can be heard (2013, p. 86)." Otherwise, the brain would be overwhelmed with incoming data and lack the mental space to do complex things with that data, such as making critical distinctions, learning lessons for future use, and imagining scenarios of future threats and opportunities. There are reasons that human perception has its limits.

A scientist is bounded by more than the limits of his or her perception. As Herbert Simon explained, our powers of rationality are similarly bounded, "where the complexity of the environment is immensely greater than the computational powers of the adaptive system (1981, p. 190)." A person can understand only so much about the world. Some facts are too strange to comprehend, at least at first. And the cumulative effect of so many things to understand can overwhelm our capabilities. People talk about their "bandwidth" as a capacity to process information. The human brain can absorb and make sense of only so much within a given timeframe. Merleau-Ponty explained that "the essence ... of all the elements lies less in their observable properties than in what they say to us (1948/2004, p. 64)." One can see and hear and taste and touch without ever comprehending. Ultimately, said Merleau-Ponty, our experience of reality is a relationship "between beings who are both embodied and limited and an enigmatic world of which we catch a glimpse ... but only ever from points of view that hide as much as they reveal (1948/2004, p. 70)."

It stands to reason, therefore, that to the extent they are scientists, leadership scholars must acknowledge their limitations, while always struggling to reach further than what is readily apparent. The idea of an "episode" can be said to set aside the rest of reality, to set parameters that are, to some extent, artificial, mostly as an accommodation for our impoverished capabilities.

The leadership episode as a unit of analysis

If indeed the most meaningful unit of analysis for leadership would be an episode, it is still unclear what constitutes an episode. The term, not unlike the terms "epoch," "era," or "event," proves to be frustratingly imprecise. The primary reason, in my opinion, is that an episode is a construct, an abstraction, taken from out of a stream of activity – plucked from the flux, you might say – isolated from the flow of history, as though bracketing everything else. One must ignore most of what led up to this episode, going back to antiquity, as well as ignoring a bevy of activities taking place simultaneously that bear no relevance to the leadership that interests the investigator. Then, looking at what transpired afterward, with the passage of time the consequences become subsumed by the torrent of other influences such that tracking the results of an episode becomes harder and harder to discern. Every episode belongs to a turbulent stream of multiple currents, eddies, twists, and waterfalls far more bewildering and more powerful than anything that takes place in the moment between the one called a leader and the one called a follower. Every episode is a confluence of countless variables, transient and oftentimes subtle. Soon, the event itself becomes lost in the current, just part of a never-ending stream.

Can anybody really say why a pebble in a creek tumbles several centimeters before settling back into the mud? The pebble tumbled; that much is observable, measurable, and incontrovertible. The challenge lies in identifying the cause. And to be sure, identifying the long-term consequences. Nobody said this would be easy. Nevertheless, there will be funding to find this out from those who aspire to toss pebbles.

Hannah Arendt once wrote that humans are incapable of foretelling the consequences of their deeds, let alone knowing the motives for doing them (1958, p. 233). The outcomes are to be hoped for, but never predicted beyond a certain point, because, in her words, action has no end. "The process of a single deed can quite literally endure throughout time until mankind itself has come to an end (1958, p. 233)." In a few swift strokes, she emphasized the limits of our ability to control or even understand what anybody does.

> [Men] have known that he who acts never quite knows what he is doing, that he always becomes "guilty" of consequences he never intended or even foresaw, that no matter how disastrous and unexpected the consequences of his deed he can never undo it, that the process he starts is never consummated unequivocally in one single deed or event, and that its very meaning never discloses itself to the actor but only to the backward glance of the historian who himself does not act.
>
> *(1958, p. 233)*

Arendt was careful to note that everybody takes action of one kind or another. Despite all of these reservations and beliefs, the risk and the uncertainty, human beings take initiative and launch new projects all of the time (1958, p. 177). It was not her contention that leadership doesn't happen. It most certainly does. If anything, it is far more prevalent than scholars of Leadership Studies might care to admit. Our social life consists of influence and counterinfluence, like a cascade, going back and forth, up and down. We might be tempted to refer to these numberless encounters as micro-leadership. And with this imagery, we find ourselves back in the torrent and onrush from which we despaired of isolating such a segregated thing as an "episode."

It would be incumbent on me to note that these claims about studying leadership by means of discrete episodes would run counter to the arguments contained in an article from 2016 written by Rian Satterwhite, Kate Sheridan, and Whitney McIntyre Miller, where they urge scholars and educators to stretch their consciousness beyond the immediate in both directions – both toward what they refer to as the deep past and the deep future, far beyond the usual horizons (p. 50, citing Plotkin, 2008).[1] Their model of a timeline resembles the classic work of Fernand Braudel on the magnitudes of history (1980; see Harter, 2020, ch. 7).

What the reader will note, however, is that I am more sympathetic to their plea than it might seem. For one thing, I agree that "we must... embrace a more nuanced and deepened sense of time that will serve to connect us not only with those who have come before us but with those who will walk this planet long after we are gone (p. 52)." For another, even though I just made the case for using the episode as a unit of analysis for leadership studies, I also have reason to problematize the very idea of an episode. I do so in a manner not unlike what Satterwhite, Sheridan, and Miller suggested, but for alternative reasons. My approach begins with the work of a philosopher named Pierre Hadot.

Inscoping and outscoping: The spiritual exercises of Pierre Hadot

Toward the end of his career, an elderly scholar by the name of Hadot composed a little book about the spiritual exercises of the German polymath Goethe.[2] From the beginning, Hadot explained that by "spiritual exercises" he did not mean anything religious or supernatural. These were activities for the imagination, intended to bring depth to one's understanding of the world and thus to one's life. His translator tells us that Hadot was aware at the time that he was dying (Chase, 2023). Poignantly, the book is dedicated to his grandson. More to the point, the first two essays address the theme of this chapter, in surprising fashion. Let me explain.

---

1 The notion of "deep time" has been credited to James Hutton (1788), one of the founders of modern geology (see Repcheck, 2003).
2 Christina Hirsch, Charlotte von Bülow, and Peter Simpson (2023) have recently explored ways in which the work of Pierre Hadot pertains to the study of leadership. My reliance on Hadot parallels theirs. For similar invocations of Hadot on the topic of leadership, see also Case and Gosling (2007) and Simpson and French (2006).

The first essay in his book explores what it means to live in the present. The past is already done. The future is unknown. All we have is the fleeting moment that is now. Hadot drew from his knowledge of antiquity to quote sages and poets about the perils of dwelling too much on times that lie beyond where we are. People are often said to live in the past, for example, nursing old grudges, missing former lovers, and regretting the sins of youth. One can take this reverie too far. It can be downright unhealthy to gaze too long backward. By the same token, folks (like me) fixate on what might happen tomorrow. They abide in expectation, if not anxiety, experiencing some mixture of hope and dread about a world that might never come to pass. Living too much in the future robs a person of his joy. All we have is this instant. And, Hadot concluded, the right mindset, the healthiest posture to assume by living in the present, promises to bring a sense of fullness, as intimations of eternity can occupy the hour. It stands as a way of being there, to be part of life as it transpires – neither before nor after, but right now.

Hadot wrote that for every person who adopts this perspective: "every instant is significant and full of meaning (2023, p. 35)." Consciousness learns to ignore the lateral fictions of past and future, while opening to the vertical dimension that the Greeks referred to as *kairos* (2023, p. 7). When a person stands unshackled to what has gone before and what might yet lie ahead, he or she understands best what it means to be free, for each moment is an opportunity for making fresh choices. On such occasions (which means at *every* moment), human beings can begin again to create a world of their choosing. Living in the present means forever beginning and thus abiding in the forge of everything ordinarily understood as leadership.

The parallels here to the example of Caesar at the Rubicon are obvious. A proven leader halts on the precipice of decision, immersed as it were in weighty deliberation about whether to stay or go. The image seems frozen. Nothing appears to be happening. As had been stated earlier, historians, like the soldiers in his retinue, can only wait. Caesar no doubt consulted the past and imagined possible futures, but suddenly everything stopped. He had a decision to make. Here was a moment pregnant with meaning.[3] According to Hadot's philosophy, then, leadership scholars would be

---

3 Hirsch, von Bülow, and Simpson (2023) state: "The pressure to act counters the requirement to take time to think more deeply and to reflect on the specific characteristics of the situation (p. 394)." Leaders must "create a space from which it is possible to carefully evaluate a situation before passing judgment or taking action (p. 398)." For this reason, they recommend that leaders develop "the capacity to tolerate the discomfort of stillness until the proper move presents itself (p. 400)." They must somehow "interrupt the impulse to act."

advised not to ignore the transient interval, as somehow too brief to bother with; but instead, we are to elevate its importance, scrutinize it, measuring its significance not by its duration, but by its worth. Leadership originates in the human capacity to initiate, to give birth to something completely new. So much ensues from each and every choice. Leadership can be said to trail after the wondrous impulse.

Hadot wrote a second essay that, superficially, might be thought to contradict the first. In these studies, he wrote about the spiritual exercise of adopting a position from above, like gazing from a mountaintop or looking back on Earth from outer space. Systems thinkers call it outscoping: zooming to a point of view above, taking in as much of the whole as might be possible, and seeing beyond the immediate. Some call this practice perspective-taking. In the literature on leadership, we call this vantage point the balcony, from which a leader might comprehend the larger patterns being cut by the dancers below. Except that for Hadot, the purpose is not to study the movements in order to improve upon them, i.e. to intervene more intelligently. Instead, the purpose is to appreciate the relative insignificance of everything people are doing, which is to say: to fit the many gross exertions that we experience day-to-day into a vast and breath-taking context that impresses upon us just how trivial we are "in the grand scheme of things."[4] *Sub specie aeternitatis.* The goal is not so much to operate more effectively. Instead, it is to question what we are doing in the first place. He called this an "exercise of detachment and distancing, to achieve impartiality, objectivity, and a critical spirit (2023, p. 79)."

Hadot explained that from a sufficient distance, the fortunes of leadership matter very little. All leadership is frankly ephemeral. Nevertheless, to the extent that one hopes to engage in leadership – or anything else, for that matter – let it accord with a wider and wider universe, as part of an immense communion. By doing so, each of us becomes lighter, casting aside the heavy weight of responsibility that burdens us. So much less will be found to ride on our shoulders. "This too shall pass," wrote the Sufi poets. The troubles of the day do not disappear altogether, to be sure; yet an individual might become buoyant, knowing how transient we all are. And the petty frets, the rivalries and slights, will shrink accordingly.

---

4 Hirsch, von Bülow, and Simpson (2023) state that taking such a perspective "helps us re-perceive how small and passing are human affairs in the scale of the Whole, helping put things in their true proportion (p. 400, citing Sharpe, 2020)."

Hadot quoted at length a passage from the work of Pascal, and it puts the argument succinctly:

> Let man therefore contemplate all of nature in its lofty, full majesty, let him remove his gaze from the base objects that surround him…let the earth appear to him as a point compared to the vast revolution described by this star [the sun], and let him be amazed at the fact that this vast revolution itself is but a most delicate point as compared to the one embraced by the stars that rotate in the firmament… All this visible world is merely an imperceptible stroke in the ample heart of nature.
>
> *(quoted in Hadot, 2023, p. 55)*

Pascal's lovely prose also suggests something of the generative power of such an exercise, for it is frequently the case that from the mountaintop leaders descend with a purpose. A person will have become reoriented. Here again, as with the previous essay, Hadot indicated that leadership often originates as a result of such experiences, for at a distance the motley – that is, the hustle and bustle of everyday lives – will seem beautiful and worth celebrating, in the exact same way that astronauts looking down at our planet felt a renewed commitment to its stewardship (Hadot, 2023, pp. 80–84). So small, so vulnerable. Hadot wrote that "it is the spectacles of the laws of nature that invites the soul to find within itself the duty of action in the service of others (p. 74)."

It would seem, in conclusion, that the twin horizons for studying leadership with which this article began – namely, the ephemeral moment and the encompassing breadth of the universe – take on a profound meaning that scholars might be advised to contemplate anew. Leadership can be construed as more than any episode, however long. It is the product of two extreme viewpoints, one of them tiny and one of them immense, one of them fleeting and one of them forever, both of which taken together tell us much about what leadership is even supposed to mean.

Perhaps Anaximander, that early Greek philosopher (610–546 BCE), had it right, namely that everything – including leadership – originates in the *apeiron*, in unlimited depths.

Leadership starting from a stop position

The imagery of three different things, namely time itself, human history, and consciousness, depict them as "flowing" in some sense, creating an expectation that at any given point, there will be antecedents and consequences, both a Before and an After, cause and effect. The object of our investigation is believed to originate in events that already occurred and to result in events that have not ... or at least not yet. No matter what story a person tells, it includes a beginning, a middle, and an end. And on either side of it, beyond the temporal horizon, we choose not to concern ourselves. Yet we stand as by a river aware that both the currents upstream and downstream exist outside of our direct experience, somewhere around the bend.

Writing in 2020, Barry Cooper pointed out that indeed anthropologists seem to find themselves with not one, but two continua: evolutionary biology and cultural history. Each of these streams can change independently. He writes, "there could be genetic change or mutation without behavioral change and behavioral change without corresponding changes in the genome.... (p. 22)." Cooper explains that this distinction can be traced back to Aristotle's teachings on *physis* and *nomos*, and one finds an equivalent distinction in the works of Martin Luther and Immanuel Kant, continuing in one form or another into the contemporary university where it has been useful to differentiate the Sciences from the Humanities.

The study known as Philosophical Anthropology often insists on there being two parallel narratives – one of them about human physiology and one of them about *Geist*, which has to do with the spiritual dimension, including reason, the arts, and tradition. Human beings can be said to stand in both streams, participants in both narratives simultaneously. This imagery presupposes that nothing denoted as leadership arises out of nowhere, *ab initio*, like the goddess Athena emerging fully formed from the forehead of Zeus. Every episode a scholar might wish to study has its roots in what has gone before, in the economic conditions, for example, or some prior trauma, the residues of individual upbringing, even of persistent archetypes; and it was this presupposition that Arendt emphatically denied. It is possible, she argued, to bring forth a new thing. We as human beings have it in our power. It is just exceedingly rare.[5]

Gabriel de Tarde (1903) called such disturbing, novel events: innovation. Often, of course, the fledgling innovation arrives stillborn and goes nowhere. Or the innovation incites such a backlash that nobody else dares to adopt it for themselves; it will have been regarded as too radical or

---

5 Caesar's march into Rome was not entirely unprecedented. He had witnessed similar events already in his lifetime (Goldsworthy, 2006, pp. 47 & 70). His biographer devoted a chapter to explaining the prior dictatorship of Lucius Cornelius Sulla, for example (Goldsworthy, 2006, ch. 3). Goldsworthy then elaborated, "At times of severe crisis the Republic had occasionally set aside its fear of the rule of one man and had appointed a dictator, a single magistrate with supreme *imperium* (2006, p. 57)." Growing up, Caesar saw that politics in Rome was often accompanied by – and resolved according to – violence (Goldsworthy, 2006, p. 60).

perverse. But human beings are truly imitative creatures who pass on much of what we see and hear from others, in a lively cascade, that it hardly ever occurs to us to stop for a moment and think things through for ourselves, authentically, with fresh eyes.

It would seem that what Pierre Hadot was urging on his readers when he wrote about (a) living in the present and (b) taking the broad view were exercises in interrupting these luxuriant flows (both nature and culture), interrupting them long enough to interject some unique idea, to decide for oneself which values to embody in the moment. From this perspective, leadership is less about the mechanics of getting other people to accomplish some specific task (on the battlefield, in parliament, at work) and more about any one person addressing the present situation – whatever that happens to look like – as a full and free agent, autonomous, capable of original clinamen.[6]

Few readers will have had reason to notice a polite disagreement dating from the 1950s between Arendt, who had argued that totalitarianism in the twentieth century was a completely new thing, and Eric Voegelin (1953/2000), who saw in it just another grotesque manifestation of a recurring theme in politics. One might be tempted to infer that Voegelin was of the persuasion that human nature never changes, so he rejected Arendt's insistence on natality. This might appear to be the essence of their quarrel. In fact, the dispute between them was more nuanced than this. Arendt was horrified by the totalitarian ambition to change human nature, inasmuch as the attempt results only in destroying lives. So, she was not saying that anyone could change human nature, no matter how comprehensive and brutal the regime. But the ambition, married to modern techniques, does present humanity with a new threat, a new temptation. And she was right to be appalled. By the same token, Voegelin expressed a version of natality that Arendt would probably have found congenial, namely that situations do indeed change. New challenges arise and new predicaments impose themselves with some regularity. But these eventualities do not, in his words, determine our response. We are able to *choose* how we respond, for such freedom belongs to our nature. So, it would seem as though they were far closer to agreement than it first appears.

The significance of this little exchange played out many years ago in the dusty annals of academe rests on the following accord between them, namely that human beings can indeed choose how to respond freely to changing conditions, for it lies at the center of human nature that with

---

6 For an examination of the origins and meaning of the term clinamen, see Fowler, Fowler, and Carus (2002).

character, passion, and prudence, we assert ourselves, i.e. our "selves." So that the crime of totalitarianism was not that it was designed to change human nature, since that is impossible, but instead to destroy it by stamping out this capability of choice, a capability on full display whenever anyone rises up to lead others, as well as when others elect to follow.

When leaders are mulling things over

Let us go back therefore to an immobile Julius Caesar, pondering the decision to cross the Rubicon that day and incite civil war. Nothing overt was happening. As a commander, his military mission had come to an end in 49 BCE. He had had a clear sense of direction while subduing Gaul, but that task was successfully completed. Caesar now had to decide what he would do next. Students of leadership would be hard-pressed to say that leadership was taking place in that moment. Nevertheless, something of tremendous historical consequence was about to occur. It strains credulity to say that scholars should have no interest whatsoever in such pregnant pauses.

Years later, the Roman historian out of Africa named Gaius Suetonius Tranquillus wrote a biography of the Caesars (2011), beginning with the life of Julius. Suetonius alleged that long before he ever left for Gaul, Caesar had dreamt of world conquest, plotting on more than one occasion to incite revolution and overthrow the senate (p. 5f). He is even reported to have said, "Civil war is clearly a necessity (2011, p. 16)." In this account, Caesar was already predisposed to disrupt the status quo, long before he conquered Gaul. He had expressed the intent to do so. This is not a trivial claim, even though subsequent historians have expressed their doubts (see Goldsworthy, 2006, pp. 70, 100f, 111, 151, 471).

Let us suppose that Suetonius is substantially correct and that Caesar had long nurtured an ambition to govern the entire world. Why then did he hesitate here, on the banks of the river? Why not simply lunge forward? Was he contemplating the timing of a revolt? Was he questioning whether this was the opportunity he was waiting for? Apparently not. Others wrote that Caesar surpassed other men in "seizing the right moment... (Plutarch, 2001, p. 217)." Or was he struggling to summon the courage, knowing the dire consequences of his action? Again, his courage was widely admired, by friend and foe alike, so that particular hypothesis does not explain the hesitation. Nevertheless, something briefly held the man in check.

At roughly the same time that Suetonius was composing his work on the Caesars, a writer from Greece named Plutarch compiled famous biographies of Greeks and Romans, including one about Caesar (2001). In this version, Caesar had created a bevy of rivals to fear his ambition, even before the Gallic Wars. They plotted to ruin his career in his absence

(Goldsworthy, 2006, p. 378). They were bent on thwarting him. It wasn't Caesar's outsized ambition that led to this moment; it was instead their jealousy. Then, during those wars abroad Caesar added to his fame back home among the people by means of his martial and diplomatic exploits, winning even more friends through stunning largesse. During his time across the Alps, he had become aware that back home there had ultimately risen two camps: one in favor of Caesar and one against. Each side had access to armies and to considerable wealth. If he marched on Rome, the two sides would inevitably clash. But it wasn't uncertainty or fear that kept him poised on the brink. For Plutarch, it was the weight of the knowledge of what his actions would mean for posterity. He seems to have savored the potential for greatness, almost as though he *just knew* that here was his opportunity for immortality. But is that what occupied Caesar's mind? History is without evidence, one way or the other.

Caesar had no way of knowing at the time that so many of his detractors would flee his approach. As it turns out, wrote Plutarch, Caesar "made himself master of all Italy without bloodshed in the space of sixty days (2001, p. 223)." The civil war continued across the Mediterranean for years before Caesar arrived at a resolution and rose to the supreme position among men, even flirting with the symbols of royalty before being cut down by his detractors. All of that was to be in the future. Plutarch indicated that back at the Rubicon Caesar was appreciating the moment, anticipating the stories that would be told about him forever after.

Mark Freeman (2010) has drawn our attention to the fact that before Augustine, who lived hundreds of years after Caesar, the West did not produce autobiographies that examined the inner workings of an author's mind (pp. 27–36). For whatever reason, people from Greece and Rome did not write about their private thoughts and feelings, except perhaps in private letters. Caesar himself did compose accounts of his exploits, so he was not above recording the story of his leadership; he eventually wrote an entire book about the Civil Wars that were to ensue. Nevertheless, he avoided passages describing his mind (e.g. Goldsworthy, 2006, pp. 80 & 187). More specifically, he did not identify a moment such as this one at the Rubicon, with hindsight, as somehow significant – weighty, consequential, portentous. (I am unaware of any evidence that he had done so.) This does not have to mean that it wasn't significant, of course. Freeman referred to such an occasion as a "monument, a commemorative psychic edifice (p. 52)." We construct them in our memory like shrines when a person encounters what he called the transcendent horizon, where a finite creature meets with some destiny or fate (p. 94). A person might say, "That's when I realized…." In that particular historical epoch, before Augustine, such things were simply not written down.

Let us accept for now the report that even a younger Caesar had harbored the ambition to rule, to accomplish for himself what Alexander the Great had accomplished in his own time. Such a feat fit some kind of inner narrative that he had been nurturing now for years. Rising to dominance was part of the story he hoped to live, and for him, that story had yet to be written. It still lay in the future. Yet scholars know that leaders understand themselves partly as participants in a narrative that extends into the future. They can be said to cast themselves ahead. Without such expectations, wrote Freeman, one suffers from what he called a narrative foreclosure (ch. 5). There is no longer any motive to exert oneself. Julius Caesar may not have known precisely how the story would unfold, but he knew which direction he still wanted it to take. And he knew that it wouldn't happen unless he did something overt. He had learned after years of politics and war that you cannot prevail by wishing for things. You must act.

And so he did.

Judging leadership within three horizons

It would seem that investigators into this phenomenon called leadership operate within certain horizons, i.e. within a range that has its limits beyond which we cannot go. One horizon is the unexpressed and inaccessible human mind, when leadership emerges like spring water out of the ground. One must infer that the reservoir is under there, even if only in episodes of leadership do the waters become manifest. Beyond a certain point, the inner workings of the mind are a black box, opaque. Another horizon is the longue durée, where leadership becomes submerged in the larger flux of historical events. Each discrete episode, like a ripple, subsides, quickly becoming part of an encompassing tumult. Yet another horizon, a third horizon suggested by Hadot, is the transcendent meaning of what transpires, its significance within the rubric of what constitutes goodness.

Each participant, not least Julius Caesar, stands at the intersection of these three things: (a) one's private intent, (b) the flow of history, and (c) the importance of taking some kind of action. Yet it is my belief that understanding leadership requires at least some appreciation of all three horizons, which are commonly examined by the academic disciplines known respectively as psychology, history, and ethics. Leadership is inherently a narrative combining elements of all three, where individuals with a purpose enter into the social dynamics by which some good might be attained.

Let me add, almost as an afterthought, that the investigators into the phenomenon of leadership also operate within their own boundaries. They will observe, comment, and ultimately judge from their own unique vantage point, their own intersection of psychology, history, and ethics – as I do now. What they are not permitted to do is deny the relevance of any one of these, to dismiss evidence and arguments about what happened and why. Accordingly, Julius Caesar on the brink of invasion in 49 BCE was a leader and quite possibly, in his own imagination, launched an episode of outsized proportions that changed the course of human experience down to the present day. It is my opinion – harsh though it might be – that if you deny such an assertion, then you cannot speak credibly of leadership at all. Whatever else you might say about leadership can safely be ignored (Goldsworthy, 2006, p. 1f).[7]

The rose and the gardener

The 2018 translation of Michel Serres' book titled *The Incandescent* borrows a saying that no rose has ever seen a gardener die.

Building outward from this homespun adage, Serres constructs an elaborate diorama in which a child holds a toy while standing in front of a house that rests at the foot of a sunlit mountain. Each layer or level in the diorama has a kind of life span, a history. The toy manufactured last year might not survive the summer. The child might live another eighty or ninety years. The house, several generations. The mountain, millions of years. The sun, billions. To the child, everything behind her seems enduring, permanent. Only the toy will seem ephemeral. The father, who is responsible for the house, knows that without occasional handiwork, the house might fall into disrepair. He also knows that without his attention, the child may not live to adulthood. Serres calls it the gardener illusion: a person will regard those items with a shorter span to be temporary, but by and large anything with a longer span he or she will regard as a backdrop, or to borrow an unusual term from Serres: immarcescible (2018, p. 3).

The sciences have found ways to date everything, including the planet and sun. They know in an academic sense that nothing persists indefinitely. Mountains erode, stars collapse, and the entire universe itself might one day contract to a single point and go out of business, with either a bang or a whimper. Yet even they (the sciences) will operate as though certain laws of nature will continue to operate for the foreseeable future. Their work relies on a range of constants. They will have adopted some version of the gardener's illusion. Otherwise, they have nothing as scientists to do. Nevertheless, ultimately everything flows toward death (for living things) and toward oblivion. Many call this process entropy. Sounds bleak, right?

---

7 Goldsworthy referred to the crossing as a "crucial episode in the history of the ancient world (2006, p. 377)."

But then Serres points out that even transient things such as toys and houses consist of durable elements. The little girl might live only so long, but the particles that make her what she is in the morning will pass on to something else. The form of the human being will eventually expire. We all know that. Its contents will become reapportioned into new constellations. Elements from the distant past persevere in us today.

Serres identified three basic types of memory (2018, p. 24f). The first and most unreliable is what a human being remembers. Every one of us remembers and misremembers only a fraction of what was ever thought, felt, or imagined. A person forgets far more than can be recalled. The second type of memory is what survives from the exertions of people who have since passed away; their creativity leaves artifacts, a culture, that will outlast what any one person happens to recall. This category includes statues, books, and musical scores. Libraries might burn to the ground. Monuments can be toppled. What remains might be partial and misleading, yet it likely goes on and on, in one form or another down through the generations. Culture is culture because it will have been transmitted from one generation to the next. The third memory is the long, slow existence of what is called nature – the rivers and trees and flakes of chalk. Every item encountered belongs to this third trajectory, even the very DNA that traces back to Lucy, the primal mother of humanity out of Africa. The memory contained by our originating stuff will last – and will be altogether true. No person, not even Caesar, is the sum of only his own experience. He bears with him the memory of his tribe. And deepest of all, the gross imperatives of physics and chemistry.

It helps to picture in one's mind the many threads that extend from the so-called Big Bang outward through the ages, so to speak, to produce the diverse objects populating our world – the harmonica, the dandelion, and the Atlantic Ocean. And each of these will grow or develop along myriad pathways. Choose any single point in time, any moment, and then plot in three dimensions the possible changes. The toy breaks or it doesn't break. The little girl grows up and marries and bears her own children – or she succumbs to some wasting disease before puberty. Nobody knows. Like a decision tree, the branches of what is possible extend in every direction, depending on a bewildering variety of variables. The same will be true of those items we take for granted, the forest, the cliff, the island. Multiple threads reach out and split and keep growing, because nobody knows what will happen, even though we expect *something* will come of it; so that if in your imagination you were to speed up the image of all these tangled tendrils, going every which way, it would look like a hand grenade exploding, not unlike the Big Bang on a much smaller scale (2018, p. 13). The present moment is ground zero for that explosion in slow motion.

With this image in mind, then, Serres could write that "the innumerable gushes forth from the instant (2018, p. 10)." He even went so far as to claim that "the present moment reveals itself to be interminable (2018, p. 11)." And he can talk this way because of a deep conviction based on his understanding of science that as a result of these countless bifurcations, the mute collision of atoms, something unpredictable is always possible. Darwin, for example, spoke of mutation. Arendt, if you recall, natality. Out of so many interactions, so many births (some of them monstrosities), so much that is strange, especially if one insists on using the ordinary timescales of daily life.

Before lamenting the limits of human memory, however, and calling humanity feeble or frail, which we certainly are when compared to a mountain, consider that the human capacity to forget makes novelty likely. To understand any one thing, a person must forget so much else. This limitation enables innovation. The individual person must constantly learn, adapt, and otherwise create, in compensation for this weakness. Behold, a new thing. Serres would say that we project our exhilaration (or negentropy) onto the gradual processes of the natural world; we dare to accelerate the rhythms of history (2018, pp. 9 & 46f). We can do this. We can *choose* to do this. And we can choose *in which direction* to begin.

Have we not characterized Caesar thus at the Rubicon?

References

Arendt, H. (1958). *The human condition*. University of Chicago Press.

Braudel, F. (1980). *On history* (S. Matthews, trans.). University of Chicago Press.

Case, P., & Gosling, J. (2007). "Wisdom of the moment: Pre-modern perspectives on organizational action." *Social Epistemology*. 21(2): 87–111.

Chase, M. "Translator's introduction." In Hadot, P. (ed.) (2023). *Don't forget to live: Goethe and the tradition of spiritual exercises* (M. Chase, trans.) (pp. xiii–xv). University of Chicago Press.

Cooper, B. (2020). *Paleolithic politics: The human community in early art*. University of Notre Dame Press.

Dawkins, R. (1991). "The ultraviolet garden: Growing up in the universe." *The Royal Institution Christmas Lectures for Children*. Retrieved 1 April 2024 from https://richarddawkins.net/2009/02/ep4-the-ultraviolet-garden-growing-up-in-the-universe-richard-dawkins-2/.

Fowler, D., Fowler, P.G., & Carus, T.L. (2002). *Lucretius on atomic motion: A commentary on De Rerum Natura, Book Two, lines 1-332*. Oxford University Press.

Freeman, M. (2010). *Hindsight: The promise and peril of looking backward*. Oxford University Press.

Goldsworthy, A. (2006). *Caesar: Life of a colossus*. Yale University Press.

Hadot, P. (2023). *Don't forget to live: Goethe and the tradition of spiritual exercises* (M. Chase, trans.). University of Chicago Press.

Harter, N. (2020). *Leadership across boundaries: Passage to Aporia*. Routledge.

Hirsch, C., von Bülow, C., & Simpson, P. (2023). "Stoicism, philosophy as a way of life, and negative capability: Developing a capacity for working in radical uncertainty." *Leadership*. *19*(5): 393–412. https://doi.org/10.1177/17427150231178092.

Hutton, J. (1788). "Theory of the earth; or an investigation of the laws observable in the composition, dissolution, and restoration of land upon the Globe." *Transactions of the Royal Society of Edinburgh*. 1(2): 209–304.

Luhmann, N. (2013). *Introduction to systems theory* (P. Gilgen, trans.). Polity.

Merleau-Ponty, M. (1948/2004). *The world of perception* (O. Davis, trans.). Routledge.

Plutarch. (2001). *Plutarch's lives* (The Dryden translation, edited with preface by Arthur Hugh Clough). The Modern Library.

Repcheck, J. (2003). *The man who found time: James Hutton and the discovery of earth's antiquity*. Perseus Books Group.

Satterwhite, R., Sheridan, K., & McIntyre Miller, W. (2016). "Rediscovering deep time: Sustainability and the need to re-engage with multiple dimensions of time in leadership studies." *Journal of Leadership Studies*. 9(4): 47–53.

Serres, M. (2018). *The incandescent* (R. Burks, trans.). Bloomsbury Academic.

Simon, H. (1981). *The sciences of the artificial* (2nd ed.). MIT Press.

Simpson, P., & French, R. (2006). "Negative capability and the capacity to think in the present moment: Some implications for leadership practice." *Leadership*. 2(2): 245–255.

Suetonius. (2011). *The Caesars* (D. Hurley, trans.). Hackett Publishing.

Tarde, G. (1903). *The laws of imitation* (E.C. Parsons, trans.). Henry Holt & Co.

Toynbee, A. (1948). *Civilization on trial*. Oxford University Press.

Voegelin, E. "The origins of totalitarianism." In Voegelin, E. (ed.) (1953/2000). *Collected works* (vol. 11; ch. 1). University of Missouri Press.

Williams, S. (2014). "Sounds you can't hear can still hurt your ears: Exposure to inaudible low-frequency pitches changes the functioning of the inner ear." *Science*. https://doi.org/10.1126/article.22362.

3

GOING BACK TO BASICS IN THE INVESTIGATION OF LEADERSHIP

The logical benefits of de-differentiating

"Zima Blue"

A simple robot circles around the swimming pool scrubbing tiles colored Zima Blue. Round and round it goes, doing its job patiently, evenly, as it had been designed to do (Pennacchioli & Valley, 2019; Swaminathan, 2023). Thus begins a brief 2019 animated film that was part of a series on Netflix titled *Love, Death and Robots*. The story unfolds like this.

With time, the cleaning robot acquires new appendages and leaves the pool to go out into the world. While exploring civilization, his delicate color sense means that the thing he does exceptionally well is paint on canvas, trying to express himself. Soon, an enthusiastic audience takes an interest in the artist known only as Zima Blue. The robot, mistaken for an eccentric human being, becomes the toast of the town. His works demand a hefty price, so that Zima can afford to continue to refine his autonomous body and mingle with the rich and famous. Now a celebrity, Zima moves through a decadent (human) culture. Agents clamber over one another to sign him to fat contracts. Desperate women throw themselves at him. Every room he enters starts to buzz.

The further he penetrates high society, he increasingly emphasizes in his paintings a patch of Zima Blue, so that it becomes like a signature. It begins with little rectangles in the center. Except that from canvas-to-canvas these blue portions get bigger and bigger, becoming dominant, blocking everything else being depicted in the frame. Finally, Zima invites the glitterati and the media to his home, promising something spectacular. Everybody who is anybody attends. The party soon gets underway, though Zima

DOI: 10.4324/9781003540526-4

brings the festivities to a halt. At the backyard pool, he thanks everybody for their interest in his career, and then in full view he starts to dismantle himself, detaching all of the false appendages, until all that is left is the humble device that starts going around the massive pool again and again, taking satisfaction from keeping those Zima Blue tiles clean, forever. The party-goers, bewildered and disappointed, gradually leave the estate … and leave the robot in peace.

Introduction to this chapter

Readers familiar with the work of Eric Voegelin are acquainted with his distinction between compactness and differentiation. A number of secondary sources have helped to explain what Voegelin intended by these terms (see e.g. Cooper, 2018). Differentiation was considered to be an advance, if not a leap in being, that enables human beings to "ascend toward what is immortal and everlasting (Voegelin, 1956, p. viii, quoting Augustine)." This is not to ignore certain risks that come with differentiation, such as retrogression back to compactness, to cite one example, and deformations.[1] Nevertheless, the experience of differentiation, standing alone, is generally regarded as a good thing, an improvement – whatever people subsequently do about it. I was struck, however, when Gregor Sebba asked a legitimate question: "what is so good about differentiation (1982, p. 64)?" I was struck in part because I had been learning a bit about the occasional merits of something called de-differentiation. What is the relationship of this process called dedifferentiation to the operation that Voegelin referred to as differentiation?

Before attempting an answer, it would be incumbent on me to acknowledge a couple of things. First, Voegelin reminded his audience at the Walgreen lectures in 1951 that political science often finds itself using language that has also been adopted for other usages. Sometimes, the meanings overlap, but often they do not. Without clarification, political science risks contributing to confusion (2000, pp. 109–111). The term "dedifferentiation" does have uses beyond political science, as I hope to show briefly, which is why one of my goals is to help clarify these terminological issues. Second, a scholar such as Voegelin who published so many books, articles, book

---

1 Pierre Schlag (2009) explained as a matter of logic that a differentiation between two things that are not in fact distinct means that one must dedifferentiate them, which is to say collapse them into a single thing and proceed from there. You refer to Mrs. Harter, and I call her Karin, but as it turns out they are one and the same person. Before we can speak meaningfully about her, we need to "dedifferentiate" who we are talking about. Otherwise, we are likely to become confused.

reviews, and substantive letters over so many years will have revised his or her thinking along the way. It can be unfair to allege what someone such as Voegelin thought, as though he always thought the same thing, from first to last. Voegelin was, if anything, conscious of his changing thoughts and ideas, even to the point of starting over on a massive project that had reached nine volumes, so I should try to anchor my remarks explicitly in specific texts (see Harter, 2019a).

This paper will begin by considering the hackneyed distinction between two complementary operations, namely Analysis and Synthesis, for they will open out shortly into the process known as differentiation. In order to explain the term "dedifferentiation" as it is being used in other fields of study, this article will then provide a few relevant examples from the fields of biology, sociology, and psychology – each of which has found uses for the term. Only then will we return to Voegelin. At the conclusion, I will offer an example of how dedifferentiation might help us to understand leadership.

Moving from analysis to synthesis (and back again)

The term "analysis" originates from the idea of separating parts of a whole for closer and discrete scrutiny. Michael Beaney (2021) explains that the etymology of the term is to loosen up or dissolve, to untie the boat from its moorings. The companion term "synthesis" originates from the idea of combining (or reconstructing) parts into an integrated whole. These operations can be said to be complementary, like moving conceptually in one direction (from the whole to its parts) or the other (from the parts to their whole). One of the classic examples is the pocket watch, which is comprised of distinct pieces that upon disassembly can be laid out in an array on a black cloth. Going from a pocket watch to an array of parts represents analysis. Assembling the parts into a pocket watch represents synthesis. The following paper depends on using this imagery of assembling and disassembling parts, as a necessary but insufficient schema for what I hope to describe below as dedifferentiation.

The pocket watch example could be misleading if the assumption is that when one speaks of analysis, the process involves only physical objects, i.e. things, composites made up of multiple parts, because the analysis can also apply to steps in an argument, working backward from the conclusion to premises, as though tracing a line of thought. For that matter, analysis might consist of defining key terms before proceeding to judgment of the meaning of a statement. In other words, according to Beaney (2021), what we end up with are at least three different understandings of the term "analysis": decompositional, interpretive, and regressive analysis. This explanation will be helpful when trying to understand the versatility of this concept called dedifferentiation, because it is a process similar to each kind of analysis: breaking a whole into its components, tracing a thing back to its origins or at least back to previous stages of development,[2] and isolating a portion for closer scrutiny – that is, for focal awareness.

For purposes of illustration, let us look closer at one of these devices for conducting dedifferentiation. In the introduction to this book, we saw that Richard McKeon had identified four distinct methods in the social sciences. One of these, which he called the logistic method, starts with that which is simple and then, step-by-step, builds a more elaborate argument. To proceed in this fashion is to "construct" knowledge (2016, p. 11). One isolates the elements first, making sure to get them right, before proceeding.[3] This might mean stating key definitions or offering clear premises, so that by the end of a linear process one arrives at a proof (2016, p. 13). What we are doing when we use logistical methods is tracing the implications of our assumptions in order to test their adequacy (2016, p. 249).

Because of its linear structure, an argument of this type depends on the adequacy of each step. To this extent, it becomes an example of dedifferentiation to go back to the beginning and scrutinize the foundations, primarily comprised of the individual building blocks out of which the entire edifice has been built. (Metaphors about building construction, such as a brick house, are not inapt.) By "going back" in this way, it might be possible to substitute other building blocks and arrive at a completely different kind of structure. The idea is that dedifferentiation in this sense is a return to the meaning of terms and the suppositions out of which the rest has been made.[4] McKeon had shown how this might unfold. He asked his students,

2 This use of analysis could mean breaking an argument into steps or stages, as Richard McKeon will explain, but as Jacques Derrida illustrated, analysis in the form of deconstruction can trace the genealogy of a concept or theme, going back in time. Jürgen Habermas (1993) explained, though, this does not mean prior in the sense of a chronology, indicated by the calendar, as for example what Plato said then what Aristotle said, etc., down through the ages, which would be one kind of analysis (historical), but instead experientially prior, by which I mean "at the root or origin of experience." What comes first *phenomenologically*? Although history and phenomenology are not identical operations, each of them would be a kind of analysis.

3 Consistent with what we found in the introduction regarding what McKeon called the dialectical method, where we listed several representatives from the history of philosophy, we can identify several representatives of the logistic method as well, namely Euclid, René Descartes, Gottfried Leibniz, and Sir Isaac Newton.

4 Irving Copi (1978) once wrote that an "efficient method of establishing the validity of an extended argument is to deduce its conclusion from its premises by a sequence of elementary arguments each of which is known to be valid (p. 310)." The technique is not unlike what Sherlock Holmes proposed for criminal detection (Copi, 1978, p. 478, quoting Arthur Conan Doyle's *A Study in Scarlet*).

for example, what authors meant by the term "freedom" (2016, lectures 2 & 6). What Hobbes meant is not the same as what Kant meant. And because they used the same term in competing ways, one must start over with this difference in mind, because their contrasting meanings shaped their contrasting conclusions. Dedifferentiation is a name one might give to checking an argument in this fashion.

James Hillman hearkened back to an old term *notitia*, meaning "an appreciative and discriminating attention to the quality of things" and also "attentive noticing" (Sipiora, 2023, p. 42). We might say "taking note" or "becoming acquainted," not with regard to oneself, i.e. the private, interior of thoughts and feelings, hopes and fears, which so many psychologists ask their clients to examine, but instead with regard to the things of this world out there, their materials and design, their character as things and their many interrelationships (Sipiora, 2023, p. 51). The investigation depends on one's focal awareness, not unlike where you cast your flashlight in a dark room. A person can de-differentiate by occluding everything else for the moment – that is, tentatively, provisionally. As we will see, this activity would be something Eric Voegelin could endorse.

Representative fields of study using the concept of "dedifferentiation"[5]

The following three examples are illustrative of how the term can be used. They are not meant to be exhaustive. (One can find uses in the psychometric research on aging, for example, as well as the role of affect in child cognition, let alone the familiar processes of bodily decomposition or Schumpeter's creative destruction.[6]) Furthermore, a lot more could be said here by experts to elaborate on these usages, so it seemed best to keep my descriptions relatively brief.

Molecular biology

In biology, a cell can transition from its differentiated purpose back, so to speak, to a prior state or condition (Child, 1915). If we were to picture a marble that can roll in any one of several directions, this marble represents the cell in its undifferentiated state or condition. At this point, we are imagining a versatile cell full of possibility but not otherwise distinctive.

---

5 Barry Oshry, writing in 1995 for business managers, dedicated one page to a poem, which he titled "An Ode to Dedifferentiation" (p. 190).
6 Michel Serres wrote briefly about the topic of dedifferentiation in his book *The Incandescent* (2018, p. 40f).

(Apparently, this is one of the primary reasons that researchers covet stem cells: they are undifferentiated, or we might say potentially to-be-differentiated.) Once the marble starts rolling down one pathway and not others, becoming specialized, it loses its capacity to become something else. Its path follows what is known as an epigenetic landscape (Wikipedia, citing Waddington, 2014). The cell develops over time to do one function and not others. Other cells develop alongside it, working together to accomplish a specialized function. Starting out, the cell was capable of doing other things, although that will not be the case once it begins rolling down its path.

De-differentiation is like rolling the marble back uphill to its earlier state or condition, so that it could develop another function next. It does not simply switch from one function to another laterally. A blood cell does not become a skin cell, jumping sideways.[7] It must go back up first and then develop in a new way. Biologists have observed this phenomenon when an animal (or plant) regenerates a new appendage. Once the old one became detached, the damaged surface left behind is comprised of specialized cells that now must be redeployed differently if the new appendage is to grow. The cells on this damaged surface return to a dedifferentiated state awaiting a new pathway and new functions. The process has been described in the following manner: "Dedifferentiation is regarded as one of the mechanisms involved in regeneration, as it enables cells, especially those without proliferative potential, to proliferate again and redifferentiate, leading to the replacement of the lost cells (Yao & Wang, 2020)."

Awarded the Nobel Prize in Physiology/Medicine, Shinya Yamanaka and John Gurdon proved that "mature specialized cells can be reprogrammed back to undifferentiated states—the process known as dedifferentiation (cited in Rabajante, Babierra, Tubay & Jose, 2015)." However, it is important for our purposes to note that "dedifferentiation may have either positive or negative consequences to tissue repair in different tissue/organs (Yao & Wang, 2020)." It is not always helpful. Nevertheless, "dedifferentiation in regenerative medicine may provide a new, rational, evolution-inspired strategy to bypass inherent limitations with therapeutic cells ... and initiate tissue development under better control (Yao & Wang, 2020)."

7 Dedifferentiation is distinct from what is known as exaptation, which is the process by which an organ originally serving one function, such as a fin for swimming, starts to be used for a different function, such as walking on dry ground (Fitch, 2018). That is a lateral move of a different kind.

Sociology

In systems thinking, a system might reorganize at a lower level of complexity. Talcott Parsons had described the process of social differentiation during which a social unit (or system) subdivides or splits into different functions, such as offense and defense in sports. Lechner (1990) noted that Parsons tended to see the positive effects of differentiation, such as the division of labor, and tended to elide possible problems with it, such as increasing detachment and isolation among the separated members or groups. Beyond a certain point, people stop interacting and create their own subcultures. Over time, they might drift apart or start working at cross purposes. In that situation, wrote Lechner (1990), the system might need to *de*-differentiate by returning to core values and the standardization of certain practices, reconnecting the parts somehow in a process of reintegration. The differentiation *of function* can continue as before; there is probably no reason to collapse the organizational structure. But the move toward dedifferentiation might pertain to other things, so that members understand how they fit into the larger system and acquire a greater sense of unity. In other words, a system can be differentiated in one respect while also being dedifferentiated in another respect. This is not inconceivable. It bears noting, however, that sometimes what sociologists mean by dedifferentiation is some kind of fusion, such as blending two different departments at the university in order to save money. This meaning of the term is regrettable. Instead, the proper meaning, according to Gary Rhoades, is a return to a previous status quo (1990, p. 192), almost like a retreat from a current position.[8]

As with other versions of the idea of dedifferentiation, this step away from complexity might enable greater complexity later, starting over with the same basic building blocks. One must break the structure apart in order to let the subsystems re-constellate in new ways. Here is a real-world example of dedifferentiation. The story is told of the firm that made exceptional buggy whips (Stross, 2010). Then, buggy whips became unnecessary, because people were buying horseless carriages. Whatever became of that buggy whip manufacturer? It had to dedifferentiate back to a simpler, more versatile condition in order to start making something customers

---

8 Dedifferentiation is thought by some to mean the death of the system itself because the only reason a system can be said to exist is because it can be differentiated from its environment. Failing that, it no longer exists. There is no system. The transition might result in total dissolution, never to return. Or the system might be resurrected in a new way. That interim phase of dedifferentiation can certainly look like the death of a system. But there is always more going on beneath the surface.

actually wanted. Or it went out of business, the individual parts of which being released to be used differently. The specialization, no matter how well done, was no longer in demand.

Back in 1959, Alvin Gouldner explained what dedifferentiation means for systems thinking. He wrote that parts of a system with a degree of functional autonomy can disassemble and reassemble in fresh configurations. He also called this "destructuring" (1967, p. 164). So temporarily, yes, a subsystem can transition by becoming no longer a system at all and then becoming a new subsystem. The integrity of the encompassing system changes, though it remains a system. He wrote that, however briefly, the system "surrenders" its "sovereignty" while this transition takes place. The city remains a city, for example, even if one family living in that city splits into two households because of a divorce. The system (city) persists, even while the subsystem (family) destructures. The two households become re-integrated into the city as separate units.

By the same token, the entire city can dissolve while the family remains intact. We might think of this as a pure case of dedifferentiation. Or the family simply moves to another city. The subsystem remains intact, but it leaves one system to join another. In the case of large-scale migrations, a community within a city, such as a religious sect, might gather up and leave, settling in a new territory in order to form a new city (Gouldner, 1967, p. 164f). In other words, for this process to make sense, one must consider systems at different levels of organization.

Part of Gouldner's message was that frequently dedifferentiation turns out to make the persistence of the larger system possible. The system is more robust if its subsystems can periodically dedifferentiate. Dedifferentiation might be an expedient (1967, p. 165f). He wrote that paradoxically "limited increases in randomness, by way of structural dedifferentiation, may be the ultimate defense of systems in the face of extremity (1967, p. 166)."

Psychology

As part of the origins of psychoanalysis, Sigmund Freud hypothesized that the distressed client might need to revisit some episode from the past in order to confront, say for example, a prior trauma. He was convinced that many conditions start in childhood (1997, p. 113). The remedy might lie in going back in the imagination to an earlier time, when the client was less developed psychologically, in order to face the episode consciously, now that the client has developed a more mature capacity to manage or cope. This kind of therapy might resemble dedifferentiation in the sense that something from the past, a memory, let us say, or a suppressed fear, has survived in a form that is proving to be dysfunctional in the present; so, the goal is to strip away the intervening years of maladaptation, isolate the dedifferentiated element, look at it in a new light, and reintegrate that element in a more functional way going forward. In a manner of speaking, one must take a giant step back now in order to gain some critical perspective. Then the work begins: the maladapted configuration of beliefs and practices must be reconfigured after starting over.

A theologian named Aarne Siirala noticed this tactic in the work of Freud where frequently "the happenings and nonhappenings [of early childhood] cause the most serious injury to human growth (1970, p. 122)." Consequently, Freud advised taking early developmental stages quite seriously, as though somewhere the child made a wrong turn and must return to that moment of decision in order to choose a different path. And for Freud, what awaits the client will be fearsome, having been suppressed for many years in a kind of wishful occlusion. The client shall have been averting his or her attention from the realization that something went wrong; instead, the client will likely resist revisiting the past, because doing so would appear to make the client vulnerable. Thus, one must overcome one's fear for the sake of the backward glance. Therapy requires such courage.

Siirala then pointed out that Martin Luther held to a similar view, namely that it would be wholesome to go back in one's mind to an earlier state, although in Luther's case, that earlier state would be a good thing, a happier time, the relative innocence of youth. Things were simpler then. The burdens of adulthood and the disappointments of life had not yet encrusted the mind, inducing us to become cynical and self-protective. For Luther, the goal was to go back before things had gone wrong. He differed from Freud in part by taking the position that this earlier state was blissful, innocent. (This, despite his belief in Original Sin.) Children have fun. They play. They sing. They exhibit a kind of purity that the world will slowly corrupt (if they let it). Siirala noted the many passages in Christian scripture where Jesus had insisted that followers become as little children themselves, abiding in faith and open to reality (1970, p. 123). Something in the mind must be dedifferentiated, returning to a simpler state.

Cognitive psychologist Howard Gardner came up with an ideal type which he called the Five-Year-Old-Mind (5YOM). He explained that the 5YOM represents the stage of cognitive development typically achieved by someone roughly ages five through seven in which the mind is relatively unformed, with only the most basic knowledge about the world. The child has probably not yet begun formal education in earnest. Nevertheless, he or she already uses a variety of symbols, which enables the child to start learning. The child has begun to build a storehouse of schemas about how the world works, even if these schemas are often simplistic, if not crude, and in many instances incorrect. Some of these schemas are more or less fixed, requiring education and experience to undo, yet the 5YOM is remarkably open to new schemas about many things. It is not so much a closed mind as an incomplete and naïve mind, with both extraordinary powers and limitations. In Gardner's words, "The five-year-old stands poised at the pinnacle of possibility (1997, p. 26)." At this stage, one might say that it is noticeably undifferentiated. Differentiation as a cognitive process usually begins in earnest at this point.

Gardner then went on to assert that with regard to any new activity, such as a skill or body of knowledge, the person still possesses a 5YOM, no matter how old they have become chronologically (see e.g. Gardner, 2011a, 2011b, pp. 118–121). That part of the brain is unformed – or as we have been calling it undifferentiated. For many purposes, adults will always possess a 5YOM. Until a student actually learns algebra, no matter when, he or she brings to it a 5YOM. An intellectual fifty years of age thoroughly trained in chemistry, for example, probably brings a 5YOM to issues of macroeconomics; there is no reason to assume that expertise in one area of study overcomes ignorance in another area of study (see Harter, 2019b; cf. Balinsky, 1940, p. 36). If anything, there is a risk that the chemist has jettisoned some of the positive aspects of the 5YOM. Adults tend to have lost much of a child's openness – the sense of wonder, curiosity, and humility that the typical five-year-old possesses. Gardner wrote about the 5YOM of "its adventurousness, its generativity, its resourcefulness, and its flashes of flexibility and creativity (2011b, p. 120)." This loss into adulthood will be especially acute in those who regard their expertise in one area of study as sufficient for everything else, an attitude that we might regard as a type of arrogance. For this reason, Gardner advises adults to "dedifferentiate" back to the 5YOM when undertaking a new intellectual project.

Moving from compact to differentiated to integrated

The philosopher Eric Voegelin adopted a simple schema to represent the structure of consciousness across time. Consciousness can be said to move from compactness through differentiation toward a comprehending integration. This transition greatly resembles the idea of analysis/synthesis. He referred to the process as making the knowable known (1956, p. 5). By moving in this direction, one also makes more apparent the distinction between that which is knowable and that which is unknowable. You and I can trace the development by which this occurs, as more and more of the knowable becomes known. In other words, the process describes a history. We say, for instance, that science makes progress.

By "compact" we mean to describe something so densely packed that an observer cannot discern its component parts. Michel Serres often referred to that which is compact as a black box, the contents of which are opaque. Systems thinking explains that if we can detect inputs and outputs without knowledge of its interior – which is to say, its "throughput" – then the system is compact. A person can regard it only from the outside and make inferences about how it works. Otherwise, its elements are indistinct (see Glanville, 2009; Bunge, 1963). So many things in daily life are experienced as compact until a person finds a way somehow to differentiate among its component parts, which is to say tease apart, unpack, separate, and disclose what had been otherwise inaccessible. Differentiation means that process by which the so-called black box is opened to scrutiny and sorted. What had been opaque has become transparent.

A glossary of technical terms used by Voegelin states that in his usage, compactness refers to "experience having distinguishable features not yet noticed as distinct" (Webster, 2006, p. 153). The corresponding explanation of his usage of "differentiation" refers to a process of noticing and also expressing these differences (Webster, 2006, p. 155).

Voegelin held that aspects of experience may become conscious, while others do not. They remain "compact" – still there, in all likelihood, but unnoticed or inarticulate. For him, differentiation means progress, a greater awareness. Until differentiation, that is, different things (objects and ideas) can easily be confused. It is a breakthrough to recognize that "this over here" is not the same as "that over there." At last, one can say, I "see" the difference. I won't be making that mistake anymore. That is the mundane way that it works. But let's be clear: Voegelin was not referring to every instance of differentiation, like learning the difference between ginger ale and root beer. These cognitive breakthroughs, such as they are, might technically be examples of differentiation, but Voegelin intended a more specific example. Differentiation, as he intended the term, signals an openness to the structure of being (Webb, 1981, p. 270f). As set forth in that glossary, his emphasis was on differentiating the transcendent as an abiding point of orientation. Any other point of orientation results in a closed existence and leads to deformation. He was less interested in ordinary moments of differentiation.

In the course of things, people can lose or reject a prior differentiation, for whatever reason, and revert or regress back to compactness. There is no guarantee of progress for individual human beings. In Voegelin's work, therefore, such regression might be judged to have been a failure and something to lament. Humanity struggles to discover what is true, and differentiation helps us to do that. Any movement away from truth is not falsehood but darkness, opacity (Webb, 1981, p. 158). And those are, in his opinion, bad things.

In response to his position, in what I am about to argue, sometimes one must de-differentiate before making further progress. This is a lot like saying that one must step back in order to get ahead, similar to a tactical retreat. Left to its own devices, differentiation may have led to a subsequent monstrosity, for example, after everything is put together; or at the very least that which has been differentiated may have become so specialized as to become vulnerable, in the way that certain dog breeds become functionally retarded.

As it happens, in addition to lamenting the loss of differentiation as a giant step backward, Voegelin did account for the occasional necessity of abandoning differentiations that fail to accord with experience. He used Xenophanes as a representative of this tactic, when Xenophanes questioned the seemliness of symbols, primarily the panoply of ancient myths (1957, pp. 171–174). The way that divinity had been presented as so many personages living on Mount Olympus was unsustainable. History records the many times that an existing equilibrium made up of multiple differentiations starts to collapse, and humanity is thrown back onto the grounding of experience, the primal layer out of which consciousness emerges. This is not so much a reversion to compactness ("I used to know X, but now I don't") as it is a reacquaintance with reality, necessitating a fresh attempt to differentiate experience all over again (Keulman, 1990, p. 135). Compactness is a kind of obliviousness, ignorance, whereas what Voegelin was urging stood in stark contrast as an intensification of one's attention, seeing the problematic nature of things, knowing there to *be* problems. One's version of reality proves to be inadequate, so one must look again at the reality itself. To that extent, yes, Voegelin was advising a kind of dedifferentiation en route to a greater depth of understanding. Dedifferentiation could serve a transient purpose, as a means of renewal.

In *The New Science of Politics* (2000), Voegelin had set forth a relatively straightforward historical lesson. He wrote, "The symbols in which a society interprets the meaning of its existence are meant to be true… (2000, p. 130)." That was always the objective. In the earliest empires, the standard by which to judge their meaning was transcendent order, exhibited foremost by the cosmos. Voegelin would call this the cosmological principle. As God orders the universe, so a king orders society. Anyone who comes to a different interpretation is mistaken. There is truth, which I will symbolize here as T_1, and anything else is False (F). There is no T_2. Except that eventually, there would be alternative truths. There would be external, rival empires, for example, competing for territory, and there would be internal rebels. When an empire finds itself confronting rival truths (T_1 versus T_2), the only standard for resolving the dispute was force of arms. In that era, might made right.

Except that Voegelin stated explicitly in his introduction to *Order and History* (1956) that this was not the case, not initially. He wrote,

> The self-interpretation of an early empire as the one and only true representative of cosmic order on earth is not in the least shaken by the existence of neighboring empires who indulge in the same type of interpretation.... [People understood] that the order of being can be represented analogically in more than one way.
>
> *(2000, p. 7)*

What I believe about the world – whatever it is – does not have to contradict what you believe. One might say that even polytheists sensed behind their panoply of divine characters a unified reality. Only later did the imagery of a jealous god – solitary and universal – emerge.

With the passage of time, another standard for determining truth arose in multiple locations. Perhaps social order was not meant to accord with the cosmos; instead, it was meant to accord with reason or revelation, i.e. something from the mind of an individual (whether a prophet or a philosopher), and the standard was no longer brute strength and force of arms. Voegelin called this the anthropological principle (2000, p. 143). As a result of this axial age, different individuals offered alternative truth claims about the meaning of society, so that once again the community would be confronted with a conflict of truths (T_1 v. T_2). In these instances, however, the resolution would have to be sought by means other than war, such as scripture (in the case of revelation) or logic (in the case of philosophy). Or, society might subdivide into religious sects or philosophical schools.

Christianity introduced into the West a third standard, which Voegelin called soteriological truth, based upon doctrines of salvation. For hundreds of years, Christianity promulgated a belief that there is one God and one universal truth (T_3). There were right answers and wrong answers, and nobody could simply split off from civilization and live separately, for to do so was wrong. It was to live in sin. Thus, when a conflict of truths eventually broke out yet again, as it no doubt would do so repeatedly, we come back to the question of how to resolve these disputes. With the passage of time, the church started to resemble the cosmological order in its reliance on prosecution (e.g. the Inquisition) and warfare (e.g. the Crusades). The church resorted to might. What interested Voegelin in these lectures (from which I am extracting these lessons), was the experience of losing faith in any truth – that is, in any symbolization of the meaning of existence. What if T_1 starts to disintegrate, without any viable alternative T_2? What then?

The understandable anxiety that accompanies this spirit of suspicion required one of two basic responses. The first was what Voegelin called at the time Gnosticism, which is a heresy that seems to have influenced politics in the West ever since. Much of *The New Science of Politics* was an explanation of this response. The second response is far less attractive, because it confronts the anxious individual with two unpleasant realizations: first, that suffering is inescapable; and disorder, a fact of life; and second, that the mystery behind the meaning of existence is beyond human understanding (1957, p. 172).

It would be unnecessary therefore to hold that Voegelin regarded all differentiation as an advance, if not a leap in being. Some differentiation, yes, constituted an advance, such as the recognition that in the hierarchy of being, there is a gulf between human beings and a transcendent deity (1956, p. 9). Human beings progressed from differentiating components of a knowable reality to differentiating that which is knowable from that which is not (1956, p. 5). The latter breakthrough accords with the basic distinction between that which is passing (such as human life) and that which is lasting (such as God) (1956, p. 3). And just as the differentiation among components that are knowable requires symbolization to reflect the various relations and tensions in the field of existence (e.g. names of things and theories about how they interact) (1956, p. 3), the differentiation between the knowable and the unknowable requires symbolization as well to reflect the tensions, frictions, and balances that result as we try to understand our situation (1956, p. 11).

Forgetting a distinction once learned in school, as for example, between poetry and pushpin, might be regrettable, but it hardly constitutes "a recession from an adequate symbolization of truth concerning the order of being (1956, p. ix)." People are exposed to thousands of minor distinctions that have no bearing on the history of order. (All one has to do is go grocery shopping to encounter hundreds of mundane distinctions. Did you want whole milk or skim milk, in the gallon size or the quart, according to a specific brand or generic, etc.?) Instead, only certain recessions interested Voegelin. And even then, like I said, the remedy is frequently an act of dedifferentiation.

Perhaps the most penetrating examination of this kind of analysis was his 1966 book *Anamnesis* and its account of "a reactualization of the path that has been traversed (Walsh, 2002, p. 5)." This sounds very much like dedifferentiation. In these pages, Voegelin had set out to remedy the tendency of symbols to congeal as doctrine or dogma – to harden into literalizations, as his editor was to put it (2002, p. 17). Rather than a return to the past, however, before things went wrong, anamnesis as a technique is a recovery of a more immediate, open encounter with the engendering experience, a no-longer-forgetting.[9] The *Collected Works* (volume 6, edited by David Walsh) brilliantly begins by reprinting remarks at the passing of Voegelin's friend Alfred Schutz, where Voegelin brings forward into the present the significance of Schutz to his own thinking. Schutz is still alive in the mind of Voegelin. What mattered was a willingness and ability to turn toward the continuing presence of his departed friend (2002, pp. 41–44). He wrote,

> Nearly four decades of shared thinking and mutual criticism do not only leave their marks upon the work, they also leave behind the habit of asking oneself, throughout that work, what the other person would say about it. One of the keenest philosophical minds of our time is still the silent partner of my thinking.
>
> *(2002, p. 44)*

Voegelin refused to forget his friend. He returned again and again to his engendering experiences of Schutz – not as a return to some prior event over the course of forty years, but instead as a return to the state or condition of being in a relationship with him now. That experience we might refer to as an encounter with transcendence (2002, p. 71), for the experience of another person is transcendent. In a previous letter to his friend Schutz, Voegelin was articulating his respect for Schutz's mentor (Edmund Husserl) with regard to phenomenology, but he was also explaining where he believed Husserl had been limited by ignoring transcendence (2002, p. 83).

The act of differentiating, however it is achieved and whatever it is that it produces, would not stand as the final step in a process (Voegelin, 1974, p. 176). Instead, one must then go back to integrate that which was differentiated, which is to say that one must explain how they are related to one another. Let us call the differentia X and Y. What then is the relationship X-Y? Together, these are constituents of one overarching reality. This step puts it all into context, by an act of synthesis – not to blend or blur them back together so that they become compact again and the differentiation lost, but instead to demonstrate their role in a comprehending system. What is X to Y? And what is Y to X?

---

9 The last chapter in this book is an equivalent exercise.

An example of dedifferentiation: The archaeology of leadership[10]

The process known as dedifferentiation occurs across many domains. What might appear to be a retreat or surrender of prior gains, the process can also prove to be wholesome, if not generative, whether we are talking about biology, sociology, psychology, logic, history, or economics. But of what use is the concept to Leadership Studies, which is the focus of this entire book? Aside from the obvious utility of thinking well, as for example, breaking down somebody's argument and prioritizing steps in social projects, I would suggest the following.

Giorgio Agamben composed a little essay on philosophical archaeology (2009) in which he explains that the history of anything begins at the moment of its emergence. Prior to that in time is its pre-history. The history of a human being, for example, begins at birth. The history of a nation begins at its founding. The history of a book begins at publication. We would not say that these things appear *ex nihilo* (out of nothing). They are not uncaused, appearing spontaneously. So, the question arises: what comes before the emergence? If there was no human being before birth, no nation before founding, and no book before publication, what in fact was there? Part of the science of any phenomenon, including leadership, is an investigation into the conditions for its emergence. How is this thing that we are studying made possible?

Agamben insists that archaeology is not a record of what happened at the moment of its emergence. That much is part of its history. Neither does a pre-history ask what happened immediately beforehand. Taking this one step further back in time in this way, archaeology does not simply look at what happened preceding the emergence either, because we would not know what to look at. Pre-history is literally before there is a history to consult. A lot of things were happening at the moment of emergence – not all of which turn out to have been relevant (a logical mistake at the root of astrology). One must have some sense of what to look for. But to have a sense of what to look for is not always possible. And in some instances, to know in advance what to look for is to pre-judge the investigation, almost as though one has already secretly answered the question and simply needed evidence to validate a hypothesis. To be sure, the scientific method often proceeds in this fashion, in a process labeled by Charles Sanders Peirce as abduction. Even then, it is a process grounded in a comprehending architecture.

---

10 The following section appeared previously in open access at Harter, 2021 (https://doi.org/10.20935/AL497).

Archaeology of the kind described by Agamben tries to isolate what the Greeks called the *archē*, something that "assures the synchronic comprehensibility and coherence of the system" (Agamben, 2009, p. 92). Agamben then explains that to some extent, this is what intellectuals such as Sigmund Freud and Michel Foucault were doing. Freud, for instance, was not slavishly arguing that events in infancy dictate the development of one's adult psyche, in a simple schema of cause-and-effect. "A" does not precede and cause "B." Instead, he was saying that already present in the infant is an emergence of certain drives that the child will go on to constellate as the years pass. "A" itself is continuous. How it participates in "B" is a question of that individual patient's peculiar attempt to integrate "A" with a bunch of other drives. "A" is there in one's psyche throughout one's life, helping to shape the personality. It is at all times a constituent part. What Freud sought in his investigations was the resulting architecture, the formation or shape of one's personality. One need not conduct research into the moment of birth to find this "A" (let alone the moment immediately preceding it), because that so-called architecture exists in the mature adult lying there at this moment on the therapist's couch. What emerged at birth is still here. In popular opinion, psychoanalysis has to do with regression back to an earlier phase, when each of us was a little baby, whereas for Freud the objective is to accompany the patient in an imaginative reconstruction from his or her present point of view. He was interested in the mind as it is today. This attempt to reconstruct an architecture reveals itself in the remembering. His method may appear to be *à reculons*, but it is not (Agamben, 2009, p. 98, quoting Melandri, 2004).

It follows that an archaeology of leadership, conducted in the same spirit, would investigate the conditions out of which the phenomenon emerges, and by this is meant the governing *archē* that assures the synchronic comprehensibility and coherence of the system. Such things were present in the phenomenon itself as an ordering principle, but they must be excavated, going beneath the surface of what transpires. And thankfully, the evidence for it persists in the present.

Leadership Studies education reflects the fact that the field of inquiry is an ongoing dialogue open to the disciplines (Levine, 2018; Andenoro et al., 2013, p. 6; Harvey & Riggio, 2012), which means that it must be opposed to reductionist thinking. Accordingly, the literature tends to reward methodological pluralism at multiple levels (e.g. Yammarino & Dionne, 2019), ranging from quantitative analysis to historical case studies (e.g. Riggio, 2019; Schyns, Hall & Neves, 2017; Klenke, 2008). Such research takes place within a theoretical framework that often requires its own focus (Levine, 2015; Andenoro et al., 2013, p. 3).

We can posit that students begin with an Implicit Leadership Theory (ILT) (see Schyns & Meindl, 2005), a theory oftentimes appropriate to what Howard Gardner (2011a) referred to as the five-year-old mind. Leadership education exists in part to make a student's ILT explicit and to complexify it as part of developing expertise. So, there is at least this one place for investigating the theory itself. Different academic disciplines often offer different theoretical frameworks. For purposes of illustration, we can apply a framework from the field of anthropology – and more specifically from the work of Ruth Benedict (1934).

The framework I am talking about begins in an act of differentiation with a dichotomy. Benedict (1934) observed that most cultural practices serve multiple impulses. A marriage is for more than reproduction, dinnertime is for more than sustenance, and war is for more than brawling. She decided to call each separate impulse a pinpoint. The cultural practice consists of multiple pinpoints she called a constellation. A classic description of an unfamiliar constellation and its many pinpoints appears in Clifford Geertz's ethnography about the Balinese cockfight (1972/2000). A cockfight can be a party, a ritual, a sport, an economic transaction, a drama, and a process for establishing dominance. Constellations for these impulses vary from one culture to another; they also change over time, with a life span. Niklas Luhmann, for example, described the recent untangling of a hidebound constellation combining lust, romantic love, and the institution of marriage (2008/2010).

Comparative study reveals that the same impulse in different cultures can be satisfied in different ways. Obviously, in a complex culture such as ours, the same impulse can be served by different practices. By the same token, two different impulses can be satisfied in the exact same way, so that to an outsider they would appear to be the same thing. It is with this framework in mind that leadership can be regarded as a cultural practice. At any given time, it serves multiple impulses simultaneously. The array of impulses constituting leadership varies across time and from one culture to another.

Complicating things, participants are ambivalent if not conflicted about these impulses (Merton, 1976) – to the extent they are even conscious of them.

Leadership Studies could launch research using Benedict's distinction. What are the originating impulses that make leadership possible? My hypothesis, inspired by Agamben and Benedict, is that an archaeology of leadership reveals an *archē* of dialogue. Behind any theory of leadership lies a pinpoint impulse to engage in discourse, i.e. to talk things out. This practice of dialogue, I would contend, serves the synchronic comprehensibility and coherence of any leadership system, whatever it happens to look like in actual practice.

Dialogue is our shared response to the demands of reality, of that-which-lies-over-and-against (to borrow a phrase from Heidegger), as we compare perceptions, entertain possible strategies, and formulate a plan. Heidegger (1981/1995) posits that social change can result from discourse (p. 99), or *logos*. An encounter with reality sets a person to striving, which begins in the imagination as an idea, to be uttered aloud in the company of others. Until that moment, leadership in the sense I intend the term has not yet occurred. It is Julius Caesar pausing at the precipice. Leadership as a formal position, as dominance or even authority may preexist this moment, and this is often how the word is used in ordinary speech, but not until the exchange of thoughts and ideas does the interaction fit the definition popularized by Joseph Rost (1991/1993) of leadership *as a process*.

There has been a separate literature regarding the emergence of systems without any conscious design by participants (see Johnson, 2001). These systems form in the absence of discourse about leadership, in much the same way that ants coordinate and cities grow. Social change can result in processes without discourse. Heidegger would not deny it (again, see e.g. 1981/1995, p. 99). Other forces shape social reality and the systems by which we function. Nevertheless, I see no reason to call any of it leadership unless and until it satisfies the condition of dialogue.

References

Agamben, G. (2009). *The signature of all things: On method* (L. D'Isanto & K. Attell, trans.). Zone Books.

Andenoro, A., Allen, S., Haber-Curran, P., Jenkins, D., Sowcik, M., Dugan, J., & Osteen, L. (2013). *National Leadership Education research agenda* 2013–2018: *Providing strategic direction for the field of leadership education*. Retrieved 15 August 2019 from https://www.leadershipeducators.org/Resources/Docu ments/NLEResearchAgenda.3.pdf.

Balinsky, B. (1940). *An analysis of the mental factors of various age groups from nine to sixty* [dissertation]. New York University.

Beaney, M. "Analysis." In Zalta, E.N. (ed.) (Summer 2021 Edition). *The Stanford Encyclopedia of philosophy*. Retrieved from https://plato.stanford.edu/archives/sum2021/entries/analysis/.

Benedict, R. (1934). *Patterns of culture*. Mariner Book.

Bunge, M. (1963, October). "A general black box theory." *Philosophy of Science*. *30*(4): 346–358.

Child, C.M. (1915). *Senescence and rejuvenescence*. The University of Chicago Press. https://doi.org/10.5962/bhl.title.57772.

Cooper, B. (2018). *Consciousness and politics: From analysis to meditation in the late work of Eric Voegelin*. St. Augustine's Press.

Copi, I. (1978). *Introduction to logic* (5th ed.). Macmillan Publishing Co.

Fitch, W.T. "Exaptation." In Brockman, J. (ed.) (2018). *This idea is brilliant: Lost, overlooked, and underappreciated scientific concepts everyone should know* (pp. 11–17). Harper Perennial.

Freud, S. "Five lectures on psycho-analysis." In Freud, S. (ed.) (1997). *Selected writings* (pp. 77–138). W.W. Norton & Co.

Gardner, H.E. (2011a). *Leading minds: An anatomy of leadership*. Basic Books.

Gardner, H.E. (2011b). *The unschooled mind: How children think and how schools should teach*. Basic Books.

Gardner, H. (1997). *Extraordinary minds: Portraits of exceptional individuals and an examination of our extraordinariness*. Basic Books.

Geertz, C. "Deep play: Notes on a Balinese cockfight." In Geertz, C. (ed.) (1972/2000). *The interpretation of cultures* (ch. 15). Basic Books.

Glanville, R. (2009). "Black boxes." *Cybernetics and Human Knowing. 16*(1–2): 153–167.

Gouldner, A. "Reciprocity and autonomy in functional theory." In Demerath N.J. & R. Peterson (eds.) (1967). *System, change, and conflict: A reader on contemporary sociological theory and the debate over functionalism*. Free Press.

Habermas, J. "Beyond a temporalized philosophy of origins: Jacques Derrida's critique of phonocentrism." In Habermas, J. (ed.) (1993). *The philosophical discourse of modernity: Twelve lectures* (F. Lawrence, trans.) (pp. 161–184). The MIT Press.

Harter, N. (2021). "An archaeology of leadership." *Academia Letters*, Article 497. https://doi.org/10.20935/AL497.

Harter, N. "Eric Voegelin's 1944 'Political Theory and the Pattern of General History': An account from the biography of a philosophizing consciousness." In Robinson, S., L. Trepanier, & D. Whitney (eds.) (2019a). *Eric Voegelin today: Voegelin's political thought in the 21st century* (ch. 9). Lexington Books.

Harter, N. (2019b). Book review. "From Benito Mussolini to Hugo Chavez: Intellectuals and a century of political hero worship." by Paul Hollander. *VoegelinView* (online journal). https://voegelinview.com/from-benito-mus-solini-to-hugo-chavez-intellectuals-and-a-century-of-political-hero-worship/

Harvey, M., & Riggio, R. (eds.) (2012). *Leadership studies: The dialogue of disciplines*. Edward Elgar.

Heidegger, M. (1981/1995). *Aristotle's Metaphysics Θ 1-3: On the essence and actuality of force* (W. Brogan & P. Warnek, trans.). Indiana University Press.

Johnson, S. (2001). *Emergence: The connected lives of ants, brains, cities, and software*. Scribner.

Keulman, K. (1990). *The balance of consciousness: Eric Voegelin's political theory*. Pennsylvania State University Press.

Klenke, K. (2008). *Qualitative research in the study of leadership*. Emerald.

Lechner, F. "Fundamentalism and sociocultural revitalization: On the logic of dedifferentiation." In Alexander, J. & P. Colomy (eds.) (1990). *Differentiation theory and social change: Comparative and historical perspectives* (ch. 3). Columbia University Press.

Levine, D. (2018). *Dialogical social theory* (H. Schneiderman, ed.). Routledge.

Levine, D. (2015). *Social theory as a vocation: Genres of theory work in sociology*. Transaction Publishers.

Luhmann, N. (2008/2010). *Love: A sketch* (K. Cross, trans.). Polity.

McKeon, R. (2016). *On knowing: The social sciences.* University of Chicago Press.

Merton, R. (1976). *Sociological ambivalence and other essays.* Free Press.

Oshry, B. (1995). *Seeing systems: Unlocking the mysteries of organizational life.* Berrett-Koehler.

Pennacchioli, G., & Valley, R. (dirs.) (2019). "Zima Blue." *Love, Death & Robots* (season 1; episode 14). Netflix.

Rabajante, J.F., Babierra, A.L., Tubay, J.M., & Jose, E.C. (2015). "Mathematical modeling of cell-fate specification: From simple to complex epigenetics." *Stem Cells Epigenetics.* 2: e752. https://doi.org/10.14800/sce.752.

Rhoades, G. "Political competition and differentiation in higher education." In Alexander, J. & P. Colomy (eds.) (1990). *Differentiation theory and social change: Comparative and historical perspectives* (ch. 6). Columbia University Press.

Riggio, R. (ed.) (2019). *What's wrong with leadership? Improving leadership research and practice* (ch. 2). Routledge.

Rost, J. (1991/1993). *Leadership for the twenty-first century.* Praeger.

Schlag, P. (2009). "The dedifferentiation problem." *Continental Philosophy Review.* 42: 35–62.

Schyns, B., Hall, R., & Neves, P. (eds.) (2017). *Handbook of methods in leadership research.* Edward Elgar.

Schyns, B., & Meindl, J.R. (eds.) (2005). *Implicit leadership theories: Essays and explorations.* Information Age Publishing.

Sebba, G. "Prelude and variations on the theme of Eric Voegelin." In Sandoz, E. (ed.) (1982). *Eric Voegelin's thought: A critical appraisal* (pp. 3–65). Duke University Press.

Serres, M. (2018). *The incandescent* (R. Burks, trans.). Bloomsbury Academic.

Siirala, A. (1970). *Divine humanness* (T.A. Kantonen, trans.). Fortress Press.

Sipiora, M. (2023). *Psychological citizenship and democracy: The political relevance of James Hillman's archetypal psychology.* Spring Publications.

Stross, R. (2010). "Failing like a buggy whip maker? Better check your simile." *New York Times.* Retrieved 26 June 2023 from https://www.nytimes.com/2010/01/10/business/10digi.html.

Swaminathan, B.K. (2023). "Zima Blue: Ending explained." *This Is Barry.* Retrieved 10 July 2023 from https://www.thisisbarry.com/film/zima-blue-ending-explained-love-death-robots/.

Voegelin, E. (2002). *Collected works* (vol. 6) (D. Walsh, ed.). University of Missouri Press.

Voegelin, E. (2000). *Collected works* (vol. 5) (M. Henningsen, ed.). University of Missouri Press.

Voegelin, E. (1974). *Order and history* (vol. IV). Louisiana State University Press.

Voegelin, E. (1957). *Order and history* (vol. II). Louisiana State University Press.

Voegelin, E. (1956). *Order and history* (vol. I). Louisiana State University Press.

Walsh, D. "Editor's introduction." In Voegelin, E. (ed.) (2002). *Collected works* (vol. 6; pp. 1–27) (D. Walsh, ed.). University of Missouri Press.

Webb, E. (1981). *Eric Voegelin: Philosopher of history.* University of Washington Press.

Webster, L. "Glossary of terms used in Eric Voegelin's writings." In Voegelin, E. (ed.) (2006). *Collected works* (vol. 34; pp. 149–186). University of Missouri Press.

Yammarino, F., & Dionne, S. "Leadership and levels of analysis." In Riggio, R. (ed.) (2019). *What's wrong with leadership? Improving leadership research and practice* (ch. 2). Routledge.

Yao, Y., & Wang, C. (2020). "Dedifferentiation: Inspiration for devising engineering strategies for regenerative medicine." *npj Regenerative Medicine*. 5: 14. https://doi.org/10.1038/s41536-020-00099-8.

4

GETTING BACK AT THEM

Grievance and resentment as a motive for leadership

Introduction to this chapter[1]

In the study of leadership, scholars investigate the motives of followers. Why would people follow a particular leader? Toward what imagined end? Much ink has been spilled over the rise of populist political leaders in recent years, oftentimes arriving at the conclusion that followers harbor some sense of resentment – or, to say it with nuance, a sense of *ressentiment* (e.g. Tomkins, 2021; Ciulla, 2020; Capriles, 2012). Academics trying to understand the emergence of Donald Trump as a political figure, for example, want to know about his voters: Who are these people? What do they want? One such study published by the Columbia University Press wrote about *Trump, the Klan, and the Mainstreaming of Resentment* (McVeigh & Estep, 2019). But of course, down through the ages followers have often been motivated by a spirit of grievance. This much is nothing new.

I would go a step further. *Ressentiment* is actually quite widespread in modernity, on every side of contemporary troubles (e.g. Schneider, 2023; Tomelleri, 2015, p. xxxf). Here is not only a populist sentiment, cultivated by demagogues on the right to rouse a basket of deplorables.[2] *Ressentiment* is something that anyone of any persuasion or identity can

---

1 The author is especially indebted to Elizabeth Fleury, Jenna McElhannon, and Norah Sheldon for their assistance with this chapter.
2 https://en.wikipedia.org/wiki/Basket_of_deplorables. This chapter will cite a number of popular idioms.

DOI: 10.4324/9781003540526-5

experience (Capelos & Demertzis, 2022, p. 122). There is enough bitter energy surrounding nearly any question that can be reduced to Us versus Them. Neither "side" of a controversy has a monopoly on it. Personally, I reject the implication that "they" are fueled by *ressentiment*, the poor fools, whereas "our side" is righteously indignant.

From individual indignation or outrage to collective forms of vengeance and retaliation, grievance has fueled leadership repeatedly. Rival parties, feuding families, warring nations, dispossessed populations – leaders have had plenty of opportunities to stir up and exploit such feelings. Francis Fukuyama stated, "[People] can be seduced by leaders who tell them that they have been betrayed and disrespected by the existing power structures, and that they are members of important communities whose greatness will again be recognized (2018, p. 165)." Leadership Studies has every reason to take a giant step back from current events, fraught though they might be, in order to ponder the role of *ressentiment* more broadly. What I would suggest in the following pages is that, in addition to asking what leadership is for, perhaps we should take just as seriously the question about what leadership is *against*.

A preliminary statement about resentment

At some point, everybody experiences insult or injury, beginning with the trauma of childbirth. And just as probably, everybody has done something to insult or injure somebody else. Speaking more broadly, everybody belongs to a group or collective that once experienced insult or injury. And by the same token, every group has done something to insult or injure members of another group. The catalogue of insults and injuries going back and forth is pretty long and widespread and frankly beyond tabulating.

Let us note that the insult or injury could be imagined, a product of misperception, such that there was in fact no insult or injury. Or such that nobody actually *caused* the insult or injury. This possibility does not mean that people do not undergo these experiences. They do. Set aside also the question of whether those insults and injuries were intended by anybody. Accidents and misunderstandings occur all of the time. In addition, set aside for a moment the question whether one person or one group engages in hurtful activities more than another, as though we could weigh them out on the imagined scales of historical justice. I see no advantage in calculating which group is "worse" than another. The empirical starting point for what I have to say is that every individual and every group has been insulted, injured, or both. Everybody is to one degree or another a victim, and everybody is to one degree or another a culprit. Peter Sloterdijk (2010) was to put it this way: "Are not all civilizations, either openly or in secret, always archives of collective trauma (p. 48)?"

For present purposes, let us refer to those who have been insulted or injured as **victims**. The claim of insult or injury is a **grievance** that the victim possesses regarding the person or group who is, in their opinion, responsible for that insult or injury. And one of the key feelings associated with having been insulted or injured is **resentment** – a feeling mixed with anger, indignation, and the like. The following pages will modify these terms slightly, making them more precise, yet they belong at the center of our deliberations.

The question to be framed is as follows: how are scholars to understand the role of resentment as a motive to follow someone as a leader? In order to begin to answer that question, our deliberations will benefit from consulting a variety of literatures ranging from psychology to sociology, politics, ethics, and philosophy. Fiction frequently depicts examples of this phenomenon. See for example Shakespeare's *Romeo and Juliet*. Ultimately, we can find evidence that leaders often rely on followers as victims with grievances, such that leadership will have been fueled in those cases by resentment. I am by no means the first to notice this possibility (see Sloterdijk, 2010). Nevertheless, I hope to inform the field of Leadership Studies about what this insight might mean, not only as an explanation about incidents from the past but also more significantly about prospects for our shared future.

What does it mean to say that every person is a victim? What does it mean to say that every person has grievances? And what does it mean to say that every person is susceptible to feelings of resentment? How then does that volatile combination fuel incidents of leadership?

The historical evidence of resentment

Marc Ferro (2010) published a short book illustrating examples from around the world and down through the ages of various instances where expressions of resentment influenced the course of history. Beginning with antiquity and running into the twentieth-first century, the author gives concrete evidence that resentment frequently drives behavior. It is not a uniquely modern phenomenon. Neither is it a product unique to the Western mind. In fact, Ferro goes so far as to allege that resentment turns out to be a recurring theme in the annals of history because it is an integral part of the human experience. Literally, everybody has grievances of one kind or another. And when resentment does not manifest in overt behavior, such as insurrections, revolts, and rebellion, it smolders nevertheless below the surface, unexpressed perhaps, surviving years and years in a latent condition. Ferro found that resentment is universal, but it becomes historically significant when it resolves itself as political, military, and criminal action (2010, p. 10).[3]

Ferro's catalogue is quite extensive, dating back to early slave uprisings. Sloterdijk concurred when he wrote, "From the furies of Orestes to the hysterics of Medea, ancient theater paid tribute to the dramatic potency of revengeful forces (2010, p. 50)." Serres wrote much the same: "History – a well of resentment (1997, p. 86)." As one group was perceived to act unjustly toward another group, resentment arose. The resulting tension, however, creates a situation in which each side harbors resentment against the other. Often, for instance, the resentful group gradually attains power and in retaliation treats the first group unfairly, beginning a pattern of mutual resentments. In fact, the grievances might be based on lies and propaganda, without any evidence of wrongdoing; it apparently doesn't matter whether the stories are true or not, so long as they are believed. Ferro even asserts that resentment does not require a specific cause, a distinctive trauma to point to (2010, p. 128). Resentment is more of a feeling, a feeling about others. Or, more precisely, a feeling about the bitter perception of one's own inferiority to others (2010, p. 127). The Roman Empire persecuted the early Christians, who eventually rose to command the empire and used the organs of power to treat heretics and Jews unfairly. Ferro concludes that in most cases, resentment is reciprocal, a simultaneous or alternating hostility that outlives the moment. Actions by one group that create resentment in another group are often a response to the second group's previous actions, which in turn may have been justified by their resentment against the first group for some prior offense, back and forth (2010, p. 129). It is a long, sad, recurrent tide.

Ferro writes about ongoing political, ethnic, and religious rivalries that would seem to fit this bipolar model, a simple Us versus Them schema, except that often there are multiple players bearing resentment against one another. We might say that resentment turns out to be multilateral. For instance, Ferro writes about the Austrians who resented the West for dismantling its empire in 1918 (2010, pp. 84–92), though even before that it had resented Hungary and the Czechs for their attempts within the empire to gain precedence. Many Austrians resented the Nazis who took over Austria in 1938 in what is known as the *Anschluss*, whereas just as many regarded the Nazis as their vindicators, their liberators against perfidious others. Throughout this period, many Austrians were generally not without a deep-seated resentment of the Jews in their midst. And after the

---

3 By implication, then, resentment often resolves itself as political, military, and criminal action *by means of somebody's leadership*.

war, a substantial number of Austrian citizens resented their own political leaders for acquiescing to the Third Reich. In short, there was plenty of resentment to go around (see also Schorske, 1981, ch. 3). And these Austrians were not unique in this regard. Poland has had reason to begrudge Germans, Slavs, and the West – not only for twentieth-century violence and oppression, but also for ingratitude dating back to 1683 (Ferro, 2010, pp. 74–84). The point is that resentment presents itself within a binary structure, when the reality is often more complex. For our purposes, I will restrict myself in these pages to that bipolar structure, with the understanding that more complex situations might require greater sensitivity.

Ferro is especially keen to describe the situation in his native France. In one section of his book, he examines the period of Vichy government between 1940 and 1944, when collaborators supported the Nazis and resented the Resistance for terrorist activities that disrupted business, inasmuch as they were thereby ruining a fragile peace that had been negotiated with the Germans specifically to *avoid* violence and conquest; obviously, the members of the Resistance resented the collaborators for, well, for collaborating (2010, pp. 61–72). On both sides, though, one can find evidence of internecine squabbling. One sub-group resents another sub-group. Ferro documents so many factions and personalities at the time that the entire nation was a veritable parfait of resentments. Unfortunately, something similar had occurred long before, during the French Revolution (1789–1799), when the poor resented the aristocracy and the wealthy, the wealthy bourgeoisie resented the aristocracy for blocking their access to status and power, and the aristocracy resented both the poor and the bourgeoisie. Plenty of resentment to go around.

Strangely, those who justify their sense of resentment and claim it as part of their identity often find themselves resenting others who also express resentment. *Their* grievances – whoever they are – are unlike *our* grievances (Ferro, 2010, p. 13). "Nobody knows the trouble I seen." Some Jews resented Serbs for trying to equate their totally unrelated grievances, just as some African-Americans find themselves resenting Jews for throwing up their troubled past. Each group seems to want to believe they are *uniquely* aggrieved. Victims resent other victims, almost as though resentment were a zero-sum game. Furthermore, victims resent those who try to say that there are grounds for resentment going both ways, precisely as Ferro has done. And as I am doing now. That is to say that apparently nobody should be permitted to take the position that both "sides" have their grievances against one another; ironically, those who try to transcend the partisan feeling and take a balanced view are themselves resented (Ferro, 2010, p. 15).

History demonstrates that conflicts can persist for centuries, one side against the other. (Witness the Middle East.) But Ferro notes that not infrequently erstwhile allies can have a falling out and generate fresh grievances. At one time, he reports, ordinary Russians believed that the Tsar would champion their cause against the aristocracy and against the wealthy, yet when the Tsar proved to be inadequate, their resentment turned against him and resolved itself in revolution. Something similar happened leading up to the French Revolution (2010, p. 22f). Czechoslovakia had high hopes that the West would intervene to thwart Hitler's predations of the Sudetenland, but that support never materialized. Furthermore, those who lead an uprising based on resentment can be resented if they go too far or use the opportunity to enrich themselves (e.g. Ferro, 2010, p. 29).

In his study of history, Ferro detected a common pattern. Personal resentments, based on various affronts and slights and indignities, fuel a subsequent animosity toward an entire group, toward those in positions of authority, such that one's complaints – whether against a parent, a teacher, a military commander, a rich neighbor, a bully – might have assumed the form of an ideology against anyone who enjoys an equivalent stature on a larger scale. Sloterdijk observed that "conceptual fixations are the best preservative for ephemeral responses. He who wants to remember his rage needs to preserve it in hate containers (2010, p. 57)." Ideology is just such a hate container. Once you adopt an ideology, you can easily replace one oppressor with another, reducing them to a caricature, saying in effect that they are all alike. Victims deftly lump them all together: anyone with privilege or power incites resentment. Thus, a rejected painter finds an outlet for his shame in the Nazi party. Such a transference can displace resentment from actual people onto institutions and symbols, for example, flags, castles, and even orange trees (Ferro, 2010, p. 31). After a point, the resentment becomes free-floating, untethered to any particular culprit; the initial move is to convert one's personal experience into a broader belief about who is to blame for one's frustrations. That is key to understanding leadership. In short, the personal becomes political and vice versa.

Ferro credits Lenin with recognizing this natural tendency of converting a private feeling into overt action against the system and using it to channel a revolution (see also Sloterdijk, 2010, p. 66ff). But then here is the interesting thing. Whatever one's private feelings and whatever one's personal experience, Lenin had to make the ideology paramount. It was his mission to use the personal for political ends. How you feel about this or that incident may have inspired an individual to join the cause, yet that precipitating experience – whatever it was – is literally incidental and potentially distracting from the doctrine. Lenin was not above using a person's feelings to get what he believed was politically necessary, though feelings had to be brought within some abiding creed against those in power. Lenin never lost sight of the political objective. As a leader, he could not trust feelings (2010, pp. 39ff). You might have good reason to resent X, but he needed you to resent an entire class of people to which X belongs. Imagine, for example, if that free-floating resentment were to be directed back at him! That would never do. One might call this process the Weaponizing of Resentment, and it has considerable value as a template when examining episodes of leadership generally.[4] The idea is to channel your feelings based on personal experience toward affirming a settled worldview in which there are specified victims and culprits.

Recently, a college football coach had to find a way to motivate his team after winning the national title in 2022, so he kept telling the players during the following season that everybody doubted them, doubting that they could repeat. He stirred up a mood of defiance against the outside world. A sportswriter observed his motivation tactics:

> If there's one thing we learned from the Georgia Bulldogs' 65-7 thrashing of TCU in the national championship game earlier this week, it's that motivation is extremely important in college football…. One of the reasons the Bulldogs went 15-0 this season is because Kirby Smart was able to keep his team motivated all season despite winning the national championship the previous year. One of the ways he did this was to make his team believe that they were doubted all year long, even though that was nowhere close to being the case. [The coach] uses various slights — real or imagined — to keep his team motivated.
>
> *(Ragan, 2023)*

The nature and types of grievance

The terms "resentment" and "ressentiment" do not mean quite the same thing. Resentment would appear to be the broader experience, whereas *ressentiment* has a narrower and more technical meaning. Nevertheless, each of them is grounded in a sense of grievance about the world – about some condition or insult that seems unfair.

Anne Reichold (2021) differentiated resentment into three kinds, resembling Ferro's analysis. There is **individual** resentment based on personal experience whereby the victim feels aggrieved at some moral wrong by the other party (pp. 159–162). There is **collective** resentment held on behalf of a group to which one belongs, not so much directed toward wrongdoers as

---

4 Military strategist John Boyd explained the essence of twentieth century guerrilla warfare as fomenting and exploiting resentment, from Lenin to Mao (Osinga, 2007, pp. 160–162). See generally Sloterdijk, 2010, ch. 1.

to institutions and structures that allow a pattern of moral wrongs against one's people (pp. 162–166). And there is this thing called *ressentiment* which perpetuates the wrong by adopting a feeling of powerlessness; it is more of a generalized attitude, an abiding search for culprits. It presupposes there must be somebody at fault for one's outrage, so that a person with *ressentiment* constantly scans the horizon for others to blame. Part of *ressentiment* is a spirit of suspicion; the guilty – that is, the persons responsible for one's outrage – are presumed to have veiled or hidden their complicity, such that their injustices will not always be obvious, yet the culprits are presumed to be out there regardless, even if they are presently undetected (pp. 166–170).[5]

And if the past is unjust, as Sloterdijk points out, then vengeance itself would appear to be eminently just (2010, p. 50).

The literature on resentment/*ressentiment* passes through three preeminent authors, namely Friedrich Nietzsche, Max Scheler, and René Girard.[6] They diagnosed the condition differently from one another (see Tomelleri, 2015). But stories about grievance go much further back in time, for example, in the *Psalms*, which plead with the Almighty at last to enact justice and redeem the persecuted. One could even construe Cain's motivation to slay his brother Abel in the book of *Genesis* as an expression of resentment. Professor Gerhard von Rad made this explicit: "Hot resentment had risen in Cain, which had distorted even his body (1972, p. 105)!" In short, the phenomenon is not new, even if the scholarly literature about it is quite recent.

In 2020, Filip Pierzchalski published a short article about the political practice of using resentment to unify people around a shared emotion and to motivate them to take action. Group resentment will tend to subordinate followers to the leader who promises to get even (p. 76). The assumption is that such leadership will be the most effective means for exacting retaliation (p. 77). He wrote that resentment is certainly affective. (That's affective with an "a.") In fact, it is in his opinion a re-feeling, and this is not a trivial claim: the aggrieved are holding on to something from the past, unwilling to let it go (Tomelleri, 2015, p. 25; Girard, 2015, p. viii; Scheler, 1972, p. 29). We say that one is nursing a grudge.[7] As it happens,

---

5 Reichold makes the curious claim that classifying somebody else's feeling or attitude as *ressentiment* as opposed to generic resentment is an ideological choice, not a scientific operation (2021, p. 170).

6 Sloterdijk (2010) traces the literature back to the Christian Carthaginian Tertullian (p. 106).

7 See https://idioms.thefreedictionary.com/nurses%20a%20grudge#:~:text=nurse%20a%20 grudge%20%28against%20one%29%20To%20harbor%20persistent,him%20in%20 front%20of%20a%20girl%20he%20liked.

collective resentment and *ressentiment* establish a relationship among the aggrieved, grounded in shared emotions such as revenge, hatred, malice, envy, and spite (p. 72).[8]

Of interest to us here, Pierzchalski points out that the politics of resentment should be understood as a reaction to something (2020, p. 72, citing Nietzsche, 1967, p. 37; see Tomelleri, 2015, p. 13), which means that it always defines itself in terms of a prior affront, so that it often creates a pattern between two sides for them to contend that each is responding to an offense perpetrated by the other (2020, p. 73). "They started it."[9] That is to say that resentment tends to polarize a community into opposing sides, each of which thinks of itself as the good guys (2020, p. 77). Pierzchalski wrote that political leadership based on resentment can be seen as "a targeted manipulation based on the activation of negative emotions, which is to lead to deliberate dichotomization imposed by the leader, and, consequently, to stigmatization of specific participants in political rivalry (2020, p. 77)." Very quickly, then, resentment shapes a group's identity relative to the other side as the victims, whereas in many instances the other side makes the same claim in reverse. Each tends to become a victim of the other. Clever leaders can sense this dynamic and use it to obtain and exercise power.

Nietzsche had written about the vengefulness of the impotent (1967, p. 37). He said that the soul of such a passive person can be said to squint (1967, p. 38). These persons are, in his words, mediocre, insipid, hopeless, sickly, dwarfed, poisoned, atrophied, and so forth (1967, p. 43). They stink. He worried that humanity, steeped in *ressentiment*, would squelch all merit out of their peers, leaving none at all to lead. Instead, they will look to heaven for succor and to the grave for their vindication. They rise to follow no one. Except of course in their laments, they do yield to

---

8 Capelos and Demertzis (2022) explain that *ressentiment* is certainly affective, involving a cluster of emotions, although they argue it is more complex than simple emotion (p. 124). It is more of a disposition, a psychic mechanism adopted to *avoid* certain negative emotions. Deleuze (2006) agreed that it is not so much a feeling as a disposition toward the world that is never adequately discharged (p. 115). Sloterdijk (2010) used the metaphor of a bank which accumulates grievances until there is enough unspent outrage to change society (p. 59). Minor withdrawals from this bank, such as hot retaliation – an uprising here and an assassination attempt there – accomplish very little and subtract from the capital necessary to bring about revolution. These brief and violent gestures actually make it harder in the long run to effectuate change. They are brief discharges of energy that reduce the overall pressure that had been building. In other words, to be useful rage must become a project.

9 https://idioms.thefreedictionary.com/they+started+it. Deleuze (2006) wrote that *ressentiment* is indeed reactive, except that it does not result in re-*action*. It renders a person passive, simmering (pp. 111, 117).

someone, as Nietzsche suspected. They yield to the ascetic priest, the one who strains to reject life itself, who glories in suffering and calls others to heroic self-abnegation (1967, pp. 116–125). Nietzsche harbored nothing but contempt for such leaders.[10]

Michael Oakeshott (1961/1991) more recently diagnosed the character of such a leader who rises to champion the aggrieved. This includes many demagogues and populists. In each epoch, there will be people who are aggrieved about one thing or another. This is not new, as I have been saying. Oakeshott concurs with Nietzsche *et alia* that modernity brings with it a relatively new type of response, which they had called *ressentiment*. People assume that somebody somewhere is at fault for their disadvantaged condition, but they do not always understand their predicament or know the details about how things might have turned out poorly, so they seek a leader to uncover the culprits and deal with them on their behalf (1961/1991, p. 371). Somebody must go to Washington and "drain the swamp."

Because of their ignorance, these bitter followers construe anybody else's relative success as proof that something is amiss (1961/1991, p. 372). If you possess what I don't, then not only is the system unfair, but you are probably the reason it is unfair.[11] Eventually, *ressentiment* becomes less of a mood and more a feature of one's personality signified by permanent frustration (Girard, 2015, p. ix). As Max Scheler pointed out, then, because of the latency period, *ressentiment* (unlike garden variety resentment) shows itself less as a transient feeling and more as a conscious choice about how to think about the world and one's place in it (1972, p. 30). One must actively suppress one's outrage in the moment and not give in to an emotion, thereby magnifying one's persisting sense of impotence (Scheler, 1972, p. 31; see Deleuze, 2006, p. 123). The emotion sometimes gets displaced later onto unrelated things, such as the family dog – things that will not fight back (Scheler, 1972, p. 51). One might say that the emotion simmers, in the background, until a more auspicious time, except that ultimately it never abates. It becomes part of who you are (Scheler, 1972, p. 55). It was

---

10 Deleuze (2006) explained that *ressentiment* means there is somebody to blame and that the ascetic priest, who is Christian, says that the person to blame is actually you. Your grievances are ultimately your own fault. Thus, the vituperation turns inward toward a spirit of self-loathing (pp. 128, 132). Nietzsche, who was by no means Christian, would have preferred outward-directed animosity, because it is at least more honest and healthier.

11 Deleuze (2006) explained that *ressentiment* resolves itself as an inability to admire. If anyone in society warrants admiration of any kind, for strength, genius, beauty, and so forth, then that person is *ipso facto* guilty and probably evil (pp. 117, 119).

in this sense that Scheler wrote about an "apparently unfounded hatred [that results in a] poisoned sense of life ..." (1972, p. 56f).

For Oakeshott, here is a twist, and that is because the so-called leader of the aggrieved cannot afford to resemble the successful. If these leaders accumulate wealth and enjoy privileges, then that just proves they are in cahoots with the bad guys. Or they have betrayed their social class to become successful. They sell out. Therefore, leaders must reject the trappings of success in order to keep the allegiance of their followers. Unless, that is, such leaders arose from out of privilege in the first place, unapologetically, and set out to use their wealth and status on behalf of their followers. Think, for example, of Julius Caesar and Franklin Delano Roosevelt, popular politicians who came from a patrician class.[12]

Ultimately, Oakeshott agreed with Nietzsche. The masses will cast themselves upon a leader, a human in their midst, but one imagined to be as bereft as they are, a fellow victim who has had enough. Nietzsche would of course never admire such a leader. He admired the excellent, lone paragon, going his own way, dancing, hunting, sailing the wayward seas, and scaling the Matterhorn. Using Nietzsche's template, therefore, the leader of the resentful is worse than those woe-begotten followers because at least the resentful know that they are weak and despised. At least they have the integrity to cringe. The leader, however, imagines he (or she, I suppose) is somehow worthy, meritorious beyond the noble beasts who go about doing what they please. That is because these leaders derive a sense of importance from assailing the select few who disdain regret and who actually do constructive things with their lives. Oakeshott's is the diagnosis familiar to fans of Ayn Rand: that leaders of the oppressed are themselves the lowest form of human.

Briefly, it has been suggested that only certain victims can harbor legitimate grievances. The claim seems to be that certain aggrieved parties are not entitled to their resentment. The grounds for their disqualification would be that these "victims" are white, heterosexual, capitalist, conservative, Christians accused of having been oppressors who cannot now complain when the tables are turned (see Reichold, 2021, p. 171f; Fukuyama 2018, p. 88). Those who are aggrieved tend to reject the possibility that the other side is even *allowed* to be aggrieved. This is not to say that these grievances on behalf of once dominant persons or groups are in any sense equivalent

---

12 Carl Schorske (1981) told the story of Georg von Schönerer (1842–1921), son of a successful entrepreneur who by virtue of his labors joined the nobility in Austria. Upon the father's death, the privileged son used his status to assail everything his father stood for – wealth, status, prestige, and interracial tolerance. In this regard, he prefigured Adolf Hitler (p. 119). But von Schönerer (unlike Hitler) came from the elite.

or justified. I agree that it does seem opportunistic for the dominant person or group to object when their stature is being correspondingly diminished relative to others. Still, a restoration of justice can still breed resentment in those whose position changes as a result. Resentment begins as an emotion, after all, based upon perception and not a rational position. In fact, the attempt to deny that these persons or groups are entitled to their grievances overlooks the burgeoning literature that asserts that such grievances are precisely what explain recent politics. You can't have it both ways. If one's disadvantages prove a permanent state or condition of victimhood, then there have to be persons who are correspondingly advantaged. We can't all be disadvantaged, because then one's sense of uniqueness evaporates. And it is one's sense of moral superiority *because of* his or her disadvantage that likewise vanishes (see Scheler, 1972). The point of adopting *ressentiment* was not to see oneself as just like everybody else.

Besides, as Reichold points out, as a practical matter resentment as a feeling is impervious to evidence and logic anyway (2021, p. 167); telling the aggrieved they are not entitled to their resentment only makes matters worse (2021, p. 164).

For purposes of classification, consider an array of scenarios. Let us begin by describing four. In the first scenario, grievances can arise between individuals, one-on-one, as a result of crime, for example, torts, and breach of trust. Leaders frequently appeal to individuals who have experienced some specific harm or disrespect. The #MeToo movement was originally born of a conviction that individual women had been victimized by individual men (Datla, 2020).[13] Speaking broadly, everybody has reason to resent *somebody* – a bad parent, a bully, a rival, a bad boss at work. In these distinct situations, the opportunistic leader will suggest some version of the following: "You are the victim; he is the perpetrator; I am an avenger."

In the second scenario, grievances are also present in situations of the scapegoat, when the Many single out an individual as a culprit (see generally Girard, 1986; Tomelleri, 2015, ch. 4). One thinks for example of lynchings and the death penalty as expressions of collective vengeance. Michelle Schwarze (2020) recommends something she calls spectatorial resentment, when a community as a group rallies around victims against a solitary malefactor in their midst, for it is that collective sentiment which so often fuels a quest for justice. The posse rides out onto the chaparral in order to track the horse thief and string him up. In some instances, of course, the scapegoat may not have done anything wrong.

13 https://en.wikipedia.org/wiki/MeToo_movement.

Regrettably, sometimes the thirst for retribution does not depend on the facts. Resentment can also originate more as envy: a group might turn against a privileged individual in their midst. As Pierzchalski puts it, resentment results from some combination of comparison, frustration, and oppression (2020, p. 74). And let us not overlook the strange recurring phenomenon of a people turning against their own leader in a symbolic act of the sort once described by Sigmund Freud, in which "the objects of veneration become objects of aversion (1918, p. 36)" He wrote, "Worshipped as a god one day, [the leader] is killed as a criminal the next (1918, p. 60)." It is surprisingly not uncommon for followers to resent their own leaders. Even then, we sometimes encounter the situation of the Many versus the One.

Here is a third scenario. In a kind of mirror image to the previous one, sometimes a lone individual sets out against the Many, as for example, certain serial killers who blame a group or entire institutions for something that might have happened previously to them. Eleanor Wilkinson (2022) recently wrote about a recent trend along these lines. She writes:

> [F]eelings of loneliness and disconnection can also turn outwards, accumulating in resentment, revenge, even violence. Think, for example, of how the figure of the 'incel' has been introduced into the popular lexicon. Incels emerged within misogynistic online cultures, where outcast male teenage 'loners' began to label themselves as 'involuntary celibates' after resentfully being unable to find girlfriends. Here, feelings of loneliness are projected outwards. This violence and hatred has been directed most forcefully towards women, with talk of an 'incel uprising' and a 'war on women'.
>
> *(p. 25, citing Nagle, 2017)*

Perhaps more often, though, the literature will examine instances when one group (not just individuals) rises up against another group, whether as an aggrieved minority against the majority (such as during a slave revolt) or as an aggrieved majority against a minority (such as during anti-colonial protests in India and South Africa). Two recent books, for example, explore what is called racial resentment (Davis & Wilson, 2021; Metzl, 2020). In such instances, we are witness to the Many-against-the-Many. This is a fourth scenario.

one culprit	<> one victim
many culprits	<> one victim
one culprit	<> many victims
many culprits	<> many victims

There are other ways to categorize grievances, i.e. other ways to sort grandma's button tin. The grounds of a person's grievance could be based on a single incident, such as an isolated terror attack, on the one hand, or on a pattern of abuse across time, such as apartheid, on the other hand. The point is that a person can summon and channel indignation to get back at the perpetrator, whatever may have happened. And as we know from the literature on conflict management, it is not necessary that the grievance be justified in fact, so long as the aggrieved party perceives the other person or group as somehow responsible. The facts might speak otherwise, but the reality is that perception drives the phenomenon, whether the outrage occurred only once or repeatedly. Or sometimes not at all (e.g. Loftus & Pickrell, 1995).

The basis for a grievance can take many forms. It could be violence, for example, abuse, ridicule, neglect, or a snub. The catalogue of possible indignities is endless. Back in 1987, the president of Stanford University's Black Student Union protested the mandatory course in Western culture because the reading list "hurt people mentally and emotionally in ways that are not even recognized (quoted in Fukuyama, 2018, p. 103)." That is to say, it hurt their feelings. On a scale from outright genocide, at one extreme, to inadequate deference, on the other, it does not really matter what the other side actually did or did not do. The slight could even be the absence of recognition, the lack of any overt action, a kind of neglect or omission – which raises another method for sorting among types of grievances.

Francis Fukuyama (2018) isolated the problem using two ancient Greek terms (see especially pp. xiii–22).[14] *Isothymia* is the desire to be recognized as a member of the group, to be regarded as an equal and not less than others. Nobody likes to suffer by comparison. Fukuyama equates this psychological drive to Abraham Maslow's social needs. Jonathan Haidt (2024) contrasts this motive for "communion" with a corresponding motive for "agency" (p. 152). *Megalothymia* is the other term adopted by Fukuyama, and it refers to the desire to be regarded as superior in some respect, for example, after winning the big game or finally passing the bar exam. Fukuyama equates this second drive to Maslow's esteem need. Both needs are ineradicable parts of human nature that would seem to clash directly: are we equals or are we not? Resentment can surface when either of these two needs is being denied, so that when they do in fact collide, resentment by *somebody* will be inevitable. Fukuyama claims that this does not have

---

14 Sloterdijk (2010) elaborated on this theme of the "thymos" as the seat of one's sensitivity to status (pp. 11–25).

to be the case, which is to say that people can find ways to satisfy each of these needs simultaneously (see Haidt, 2024, p. 152, citing Guisinger and Blatt, 1994), but he makes a powerful argument that *Isothymia* and *Megalothymia* do indeed frequently clash. In support, he cites a broad range of historical examples, such as the following:

- The quest for a German identity (*gesellschaft*) that led to ethnonationalism and ultimately to Nazism (Fukuyama, 2018, pp. 65–67),
- The emergence of Islamism (Fukuyama, 2018, pp. 67ff; see also pp. 146–149); for instance, he cites Al-Qaeda's attempts to restore an Islamic civilization (2018, p. 8),
- Large-scale immigration of any type generally stirs up the native populace against them (Fukuyama, 2018, p. 132),
- Vladimir Putin hopes to reestablish the Soviet Empire (Fukuyama, 2018, p. 7),
- Xi Jinping hopes to overcome "one hundred years of humiliation" (Fukuyama, 2018, p. 7),
- BLM came into existence on behalf of African Americans after a pattern of troubling treatment by law enforcement (Fukuyama, 2018, p. 8),
- The #MeToo arose on behalf of victims of sexual abuse (Fukuyama, 2018, p. 8),
- The campaign for Gay marriage to secure rights available to heterosexual couples (Fukuyama, 2018, p. 19),
- Arab Spring (Fukuyama, 2018, p. 42f),
- And even the struggle for Ukrainian independence, before Russia's invasion, began as an uprising fueled by resentment (Fukuyama, 2018, p. 44f).

Of particular relevance to leadership scholars and the topic of this paper, Fukuyama indicates that, more often than not, the leader satisfies his or her own Megalothymia by promising to satisfy the Isothymia of the followers (Fukuyama, 2018, pp. xv & 22f).[15]

What follows is yet another way to categorize grievances. We can ask ourselves: what exactly does the aggrieved want? The aggrieved might simply want some kind of accounting, maybe an admission, perhaps even a restoration of something lost. The aggrieved might seek vindication or recompense. But it's also possible that the objective is more troubling, such

---

15 Nietzsche alludes to the remedy for all this striving as *Rhathymia*, which is a studied indifference to how one is estimated by others, one way or the other (1967, p. 41).

as vengeance and retribution: an eye for an eye.[16] These are deep, even primordial motives. Yet it might be something so anodyne as memorializing the victims. That is to say, some groups make a point of cultivating these grievances through commemoration, "lest we forget."[17] Survivors visit graveyards, lower the flag to half-mast, and sit around telling old stories. As a practical matter, the aggrieved might keep their *ressentiment* alive in order to preserve some discrete lessons learned, as in "never again." "Beware Greeks bearing gifts."[18] "Remember the Alamo."[19] It may not be one's purpose to retaliate so much as it is to guard against a repeat of the prior outrage.

At an inchoate level, those who suffered something at the hands of another will likely alter their words and behavior as a result of their trauma, avoiding certain parts of town or refusing to speak of specific incidents, such that descendants pick up on this sense of unarticulated unease, even if they remain vague as to why. The victim may never speak aloud of their grievance, but their peculiar behavior speaks loudly. Carl Jung and many who draw from his work go so far as to allege that some grievances in one generation will pass through a collective unconscious and indirectly injure subsequent generations as a result of what is called phantom or ancestral trauma (e.g. Kimbles, 2014; Abraham, 1975/1994) – although, to be honest, how that feeling transmits is unclear. The point is that regardless of how the grievance is transmitted from one person to another, the fact that a grievance can seem remote in time doesn't mean that ancestral trauma would not inspire any kind of leadership today. Group cohesiveness often intensifies in response to the recitation of past grievances. Shrewd leaders know this.

As we did earlier in this chapter, we can look to the study of history (Ferro, 2007/2010). Many important episodes from the past began as a response to an affront or injustice. We have for example accounts of slave revolts in Laurium (Greece) 429 and in Capua (Rome) 73 BCE. Boudicca (60 CE) raised an army to burn down Londinium in part to repay the abuse of her and her daughters at the hands of the Romans. Today, there is a statue of her in London itself.[20] Hitler capitalized on German shame after the Treaty of Versailles. Revolutions generally rely on a simmering mood against the powers that be. Labor unions need to concentrate the *ressentiment* of labor against their perennial nemesis Management. Opponents of

16 https://en.wikipedia.org/wiki/Eye_for_an_eye.
17 https://en.wikipedia.org/wiki/Lest_We_Forget.
18 https://en.wikipedia.org/wiki/Beware_of_Greeks_bearing_gifts.
19 https://en.wikipedia.org/wiki/Remember_the_Alamo_(song).
20 https://en.wikipedia.org/wiki/Boudica.

nearly any regime will cite former atrocities to make their case, whether it be slavery, colonization, conquest, exploitation, or genocide. Today, we are witness to aggrieved identity groups, such as those based on race, religion, gender and sex, orientation, ethnicity, and wealth. Not surprisingly, then, the aggrieved set out to retaliate against their oppressors – flipping the script, so to speak, and creating a record of victimization on each side (Ferro, 2007/2010, p. 5f). They might justify their actions as payback.

We would go so far as to say that to a great extent what is known as Critical Theory, a school of thought originally attributable to such theorists as Theodor Adorno, Walter Benjamin, Erich Fromm, Max Horkheimer, and Herbert Marcuse, relies on a never-ending spirit of grievance against the past, in whatever form it happens to manifest in the present.[21] Critical Theory takes up an emotional burden to indict history for nearly everything said to be wrong in the world today. Critical Theory can be understood as institutionalized resentment. Not surprisingly, grievances rebounding *against* Critical Theory are themselves not unheard of (e.g. Mitchell, 2020; Walsh, 2017; Jeffries, 2016). Again, one finds that resentment can swing both ways. Grievance would seem to be constitutive of inter-group hostilities.

One of the consistent themes in wartime propaganda is the monstrous behavior of the other side – oftentimes too true, alas, but not always. Ill-treatment of our women. Stabbing babies with bayonets. Secret plots. Senseless slaughter. Forbidden weapons. Spies and traitors and stealth. Broken treaties. Dishonorable treatment of the prisoners and the wounded in their custody. Ridicule, blasphemy, and sacrilege. Leaders want both their soldiers and the home front to understand "why we fight."[22]

Acquaintance with rhetoric supplies plenty of tropes, such as something known as victimage and a curative rhetoric that occasionally extends rather than eases the hurt (Engels, 2010). The lieutenant of an assassinated leader waving the bloody shirt.[23] Horsemen charging forth shouting the names of their fallen comrades. Attorneys on the courthouse steps in front of a bank of microphones expressing their grim satisfaction after the trial that justice at last prevailed. Politicians in the public square urging the people to war because of some perfidy. Presidents at the grave site assuring the assembled mourners their sacrifice will not have been in vain. Even the coach in the locker room after a loss growling to his team, "Get 'em next time."

21 https://en.wikipedia.org/wiki/Critical_theory.
22 https://en.wikipedia.org/wiki/Why_We_Fight.
23 https://en.wikipedia.org/wiki/Waving_the_bloody_shirt.

Combatants and partisans want as much to see the adversary lose as to win anything for themselves. Accordingly, folks want a champion, a representative of "our" side, someone to exact the due penalty. Part of the visceral thrill of the Battle of the Pelennor Fields in *The Return of the King* (Jackson, 2003) comes when the desperate battle is finally joined by two waves of furies: (a) the Rohirrim on horseback sweeping down the slope against the enemy's flank and (b) the Army of the Dead, ghostly warriors hoping as spirits to atone for their shameful cowardice as men, swarming the waterfront.[24] Storytellers have known since before Aristotle that there is something satisfying at the final trumpet about the hero putting things to right.

Leaders in the real world often arise precisely because they stoke the fires of vengeance. Other leaders already in office find themselves besieged by their constituents to take up some cause or other on their behalf. Followers are hoping for someone to champion their cause and restore order. It would be naïve, as I said, to pretend otherwise. Leadership is often grounded in grievance, and make no mistake. So why not say so?

Concluding remarks

Resentment itself is an understandable response to injury or insult. The sense of outrage originates in the perception of some injustice, which the aggrieved sometimes expect their leader to correct. At the collective level, it has not been uncommon for both sides in a conflict to harbor resentment about one another so that leadership on behalf of one side contributes to the cycle of mutual resentments. A natural insistence on restoring justice by means of retaliation doesn't usually work and likely condemns the parties to an enduring feud. In that sense, grievances can accumulate.

As victims internalize their grievances, nurturing their hostilities, cataloguing evidence of the world's unfairness, they interpret their fate as somebody else's fault. They can be tempted to see the world as fundamentally against them. Their resentment becomes generalized against reality itself, without any genuine hope of vindication. At this degree, we see the emergence of *ressentiment* as a posture, a worldview, indicative of who they are: victims in need of a savior.

Archetypal psychologist James Hillman diagnosed too many clients as pathologically furious at injustice (2006, pp. 207–216; see Sipiora, 2023, p. 32). This might sound strange, so he explained. What does it mean to be pathologically furious at injustice? Shouldn't a person become furious

---

24 https://en.wikipedia.org/wiki/Battle_of_the_Pelennor_Fields.

about injustice? Too many things about the world incite these clients. Many of these grievances bear no relation to their lives directly, which does not prevent them from reacting with indignation toward reality – toward the wealthy, toward the powerful, toward the beautiful, toward the healthy. These clients retain such negative feelings for too long, beyond necessity, and gradually adopt an attitude of vague, persistent, and immobilizing fury at life. The problem, as Hillman saw it, is that they are not wrong to notice and declaim against injustice. The world is indeed unjust. But their transference of this awareness into a persistent, if not all-consuming quest for vengeance is not the remedy and only exacerbates the sum total of suffering.

The aggrieved will await their champion. And those who are ambitious to lead will promise them vengeance. It happens too often for Leadership Studies to ignore. Rather than weigh the merits of these historical claims, (a) chiding victims in the spirit of Nietzsche and his successors, who look down their noses at such creatures, let alone (b) despising only those we disagree with, our job as scholars is to record when it happens and dissect its tissue. And where we are able, extrude its venom from our own practice. Nothing dismays me personally more than scholars who are themselves filled with *ressentiment*, as so many seem to be nowadays. And as I am also. We can all do better.

References

Abraham, N. "Notes on the phantom: A complement to Freud's metapsychology." In Abraham, N. & M. Torok. (eds.) (1975/1994). *The shell and the kernel: Renewals of psychoanalysis* (ch. 9). University of Chicago Press.

Capelos, T., & N. Demertzis. (2022). "Sour grapes: Ressentiment as the affective response of grievance politics." *Innovation: The European Journal of Social Science Research*. 35(1): 107–129. https://doi.org/10.1080/13511610.2021.20 23005.

Capriles, R. (2012). *Leadership by resentment: From 'ressentiment' to redemption.* Edward Elgar Publishing.

Ciulla, J.B. (2020). "Leadership and the power of resentment/ressentiment." *Leadership*. 16(1): 25–38.

Datla, A. (2020). "Leading with empathy: Tarana Burke and the making of the Me Too movement." *Harvard Kennedy School*. Retrieved 20 November 2022 from https://case.hks.harvard.edu/leading-with-empathy-tarana-burke-and-the-making-of-the-me-too-movement/.

Davis, D.W., & Wilson, D.C. (2021). *Racial resentment in the political mind.* University of Chicago Press.

Deleuze, G. (2006). *Nietzsche and philosophy* (H. Tomlinson, trans.). Columbia University Press.

Engels, J. (2010). "The politics of resentment and the tyranny of the minority: Rethinking victimage for resentful times." *Rhetoric Society Quarterly*. 40(4): 303–325. https://doi.org/10.1080/02773941003785652.

Ferro, M. (2010). *Resentment in history* (S. Rendall, trans.). Polity Press.

Freud, S. (1918). *Totem and taboo: Resemblances between the psychic lives of savages and neurotics* (A.A. Brill, trans.). Vintage Books.

Fukuyama, F. (2018). *Identity: The demand for dignity and the politics of resentment*. Farrar, Straus and Giroux.

Girard, R. (1986). *The scapegoat* (Y. Freccero, trans.). Johns Hopkins University Press.

Girard, R. "Foreword." In Tomelleri, S. (ed.) (2015). *Ressentiment: Reflections on mimetic desire and society* (pp. vii–xiv). Michigan State University Press.

Haidt, J. (2024). *The anxious generation: How the great rewiring of childhood is causing an epidemic of mental illness*. Penguin Press.

Hillman, J. (2006). *Uniform edition of the writings of James Hillman* (vol. 2). Spring Publications.

Jackson, P. (2003). *The lord of the rings: The return of the king*. New Line Cinema.

Jeffries, S. (2016). *Grand hotel abyss: The lives of the Frankfurt School*. Verso.

Kimbles, S. (2014). *Phantom narratives: The unseen contributions of culture to psyche*. Rowman & Littlefield.

Loftus, E.F., & Pickrell, J.E. (1995). "The formation of false memories." *Psychiatric Annals*. 25(12): 720–725.

McVeigh, R., & Estep, K. (2019). *Trump, the Klan, and the mainstreaming of resentment*. Columbia University Press.

Metzl, J.M. (2020). *Dying of whiteness: How the politics of racial resentment is killing America's heartland* (updated edition). Basic Books.

Mitchell, M. (2020). *Power and purity: The unholy marriage that spawned America's social justice warriors*. Regnery Gateway.

Nietzsche, F. (1967). *On the genealogy of morals and Ecce Homo* (W. Kaufmann, ed. & trans.). Vintage Books.

Oakeshott, M. "The masses in representative democracy." In Oakeshott, M. (1961/1991). *Rationalism in politics and other essays* (pp. 363–383). Liberty Press.

Osinga, F. (2007). *Science, strategy and war: The strategic theory of John Boyd*. Routledge.

Pierzchalski, F. (2020). "Class resentment and leadership: Manipulation of negative emotions in political leadership practices." *Politeja*. 5(68): 63–82.

Ragan, Z. (2023, January 12). "How Kirby Smart gave Josh Heupel and the Vols some extra motivation this offseason." *AtoZ Sports*. Retrieved 15 January 2023 from https://atozsports.com/nashville/kirby-smart-josh-heupel-tennessee-vols-some-extra-motivation/.

Reichold, A. "Varieties of resentment." In Siegetsleitner, A., A. Oberprantacher, M. Frick, & U. Metschl (eds.) (2021). *Crisis and critique: Philosophical analysis and current events* (pp. 157–173). De Gruyter.

Scheler, M. (1972). *Ressentiment* (W. Holdheim, trans.). Schocken.

Schneider, R.A. (2023). *The return of resentment*. University of Chicago Press.

Schorske, C. (1981). *Fin-de-siècle Vienna: Politics and culture*. Vintage Books.

Schwarze, M. (2020). *Recognizing resentment: Sympathy, injustice, and liberal political thought.* Cambridge University Press.

Serres, M. (1997). *The troubadour of knowledge* (S.F. Glaser & W. Paulson, trans.). University of Michigan Press.

Sipiora, M. (2023). *Psychological citizenship and democracy: The political relevance of James Hillman's archetypal psychology.* Spring Publications.

Sloterdijk, P. (2010). *Rage and time: A psychopolitical investigation.* (M. Wenning, trans.). Columbia University Press.

Tomelleri, S. (2015). *Ressentiment: Reflections on mimetic desire and society.* Michigan State University Press.

Tomkins, L. (2021). "Caring leadership as Nietzschean slave morality." *Leadership. 17*(3): 278–295.

von Rad, G. (1972). *Genesis: A commentary* (revised ed.). Westminster Press.

Walsh, M. (2017). *The devil's pleasure palace: The cult of Critical Theory and the subversion of the West.* Encounter Books.

Wilkinson, E. (2022). "Loneliness is a feminist issue." *Feminist Theory. 23*(1): 23–38. https://doi.org/10.1177/14647001211062739.

5

THE GENERATIVE PRESENCE OF NOISE IN DECISION-MAKING

Long-range acoustic devices, or LRAD[1]

Using a long-range acoustic device, or LRAD, law enforcement officers create powerful sound waves to disorient and injure humans in its narrow target beam. This, according to an article in *Popular Mechanics* by Lynne Peskoe-Yang (2020). She added:

> LRADs concentrate the waves in a narrow cone of sound, extending about 15 degrees in every direction from the axis, like a flashlight. This 'directional' sound wave packs the typically diffuse kinetic energy into a tight space, bombarding those in its vicinity with a powerful tone that's an annoyance at a distance … and a serious medical threat up close.

CNN reported in 2017, "A US government official said an acoustic device may have been used to attack State Department employees at the US Embassy in Havana (Chavez, 2017; see Niiler, 2018; Cunliffe, 2023)."[2]

---

1 The author appreciates the contributions to this chapter of my colleague Ben Redekop, who raised the important question this chapter was designed to address.
2 As I was writing this chapter came news about what is known as:
Havana Syndrome, the phenomenon of mysterious brain injuries to U.S. national security officials and diplomats, and their families, both abroad and at home, that in some cases have led to major health conditions, like blindness, memory loss, and vestibular damage. [Investigators found] a suspected link between attacks in Tbilisi, Georgia and a top-secret Russian intelligence unit, and new evidence that a reliable source calls "a receipt" for acoustic weapons testing done by the same Russian intelligence unit (Croxton, 2024).

DOI: 10.4324/9781003540526-6

Just to put the accusation into perspective, one article reported, "Sonic weapons have been used for literally thousands of years to disrupt, confuse and even injure opponents (Niiler, 2018)." Nevertheless, the second half of the twentieth century saw a concerted effort to investigate and even deploy sound to do physical harm (Volcler, 2013). At certain frequencies and intensities, noise can injure a person.

Introduction to the chapter

The human mind can manage only so much of the reality it exists to understand. Beyond a certain point, the mind will stumble and fail. As I have had reason to mention elsewhere, based on the work of Herbert Simon, human beings operate with **bounded rationality**. For this reason, it is a function of mental hygiene to keep that overwhelming reality at some distance, paying attention to only so much of the world in order to concentrate our powers. We simply cannot afford to account for it all. On this, the phenomenologists were quite right to emphasize that in order to make any sense, a person must bracket most of reality, setting it aside temporarily. Given our limitations, this is how humans function.

Of course, reality cannot be bracketed forever. The world is indeed too much with us, as the poet lamented, intruding on our attempts to ignore it. Thoughts and ideas that neglect the encompassing facts will quickly fail or spiral into ideology and madness. A leader can always hope for a better world, but first he or she has to reckon with the world as it is, warts and all, because at some point there will be a test: will the vision you articulate actually come to pass? Will it work?

In order to be successful, decision-makers must account for these incursions from paramount reality. Yes, scientists can create artificial conditions for the sake of conducting experiments, and economists can imagine totally efficient markets. The architect can sketch elaborate blueprints, and the physician can preach perfect health. Nevertheless, their labors will ultimately fail unless they account for conditions on the ground. In the so-called real world, for instance, a chemical will be adulterated; the house will collapse during an earthquake. For various and sundry reasons, the best laid schemes o' Mice an' Men / Gang aft agley.... Or as Robert Merton (1936) tirelessly warned leaders, their actions will inevitably result in unintended consequences.

Here is a typical example. The concept of streaklines in fluid dynamics accounts for the interference of reality downstream, as for example, paratroopers carried sideways from the flight path. They will land somewhere over there because of the influence on the way down of crosswinds. In the same manner, a leader might issue a decision, but it must drift through the organizational hierarchy, being filtered along the way by intermediate managers. And even then, with the passage of time, conditions will change, possibly requiring further adaptation. All of which assumes that the original decision was clearly stated, requiring no subsequent interpretation.

Something always seems to happen between issuing a message and its implementation. One of those possibilities is called Noise.

This chapter will take up the topic of noise and equivalent phenomena such as friction, irritations, static, parasites, and lags or delays in system processes. These phenomena are similar in important respects. This is not to say that they are altogether identical; I do not have to go that far. Two things can be very different from one another yet share in at least one resemblance. And that resemblance might be instructive. Poets often rely on metaphor to explain how the moon can be said to gaze down upon us or the human heart opens like a blossom when it loves. Yet I am going further than mere metaphor. I am going beyond poetry. These phenomena (noise, friction, and so forth) are not just metaphorically alike; they share certain significant properties, which it will be my purpose to reveal in the following pages.

To begin, I posit that noise is inevitable. It is simply part of reality. That is a fact.[3] The next thing for me to say is a judgment. I posit that noise is inherently neutral, neither altogether good nor altogether bad. It can have its uses. Thus, sometimes noise is a problem, though not always. The resulting advice for prospective leaders is to accept this particular fact (i.e. that noise is inevitable) as well as this particular judgment (i.e. that noise is neither altogether good nor altogether bad) and then get to work finding the good in noise while reducing the bad.

Voices against noise in decision-making

Daniel Kahneman, Olivier Sibony, and Cass Sunstein wrote against noise. In their book *Noise: A Flaw in Human Judgment* (2022), they use the analogy of an array of decisions. When the array is relatively tight, within a tolerable range, then it exhibits less noise, as they are using the term. Noise is the extent of the variation within an array. At its worst, of course, the array would be little more than a random scatter. Such variation, you

---

3 Biologist R. Haven Wiley (2015) opens his study of noise by making the same assertion. Noise is inescapable. And in his studies, noise would appear to change the world, which is to say that it has causal properties. Organisms react, change, and adapt in response to noise – for better or worse. They can limit their exposure to noise only up to a certain point.

see, indicates that there is a problem. A random scatter is unhelpful. These authors argue that the tighter the array, the better. Noise in this sense is a problem to be overcome (p. 7). To be sure, they say, the right level of noise is not zero. Reducing noise might be impossible, expensive, or contrary to the values of the people within the system trying to make a decision (p. 9). Nevertheless, these authors define noise as "unwanted variability" (p. 12). It is this problem their book was designed to address.

As the argument unfolds, though, this "array" is to be compared to a target. In other words, there is some ideal, a goal, a bull's eye, such that we should all want to cluster our judgments as close as possible to one another around what we consider to have been the right answer. The authors are interested in questions that have a right answer. Noise indicates inconsistency. This is to say that judgments are to be compared to one another, as well as being compared to some ideal. Kahneman, Sibony, and Sunstein admit that on some occasions variation is not always unwanted (p. 27). Nevertheless, their book addresses situations in which variation is in fact unwanted. When multiple people judge the same thing differently, that raises profound questions about the legitimacy and usefulness of any one of these judgments. How is it fair to entertain divergent judgments? In their opinion, systems frequently require the "right" decision, similar to other decisions about equivalent things. An example they emphasize is sentencing of different criminal defendants for the same crime; too much variation across the judicial system suggests unfairness. One does not need to know which criminal sentence is "right" to realize that the variation itself is a problem. The general principle is that equivalent examples should be treated in equivalent ways.

Noise is universal, these authors admit (p. 40), but that does not mean that it is in any sense good. The objective is to minimize unwanted noise where two different judgments cannot both be right. Notice the qualifying language. Yes, noise exists. Sometimes, it is not disruptive; sometimes, it is even useful. Yet on those occasions when the purpose is to arrive at the so-called "right answer" noise would indicate unwanted variation and therefore a bad thing. The rest of their book is devoted to defending their position and explaining how to avoid (or at least minimize) noise.

Wanting to limit if not eradicate noise means wanting to limit or eradicate variability. When two decisions about the same situation differ, at least one of them cannot be correct (p. 41). This is what they contend. Nevertheless, human systems must tolerate a degree of variation because we are imperfect creatures. And to be fair, many differences are a matter of taste or preference. It might be enough to reach what they call an "expectation of bounded disagreement" (p. 44). Something of the sort is being used in judgments after the fact, as for example, reviews of battlefield orders *ex post facto*. A superior officer or a review board looks at what happened in retrospect or hindsight in order to determine whether the commander had made adequate decisions under the prevailing circumstances.

The usage of the term "noise" to indicate unwanted variation might seem peculiar to anyone outside the academic field of statistics, yet as we shall see their definition will in many ways fit what the rest of us mean in ordinary usage by noise. The topic of noise has been addressed in a variety of other contexts as well. Yet a definition of the word itself is not always certain.

Jacques Attali wrote a small book where he defined noise as "a reso-nance that interferes with the audition of a message in the process of emis-sion (1985, p. 26)" and thus "a signal that interferes with the reception of a message by the receiver... (1985, p. 27)." What this implies is that one man's noise is another man's data.[4] The determination of what con-stitutes noise is, from this point of view, subjective. In 2013, Greg Hainge published his own account titled *Noise Matters: Towards an Ontology of Noise*. He contends that noise can arise as a distortion of a signal, as with an error in transmission (2013, p. 3). It can also include all sounds that are not received as a signal (2013, p. 4), namely unwanted sound (2013, p. 6). In other words, noise serves as the ground (as in "background") to the figure (2013, p. 42). Even a signal that is wanted can become noise when it is too loud or otherwise abrasive (2013, p. 9). All of which is to say that noise competes with other kinds of sounds that the receiver is struggling to listen to. To be succinct, every open system requires input of one kind or another in order to function, yet not all input is meaningful. Meaning-ful input we might label as **Signal**. Everything else is **Noise**. Kahneman, Sibony, and Sunstein (2022) offered to help social systems differentiate between the two.

To be fair, noise pertains to more than audible sensations. A visual field can be noisy. When there are unwanted stimuli interfering with a signal, such as visual clutter, we can speak of noise. But it even goes beyond sense perception. One can say that the noise in one's own mind interferes with reception, as the listener is distracted by other thoughts (Wiley, 2015, p. 3). In other words, the idea of noise presupposes a linear pathway from (a) the outside world being disturbed by (b) extraneous input, a kind of turbulence in an otherwise laminar flow of information. As Hainge put it,

---

4 Writers have enjoyed creating variations on this adage. "One man's noise can be another man's signal" or "One man's noise is another man's music" or "One man's noise is another man's information."

noise has been considered to be the intrusion of disorder into an ordered reality (2013, p. 46f). The contrast seems simple:

- Sounds I want to hear and sounds I don't.
- Stimuli of use to me and stimuli that isn't.
- Order and disorder.

The initial problem with this simple contrast is that noise turns out to be ubiquitous. It is not as though one can completely eradicate it or block it. Noise occurs at many levels, often beneath our powers to discern. Just because you cannot hear it doesn't mean it isn't there. There is such a thing as quiet noise or noise that blends into the background. White noise. The thrum a person can (for the most part) ignore. It is unhelpful input that can be disregarded. It doesn't really qualify as noise in the conventional sense unless and until it interferes with a system's capability of discerning signals. If the signal is distorted, dramatically amplified, drowned out, or lost in a welter of gibberish, then the system can be said to experience noise. Sounds and other stimuli have to be processed *somehow* by the system in order to qualify as meaningful. Otherwise, noise is potentially disruptive, an intrusion. Again, though, this way of talking makes noise into something entirely subjective (see Wiley, 2015, p. 10). The listener's purposes determine what constitutes noise.

The sociologist Niklas Luhmann said that an open system must expose itself continually to irritations, i.e. to information that might have no value whatsoever and might even cause harm (2013, p. 88). The system must be routinely disturbed. That is the price one pays for being open to an environment over which one has no control. Luhmann said that an open system must decide what to do about noise (pp. 87ff). What information can it use? What is proving to be a distraction? Closing oneself off from these risks converts the system into a **closed** system, and – according to systems thinking – entropy (or death) will soon follow. So, in Luhmann's judgment, being open to the risk of noise is necessary for the ongoing health of the system, even when that noise might be injurious. His recommendation sounds counterintuitive. If noise interferes with the communication we prefer, then surely the goal should be to avoid or minimize the disruptions, as Kahneman, Sibony, and Sunstein have indicated in their book. At this point, we should turn to the question of whether noise is really such a bad thing after all.

Before we turn to that question, however, we should accept, even if only for the sake of argument, that Hainge was correct to establish as an empirical premise that noise is in everything and everything is in noise

(2013, p. 2). And it is noise only to the extent that the system cannot handle it.[5] Let us now see where this set of propositions takes us.

Voices in favor of noise in decision-making

Attali had argued that noise might be useful to somebody – "even music to a new system (1985, p. 35)." The stimuli, in and of itself, are neither good nor bad. Only systems can determine what constitutes noise. And Attali took the position that a system cannot always know in advance which stimuli are signal and which are noise. You might be surprised.

Where Attali came out in his reasoning is that, in his opinion, there should be a legal or political right to make noise, which is the right to emit what the listener would not prefer or understand (1985, p. 132). Rather than seeking to control noise for the sake of one's systems (limiting and monopolizing it), the ideal in his opinion would be tolerance for one another's noises, as well as the autonomy to emit noise with minimal external control (1985, p. 145). For this to work, of course, one must accept the likelihood of noise coming from all directions – which includes sounds one cannot even comprehend (1985, p. 147). I suspect that his pro-noise viewpoint is not widely shared.

It is probably no accident that he wrote in the spirit of Arnold Schoenberg, that *fin-de-siecle* composer from Vienna who sought to bring about the so-called emancipation of dissonance (Schorske, 1981, p. 345). By defying traditional musical forms, Schoenberg thought he was "democratizing" the art (Schorske, 1981, p. 351). He understood himself to be giving voice to derangement, not unlike what Attali seemed to favor, except that the listening audience in Vienna could not follow along (Schorske, 1981, p. 355). They stayed away from his concerts in droves. Dissonance was all too strange and not a little disturbing to their sensibilities. To most folks, his so-called music was treated as noise and thus rejected.

If noise might be the music of others, we should probably articulate some of the reasons that noise deserves its opprobrium. Even though he favored widespread noise, Attali admitted that noise can be a source of pain (1985, p. 27) and even a type of violence (1985, p. 26). He wrote,

---

5 Elsewhere in these pages, I will refer to noise as a form of friction, yet Luciano Floridi referred to informational friction as the forces *opposing* the flow of information within some region of what he calls the infosphere (2014, pp. 103–105). When somebody is trying to filter or block information from getting in, he calls that informational friction. Yet I am referring to noise, which is unpreferred and frankly is precisely what informational friction is designed to prevent, as itself friction. How can it be both? In either case, friction is an interference with the flow of information, whether it comes from trying to keep it out to avoid disrupting the system or getting in to disrupt the system. It figuratively depends on whose ox is being gored.

"A network can be destroyed by noises that attack and transform it, if the codes in place are unable to normalize and repress them (1985, p. 33)." The existing system must possess the means of excluding (blocking) or interpreting the sounds. If it cannot do either one of these things, then the noise will prove to be an annoyance, a hindrance, or even an assault on smooth operations. The congregation at worship might need to suspend its services, for instance, until the clamor goes away. The university lecture might be brought to a standstill. It depends upon the system. Often, the noise will not be appropriate for the existing system.

One of the ways that a system can display its power is by regulating or controlling noise (1985, p. 122). It can increase the volume of its own sounds, for example, or remove and isolate the source of the intruding sounds. In fact, it is not unheard of for authorities to regard the emission of noise as a crime (1985, p. 24). Under modern conditions, the state has become, in Attali's words, "a gigantic, monopolizing noise emitter, and at the same time, a generalized eavesdropping device (1985, p. 7)." Only the state can legally emit "noise" or permit noise to be made. Think, for example, of government attempts to quash "disinformation" online.

Implicit within this schema is the possibility that regarding noise as opposed to signals ignores the possibility that **the signal itself is noise** (Hainge, 2013, p. 246). Signal and noise are not necessarily two distinct things. Picture in your imagination two mothers standing at their respective back doors and simultaneously calling their children home for supper. Each shout is a signal, though it is intended for different auditors. The signals can be said to cross each other out. If none of the children can discern the message because the two mothers shouted at the same instant, they must consider the garbled shouts as noise, even though both were intended as signals. Neither message got through. Imagine a ballroom populated by people milling about, socializing, chatting, laughing. The space is filled with signals which, when combined, create a din difficult for some people to manage. Signals can be noise.

On a standard transistor radio, multiple stations transmit their broadcasts at different frequencies, precisely in order to avoid unwanted static. In fact, government regulators see to it that stations do not bleed over one another, which is why they assign them distinct frequencies sufficiently far apart on the radio spectrum so that each audience can find its programing (3 Hz–3,000 GHz). When I am searching for my favorite talk show, the rest is just noise to me. But to the guy in the next car, my station would be noise to him.[6]

6 The "United States Frequency Allocations: The Radio Spectrum Chart" can be found at https://www.ntia.gov/sites/default/files/publications/january_2016_spectrum_wall_chart_0.pdf.

What we are talking about is monitoring salience. The system must discern what is signal and what is noise, because noise itself might be the product of signals. But I would go further than this. In many instances, noise itself is a signal. It is evidence of chaos, a possible outbreak, a warning from the occluded environment that might warrant further attention, like the scream of a neighbor or the squeal of brakes. Or the growl of a predator in the bushes. Your "system" might need to perk up and notice – not because it mistook a signal for noise, but because the noise is a signal.

Blocking noise might prevent opportunities. Stereotypically, male bosses were notorious for ignoring what women on the job had to say. They cut them off or paid them no heed (until, that is, one of their male counterparts said the exact same thing). Marginalized people often complain that they aren't heard, and the use of acoustic terminology ("being heard") is not accidental. These folks are sending their signals. The signals just don't get through. The groupthink hypothesis, for instance, identifies what are known as mindguards which are group members who see it as their job to reduce the noise coming up the chain of command so that leaders can concentrate on leading. These intermediaries explicitly prevent certain signals from reaching their intended audience.

In parliamentary procedure and in judicial processes, somebody must rule on whether certain signals are germane or out of order. Attorneys can, like mindguards, leap from their chairs objecting to certain questions as irrelevant, for example, or prejudicial. Some noise is properly stricken for the sake of the decision-making process. That is to say that somebody in a position of authority at these proceedings is entrusted with determining the value (if any) of noise, because beyond a certain point, the very purpose of the assembly is otherwise defeated.

The ambivalence of Michel Serres about noise

Michel Serres published a book in 1980 titled *The Parasite*, which was subsequently translated into English by the University of Minnesota Press in 2007. His reflections on the role of noise in the functioning of systems exhibit a deep ambivalence. Serres understood the problem posed by noise. He was not unmindful of its destructive potential. Yet he repeatedly asserted that noise is everywhere and indeed far more prevalent than most of us suppose. For him, every relationship generates noise, and every signal is accompanied by noise. Noise is the price one pays for communication. In most cases, that noise is benign, beneath notice. Or at least we treat it as though it were benign, to the extent we notice it at all.

Perhaps we should notice the noise around us more often. Rather than block or ignore, maybe we should investigate the price that noise exacts from us. In this sense, he sounds a lot like Kahneman, Sibony, and Sunstein (2021). He seems to be in favor of noise audits. Except that such a task is overwhelming, even futile. Frankly, he wrote, the alternative in which we strive to eradicate noise altogether will end up being cruel and short-lived (2007, p. 14). One cannot police the level of noise beyond a certain point, for even in the interpretation of evidence there will be noise. As soon as a person delivers a report on such findings, there will be an accompanying noise. No matter how scrupulously one scrubs communication, it will be there in one form or another. Noise is endemic.

Serres took this one step further when he asserted that in fact noise is constitutive of relationships. It is itself the system (2007, pp. 12 & 79). Now, to be sure saying this is a more extravagant claim. Systems are what they are because of noise, he wrote. Noise makes the system what it is. Noise is frankly generative (2007, p. 184). This is a difficult lesson to hear. He offered the example of organisms in the human digestive system, parasites that rely on the human body as their host. We evolved to rely on them in order to live, and they rely on us. Symbiosis is the rule among systems. Ultimately, the distinction between signal and noise is thrown into doubt – all of which sounds highly theoretical and untethered to the real world. Yet he made the argument in a variety of ways using multiple examples.

In effect, a signal is noise working against other noises for attention (2007, p. 6). And if we are being honest with ourselves, each of us reciprocates with noise. The noise flows both ways. Each of us is a parasite to one another. That is how we persist. That is how we survive. Systems are not just the recipients of signals as input. They emit signals also. And they generate noise. Most uses of the language of noise presuppose unidirectional and laminar flow, from point A to point B, with B in a position to judge that which is noise (2007, p. 5). This is why we hypothesized that noise is subjective. The reality is far more complex, Serres reminded us, both multidirectional and turbulent (see Serres, 2023, pp. 5–15). Noise goes back and forth, up and down, round and round, repeatedly and often obliquely distorting things. The system exists because of that confusing tangle of garbled messages. If a given firm were able *per impossible* to eradicate noise completely, it would cease to exist. Poof! You certainly wouldn't be able to recognize it anymore. Shell Oil Company is the way that it is precisely because of its noise.

The farmer is a parasite to the land. The tax man is a parasite to the farmer. The rats are a parasite to the tax man. On and on and on (2007, pp. 3–14). There is no system without noise (2007, p. 12). **The system is noise.** Every irruption, every burp, has the potential to alter the future (2007, p. 21). See the butterfly effect. How can that be? Because noise relates not to persons but to relationships among persons. Noise pertains to the links between nodes and not to the nodes themselves (2007, p. 33). Noise is intermediate, the medium through which we communicate. No medium, no communication. No communication, no system.[7]

When the committee chair instructs its members to restrict themselves to a limited, preapproved list of considerations, first of all, that isn't possible. Regardless of what is said out loud during a meeting, a thousand other considerations swim through everybody's minds. Furthermore, what is being said at the meeting is noise *of which the chair approves*. Not everybody will agree with one another. Perfectly reasonable considerations might pop up out of nowhere, altering everybody's judgment, if only they could be heard. Not to make a joke of this, but if somebody hears the fire alarm during the meeting and urges everybody to get up and flee, the committee chair would not say that this "noise" is out of order and therefore to be ignored because it comes from outside the set of approved considerations. I think it was Wittgenstein who explained that every decision relies on a basket full of implicit considerations that are potentially useful and appropriate.[8]

For somebody within a given system, he or she will understandably struggle to identify and then isolate the pertinent signals (2007, p. 68). Every system survives by struggling against noise (2007, p. 87). Serres even wrote, "Noise destroys and horrifies. But order and flat repetition are in the vicinity of death. Noise nourishes a new order (2007, p. 127)." So, is this philosopher against noise? He is plainly ambivalent. Systems try to persist, to maintain pattern integrity, primarily for the sake of an established equilibrium. Yet every equilibrium squelches vitality, preventing the search for a new equilibrium...perhaps a better one (2007, p. 168). He even schematized the possibilities. We imagine that by sustaining the system, we can perpetuate a cycle (going around) and prevent entropy (sinking downward), yet the real remedy is to supplant the system periodically and evolve toward greater complexity (transcend upward) (2007, p. 186). "Noise destroys an order, the order of discourse; it also announces another order (2007, p. 243)."

---

7 Serres even wrote the following: "Without communication, there can be no life.... Without communication, there can be no society.... Without communication, there can be no self (2019, p. 159f).

8 On a Hermitix Podcast dated 22 May 2020, Bill Ross claimed that Serres was not so effective at incorporating what Paul Grice called implicatures, which refers to that unspoken reservoir of understandings between two people. Retrieved 5 March 2024 from https://podcasters.spotify.com/pod/show/hermitix/episodes/Hermes-with-Bill-Ross---The-Michel-Serres-Project-e14qi4e/a-a66fc03.

Serres went so far as to allege that leadership implies an arrangement in which the employer renders the subordinates blind (or, to retain the language of what one hears, deaf). Workers are not to look to the left or the right. "Looking" in this sense is the leader's prerogative. He (or she) is like the disabled man being carried around by the healthy blind man. The leader instructs the blind where to go (2007, p. 37). Each has a designated role. And for the leader to succeed, he (or she) must regulate the noise. This is to say that power lies in presuming to control the interstices, the pathways, and the space between us. I don't have to control you directly if I can control what you hear and see and say (2007, p. 64).

Serres then added that beyond a certain point, an unrelenting signal *becomes* noise, like the street sign you pass every day and no longer notice. It no longer accomplishes anything. It recedes into the background of consciousness (2007, p. 52). In fact, it can start to detract from the relationship, like a nagging spouse or an interlocutor who eventually starts beating the proverbial dead horse. The "signal" is not only ineffective; it has now become distracting, annoying, conveying to the recipient something that was never intended – that you are a boor, for example, or a shrew.

Given this ambivalence toward noise, Serres offered a way of imagining how we are to manage. First, he described instances at four magnitudes where peers on the same level are recruited to combat that which is unwanted. At the cellular level, white blood cells seek out and render rogue cells in the body harmless. At the community level, police and the justice system set out to correct or immobilize criminals. At the international level, allies assemble to make war against invasive regimes, such as the Nazis. And at the planetary level, the earth periodically rids itself of unwanted species, besetting them with predators or biological diseases in order to bring their numbers under control or even bring them to the brink of extinction. Again, this is only a way of imagining. In the case of noise, the implication is that we must use sounds to minimize disturbances, such as playing white noise as we sleep. This is not unlike fighting fire with fire. Or covering up one's bodily odor with perfume. For Serres, resorting to such oppositions is less than desirable. Trying to thwart inevitable noise can become wearisome and even expensive. Remember, he spoke in favor of symbiosis, so the preferable tactic would be to learn to live with noise and try to make it work for you.

At a very practical level, then, the factory supervisor might purchase ear buds for employees that each person can set to whatever music or radio station he or she desires, in part to protect their hearing, but also to indulge their disparate wishes, yet the supervisor can do so with at least these two provisos: (a) an emergency might necessitate shutting them off and (b) the supervisor should expect to see a corresponding increase in productivity on the shop floor.[9] The logic is not dissimilar to making some allowance for employees to use their workplace laptops sparingly to check personal email; this policy would allow for a tolerable "noise" hardly worth monitoring within certain parameters.

In other words, Serres was asking how we might *work with* the noise.

Lags/delays in systems: Another meaning of noise

Michel Serres was often willing to connect two or more things that are superficially unlike one another in order to determine whether they share any underlying principles. As we just saw, he did this regarding noise and parasites. Because he was familiar with systems thinking, Serres found ways to analogize principles from (a) parasites and noise of the sort we have already discussed to (b) processual lags or delays. This is to say that a lag or delay in the crisp execution of a system's functions resembles noise. Every hesitation, every disruption, every interruption, every stutter can be understood as a species of noise.

Systems operate across time, such that input results in an output of some kind, but not always right away. The actual processes need time to work. For one thing, the system might experience a **perceptual** lag, which is the time it takes for the system to recognize what is going on, to begin with. Then, there is frequently a **decision-making** lag, during which participants come up with a response. Once a decision has been made, of course, there will be an **execution** lag, as the system goes about carrying out the plan. Finally, there will be a lag until the consequences of the response take effect. It might take a while for the environment to react. Maybe we can call this the **impact** lag. Each of these lags (or delays) can take a split second or many years to complete. It all depends.

Suppose for example that you notice your pants no longer fit around the waist. (I'm sure this never happened to you personally, but just imagine it for a moment.) You ask yourself, "How long has this been going on? Have I been ignoring the evidence?" Once you do notice, then, what will you do about it? Will you buy new pants that fit? Keep the pants but exercise more? Eat less? Let's say you decide to change your habits and not replace the pants. So, you alter your diet and start taking brisk walks around the neighborhood daily. It will still take some time to see

---

9 One might consider *el lector de tabaqueros*, which refers to those persons employed to read to the cigar factory workers throughout the workday (Maatta, 2011). The same can be said of the practice of oral reading in the refectory of the monastery (e.g. Dial, 1972). The field of marketing has been interested in the use of sounds and other stimuli to influence behavior subconsciously (e.g. Lindblom, 2023). An interesting variation is using classical music to discourage loitering (Hyson, 2023).

the results. Change doesn't happen overnight. Lags are inevitable, but they can sometimes be shortened. During the twentieth century, for instance, there was a push to shorten each of these lags in the manufacturing sector for the sake of efficiency.[10] Detect a problem quickly, jump into action, and correct the problem as fast as you can, because delays cost money. Time is money. Since the firm must cycle through problem solving anyway, the trick is to do so faster than before and faster than competitors. A lag is therefore a bad thing, even if it is inevitable. Best to minimize the harm.

This approach should resemble the approach to noise championed by Kahneman, Sibony, and Sunstein (2022), i.e. to minimize if not eradicate delays completely.

Again, a lag or delay, like noise, proves to be a disruption in the laminar flow of production. It signals an *inter*-ruption. Ordinarily, engineers should want to minimize these intervals as much as possible. Interestingly, though, a lag or delay presents the manufacturer with an opportunity. First, of course, the lag draws attention to a flaw in the system; it serves as a kind of gift by exposing inefficiencies that can then be fixed. In that sense, then, a lag can be instructive (Virilio, 2007). Second, a lag gives the system an opportunity to re-think its entire process. Maybe in the interim, while the system is trying to play catch up, the participants can ponder the situation as a whole. Should we consider doing things in a different way? Are we even doing the right thing to begin with? A lag makes time available for a person to imagine possibly going in a different direction. A pause can be regarded as an opportunity for reflection. It might be the case that the process can be revised to skip the bottleneck altogether, thereby rendering the laminar flow all the more efficient.[11] Third, a lag does give a system an opportunity to adjust on its own. "Let's see what happens...." The adjustment might be an improvement, to be sure, but the mere fact that the system itself adapts (i.e. learns) should be a good thing. Maybe as it draws lessons from these lags, it demonstrates a kind of emergent intelligence. The perceived cost of delays might be offset by the growth in maturity that the system achieves. Workers often devise workarounds. Or unnecessary steps can be eliminated. The hiccup might be worth the struggle for

---

10 Lean manufacturing and its concomitant philosophy known as JIT (just-in-time) traces its origin to Benjamin Franklin, through Frederick Taylor and Henry Ford, to the Japanese engineer Taiichi Ohno at Toyota (Dilanthi, 2015; see also Vokurka & Davis, 1996; Oshima, 1979; Sugimori, Kusunoki, Cho & Uchikawa, 1977).

11 The story is told about an arctic explorer who woke up and initially recorded his starting point, then mushed his sled for hours in a straight line, taking a break to record his progress. Come to find out, he had actually moved further away from his intended destination. How could that be? He had been drifting all day on an enormous sheet of ice that was shifting underneath him undetected. The pause gave him a chance to discover the changing conditions and correct for them.

a system that can learn. Another way of saying this is that a lag might provide or disclose information of some value to the system as a whole.

In other words, we find ourselves in social systems advised to work *with* these lags, using them to our advantage. Most of the time, yes, they ought to be minimized or removed. But a completely efficient process is impossible. More importantly, a lag might prove beneficial, if that expenditure of time is employed intelligently. In this respect, we will have adopted a posture toward lags similar to the posture Serres would have us adopt toward noise.

Friction: Another meaning of noise

The field of physics tells us about the phenomenon known as friction, which impedes the flow of an object. **Friction** is resistance to motion of one object along the surface of another. In mechanics, of course, friction has its uses. Think, for example, of belts on a pulley. The wheels do not rotate if the belt experiences no friction as it rolls around them. Human beings need friction just to walk. Automobiles need friction to steer and to brake. Friction generates heat, as when rubbing your cold hands together or rubbing two sticks together in order to start a fire. Here, as with noise and system lags, we discover that the pure transference or flow encounters opposition of some sort, requiring exertion to overcome. We know that friction can be overcome with superior force, but only at the expense of the eventual destruction of the surfaces themselves, as with abrasions. You use a coarse pad to scour the pan, let us say. The friction tells you that you are succeeding at your chore. But eventually, if you persist too long or scrub too hard, you can leave scratches on the Teflon or wear the pad down to nothing.

Carl von Clausewitz introduced the idea that military battles experience friction as well (see generally, Watts, 2004). Here, the concept of friction served as a handy metaphor. The commander cannot simply deploy his units anywhere he likes at the time of his choosing – not without expending resources to get there and not without encountering opposition from the other side. In the real world, armed forces meet with other types of forces, such as long distances, tall mountains, dense forests, broad rivers, miserable weather, as well as the enemy itself. Friction in these contexts would appear to be a bad thing, a source of some frustration, ideally to be minimized or eradicated. Except that – like noise and lags – a military commander can use friction to advantage.

John Boyd understood what Clausewitz was trying to say. He had found it handy when flying planes. The Pentagon constantly asked manufacturers to build sleek jets, faster, more aerodynamic, and therefore less vulnerable to what is known as drag. But as a pilot Boyd knew how to fly these aircraft. More importantly, he knew how to fly these aircraft during aerial dogfights. And he had learned that friction (or drag) can make his aircraft more maneuverable, banking more quickly, slowing more abruptly, obtaining lift. He could demonstrate in the air that the faster of two jets in hot pursuit would fatally overshoot one that is nimbler. In other words, the measure of effectiveness was not its rapidity in relation to the ground below, which holds steady. Instead, it had to account for all of the other aircraft flying every which way, some on your side of the battle and some not on your side.

This is not to say that Boyd encouraged friction. A plane has to overcome friction in order to fly anywhere. He had simply accepted it as the reality in which pilots must operate, and he decided that the clever pilot can use this friction – tactically – to gain a competitive advantage. He asked himself, How can I use the limits imposed upon me by reality to achieve my purpose?

Later, Boyd transferred his knowledge about aerial combat to war fighting broadly speaking. He started teaching military strategy. In that pursuit, he developed the idea further that friction, while inevitable, is not always a bad thing. At one point, he made the following assertions (1987):

a the atmosphere of war is friction;
b friction is generated and magnified by menace, ambiguity, deception, rapidity, uncertainty, mistrust, etc.;
c friction is diminished by implicit understanding, trust, cooperation, simplicity, focus, etc.; and
d in this sense, variety and rapidity tend to magnify friction, while harmony and initiative tend to diminish friction.

What he concluded is that at one extreme stasis means death. Nevertheless, in the world we occupy, which the philosophers call paramount reality, overcoming stasis (i.e. life) exacts a penalty or cost in the form of energy. The expenditure of energy to overcome inertia is what signifies living things. But that expenditure must be directed toward some purpose. Otherwise, the burst and sparkle of random expenditures accomplishes nothing and eventually flickers out. What we end up with, if we are successful, is an exchange, a syncopation, open and shut, in and out, back and forth, act and reflect, for only in that way (given our constraints) can we sustain progress.

Leadership therefore limits these various constraints such as noise, lags, friction, etc. But it also learns to live within them. And then, ultimately, leadership finds uses for these constraints, capitalizing (we might say) on the boundaries of our existence to advance our shared purpose. Leaders move between two dysfunctional extremes, namely suppressing noise altogether toward zero or indulging noise to such an extent there is no such thing as a signal. All or none: these are the fatal options between which we must all do our work … perhaps leaders foremost.

Concluding remarks

In the original book proposal submitted to Routledge and its gracious editors, this chapter was titled as follows: Noise in Decision-making, Dialogue, and Deliberation: An Inevitable, Distracting, and Generative Parasite. That original title about says it all.

Leaders bear responsibility for monitoring and to some extent controlling noise in the organization. This means that leaders must expose themselves to noise. Noise itself, in whatever form it takes, threatens to interfere with the smooth operation of social systems, yet at the same time it also provides the impetus to adapt and grow. While managers busy themselves hoping to eradicate noise for the sake of some corporate doctrine, prioritizing efficiency at all costs, leaders will occasionally pause, listen, allow, and perhaps introduce noise into their processes. Oftentimes, *leadership is the noise.* Whether it is wanted by anyone else is beside the point. Just ask Socrates, Galileo, or Gandhi.

References

Attali, J. (1985). *Noise: The political economy of music* (B. Massumi, trans.). University of Minnesota Press.

Boyd, J. (1987a). "Organic design for command and control." Unpublished presentation. Retrieved 9 March 2022 from https://www.ausairpower.net/JRB/c&c.pdf.

Chavez, N. (2017, September 27). "Using sound to attack: The diverse world of acoustic devices." *CNN.* Retrieved 4 October 2023 from https://www.cnn.com/2017/08/10/health/acoustic-weapons-explainer/index.html.

Croxton, W. (2024, March 31). "5-year Havana Syndrome investigation finds new evidence of who might be responsible." *60 Minutes Overtime.* Retrieved 1 April 2024 from https://www.cbsnews.com/news/5-year-havana-syndrome-investigation-finds-new-evidence-of-who-might-be-responsible-60-minutes/.

Cunliffe, R. (2023, January 27). "The mystery of Havana syndrome." *New Statesman.* 152(5701): 57. Retrieved 4 October 2023 from https://link.gale.com/apps/doc/A738753391/LitRC?u=anon~a6ff1cd4&sid=googleScholar&xid=8140d627.

Dial, V.L. (1972). *A descriptive study of the tradition of oral reading in the Benedictine Order* (Order No. 7306818). Available from ProQuest Dissertations & Theses Global; ProQuest One Academic. (302705725). Retrieved from https://cnu.idm.oclc.org/login?url=https://www.proquest.com/dissertations-theses/descriptive-study-tradition-oral-reading/docview/302705725/se-2.

Dilanthi, M.G.S. (2015, October). "Conceptual evolution lean manufacturing: A review of literature." *International Journal of Economics, Commerce and Management.* 3(10): 574–585. Retrieved 22 January 2024 from https://ssrn.com/abstract=2678896.

Floridi, L. (2014). *The fourth revolution: How the infosphere is reshaping human reality*. Oxford University Press.

Hainge, G. (2013). *Noise matters: Towards an ontology of noise*. Bloomsbury.

Hyson, K. (2023, April 14). "Why are San Diego 7-Elevens playing opera?" *KPBS*. Retrieved 9 March 2024 from https://www.kpbs.org/news/2023/04/14/why-are-san-diego-7-elevens-playing-opera.

Kahneman, D., Sibony, O., & Sunstein, C.R. (2022). *Noise: A flaw in human judgment*. Little, Brown and Company.

Lindblom, A. (2023). *Sensory marketing in retail: An introduction to the multisensory nature of retail stores*. Palgrave Macmillan.

Luhmann, N. (2013). *Introduction to systems theory* (P. Gilgen, trans.). Polity.

Maatta, S.L. (2011). "El Lector's Canon: Social dynamics of reading from Havana to Tampa." *77th World Library and Information Congress*. International Federation of Library Associations and Institutions, San Juan, Puerto-Rico. Retrieved from https://cdn.ifla.org/past-wlic/2011/81-maatta-en.pdf.

Merton, R. (1936). "The unanticipated consequences of purposive social action." *American Sociological Review. 1*(6): 894–904.

Niiler, E. (2018, May 25). "Sonic weapons' long, noisy history." *History*. Retrieved 4 October 2023 from https://www.history.com/news/sonic-weapons-warfare-acoustic.

Oshima, Y. (1979). "Recent trends of manufacturing technology in Japan." *IFAC Proceedings. 12*(10): 53–71.

Peskoe-Yang, L. (2020, June 17). "How to dodge the sonic weapon used by police: The LRAD is like a car alarm from hell—and if you aren't careful, it could permanently damage your hearing." *Popular Mechanics*. Retrieved 4 October 2023 from https://www.popularmechanics.com/military/weapons/a32892398/what-is-lrad-sonic-weapon-protests/.

Schorske, C. (1981). *Fin-de-siècle Vienna: Politics and culture*. Vintage Books.

Serres, M. (2023). *Hermes I: Communication* (L. Burchill, trans.). University of Minnesota Press.

Serres, M. (2019). *Hominescence* (R. Burks, trans.). Bloomsbury Academic.

Serres, M. (2007). *The parasite* (L. Schehr, trans.). University of Minnesota Press.

Sugimori, Y., Kusunoki, K., Cho, F., & Uchikawa, S. (1977). "Toyota production system and kanban system materialization of just-in-time and respect-for-human system." *The International Journal of Production Research. 15*(6): 553–564.

Virilio, P. (2007). *The original accident*. Polity.

Vokurka, R.J., & Davis, R.A. (1996). "Just-in-time: The evolution of a philosophy." *Production and Inventory Management Journal. 37*(2): 56.

Volcler, J. (2013). *Extremely loud: Sound as a weapon* (C. Volk, trans.). The New Press.

Watts, B.D. (2004). *Clausewitzian friction and future war* (No. 68). Institute for National Strategic Studies, National Defense University.

Wiley, R.H. (2015). *Noise matters: The evolution of communication*. Harvard University Press.

6

JOHN BOYD AND THE IDEA OF OODA LOOPS

Introduction to the chapter[1]

An underlying theme of this book is managing uncertainty. Leaders must work within a variety of constraints, rarely knowing completely what is going on and what to expect in the future. Many authors have pointed out that a large part of leadership is managing uncertainty, and their efforts deserve to be shared widely, so that leaders especially, but more importantly followers as well, make prudent decisions in a complex world (e.g. Weick, 1995). Another theme of this book, though, is about the fallow fields, the undeveloped portions of reality that remain to be understood. Don Levine classified this kind of scholarship as "heuristic work internal to the discipline" and more specifically "constructing new analytical angles" (2015, p. xxviii). This chapter was designed to add to the existing literature another voice, a neglected voice, by the name of John Boyd.

Colonel John Boyd shaped military strategy for a generation, claiming that his conclusions would work in any competitive activity (Coram, 2002, p. 429). Eventually, others applied Boyd's conclusions to business (e.g. Richards, 2004), where the idea of the OODA loop became familiar. This chapter attempts to bring the idea of the OODA loop to the forefront and consider its implications for leadership in any context, without merely duplicating what has already been said. Some duplication will be necessary, of course, as we attempt to anchor the chapter in an existing

---

1 The author appreciates the contributions to this chapter from John Hyland and Thomas Williams.

DOI: 10.4324/9781003540526-7

literature and not ignore the writers who have already tried to make sense of this idea.[2]

It might be helpful to learn that Boyd was originally trained as a fighter pilot, a combat veteran,

- who then became a trainer of other pilots,
- who because of this experience was consulted by aircraft designers,
- who then applied what he had been learning throughout his career to military strategy more broadly.[3]

It all derived from the same basic principles, which he had applied at each level. It might be helpful to know that Boyd recorded barely any of his breakthrough ideas, except for slideshows that he would present to anyone who would listen (see Richards, 2009). Much of what survives depends on the recollection of his peers. He was apparently just too busy to write it all down.[4] Besides, he continuously revised his thinking, so that trying to understand the work of Boyd gives to the conscientious student a moving target (Osinga, 2007, p. 46). Nevertheless, he acquired a reputation throughout the Pentagon as a maverick, collecting a small number of collaborators who tended to support what he was saying. As subsequent authors will attest, Boyd's approach – especially the idea of the OODA loop – has gradually become standard throughout the military.

What is an OODA loop?

One of Boyd's lessons that has also been applied to the non-military world, primarily to business, is known as the OODA loop. It works something like this.

---

2 In my opinion, the most thorough study of the work of John Boyd is Osinga's 2007 book *Science, Strategy and War* (Routledge).

3 Purportedly an autodidact, quirky and profane, Boyd's conclusions pertain primarily to tactics during a dogfight, which is where he first noticed the principles he would spend a lifetime developing, yet he extended these principles to apply as well to fighting wars more broadly (e.g. Osinga, 2007, p. 237). He claimed that they would even work in any competitive activity, including chess, sports, politics, and management (Coram, 2002, p. 429; Hammond, 2001, p. 194).

4 Biographer Coram reveals that one short paper authored by Boyd titled "Destruction and Creation" went unpublished even though it was arguably "his most significant intellectual achievement" (2002, pp. 275 & 323). Grant Hammond even called it "a sacred text" (2001, p. 118). The result of his failure to publish is, as his biographer Robert Coram wrote, that "there is almost nothing for academics to pore over and expound upon (2002, pp. 7 & 445)."

The acronym OODA stands for: Observe, Orient, Decide, then Act. First, a pilot must **Observe** the situation accurately and quickly. Otherwise, he or she is blind. Based on these observations, the pilot must process what it all might mean. This second stage Boyd called **Orientation**.[5] Another way to say this is that one must put these observations together into a configuration that explains where one is in relation to the adversary, as well as in relation to other aircraft, the sun, the ground, and so forth (Boyd, 1987a, p. 16). Equipped with this knowledge, the pilot must then make a **Decision** about what to do. This process already entails a lag in the system as the pilot puts this information together into some kind of image, yet it means little until the pilot executes that decision in **Action**.[6] The entire sequence is described as a loop because after taking action, whatever it happens to be, the pilot faces a new situation, requiring another OODA loop, over and over, until the battle ends.

The quicker you cycle through the loop in comparison to your adversary, you should enjoy a competitive advantage. This is known as "getting inside" the adversary's OODA loop (Boyd, 1987a, p. 7). If it takes you less time to process, then you can act before the other person is ready. At which point, the other pilot must begin his or her OODA loop all over again in light of your latest behavior, which slows them down further. Eventually, the advantage will allow the nimble pilot to destroy or demoralize the adversary who cannot figure out what is happening. They become stuck in perpetual orientation, like a mental paralysis. All other things being equal, being more agile is better.[7] The objective is to "render the adversary powerless by denying him the opportunity to cope with unfolding circumstances" (Boyd, 1986, p. 136).

By the same token, the longer you can keep the adversary slowed down in its own execution of its OODA loops, you accomplish the same purpose. Whether you speed yourself up or slow them down, it amounts to the same thing. If you deny them access to key information, for example, by shutting down certain instrumentation, then they find themselves just as frustrated, even if you are not any quicker otherwise. Another way to overwhelm

---

5 Boyd referred to orientation as the most important part of the OODA loop (1987, p. 26).
6 Osinga (2007) highlighted the way that deciding (D) and acting (A) resemble the scientific method by which a person formulates a hypothesis and then tests that hypothesis, revising the hypothesis afterwards in light of the experiment's results (p. 232).
7 When the adversary has given up trying to make sense of the situation, they will lose. In another chapter of this book, I describe a type of person who will have given up and turned to somebody else in order to lead them. We might consider followers who experience *ressentiment* as having become incapable of cycling through their own OODA loops … or unwilling to do so, for whatever reason (see ch. 4).

the adversary's capacity to orient is to flood the intake, generating what Boyd called "many non-cooperative centers of gravity" – so many that the adversary cannot digest them all in a timely fashion (1987a, slide 20; see generally Proctor & Schneider, 2018). Later, Boyd would speak about deception, unpredictability, and surprise as elements in keeping the other side off-balance – that is, to unstructure the adversary's "system" (Ford, 2010, p. 19). Ideally, the actions of the pilot ought to be "more subtle, more indistinct, more irregular, and quicker – yet appear to be otherwise (Ford, 2010, p. 29, quoting Boyd, 1986)." In short, you desire both to speed up your own process and slow down the adversary's (see Coram, 2002, pp. 332 & 336).[8]

At the root of this strategy is the premise that each side must cope with uncertainty. "The fundamental, unavoidable and all-pervasive presence of uncertainty is the starting point (Ford, 2010, p. 17, quoting Osinga, 2007; see Boyd, 2018, p. 14)." Each participant must arrive at some conceptualization of what is going on, without which decisions become inapt or random. Obviously, the more accurate one's conceptualization, the better. Erroneous interpretations could lead to fatal errors.[9] But no matter how successful in the moment, that conceptualization must be revised continuously. You cannot cling to a conceptualization that no longer fits the facts. Boyd called the OODA loop a self-correcting process (Ford, 2010, p. 26). What worked a moment ago might be obsolete in just a matter of minutes. Thus, orientation requires a considerable degree of openness and conceptual elasticity. As Daniel Ford wrote, change is inevitable, but more importantly one must catch up with the rate of change, repeatedly. And by taking action, one is accelerating the rate of change during combat. Ford referred to this as the tempo of change (2010, p. 19). The goal is to transform a sequence of "Change and Change and Change" into "Change-Change-Change," and then into "ChangeChangeChange."

Boyd insisted that there is a fractal quality to these OODA loops. The pilot's processes are part of a larger effort by the squadron, where the commander undergoes his or her own OODA loops. We can then outscope to the entire Air Force, which has its own OODA loops, outward to the

---

8 For instance, Palaoro (2010) demonstrates how to use information operations tools to disrupt OODA loops.

9 The pilot must pay attention both to internal processes and to external processes, within the system and out in the environment. A fixation on either one, to the exclusion of the other, can be dangerous. And these understandings of the interior and the exterior must align with one another to make a coherent and true-to-life whole (Coram, 2002, p. 326). Once a pilot labors under a misapprehension, whatever it is, one error can contribute to a feedback loop that becomes increasingly distorted until it is fixed.

military generally, and ultimately to civilian leadership. Any OODA loop takes place within a context of other OODA loops, nested within a hierarchy of decision-making (Robinson, 2021, p. 44; Osinga, 2007, p. 155). The pilot who understands the whole architecture up and down the chain of command should have an additional advantage (e.g. Coram, 2002, p. 337). These multiple OODA loops form the context for action.

Furthermore, an isolated OODA loop is not isolated at all. One OODA loop triggers another one sequentially. So the pilot needs a fresh orientation each time through the cycle. It helps to have an encompassing orientation about the encounter as a whole, a kind of "framework" about the whole for each separate loop. That is to say that the pilot should not have to invent a completely new conceptualization at every moment. A broad conceptualization that continues to apply, with variations, can be said to be "durable." Adjustments to a durable conceptualization will be minor, requiring less effort (and less time). A superior conceptualization of the situation as a whole therefore will be useful throughout the engagement.

Boyd believed that a pilot must not only cycle through an OODA loop quickly and accurately but do so also from the point of view of the adversary (Coram, 2002, p. 335). What do *they* see? What must *they* now believe? What is going through *their* mind? How is the foe working through his own OODA loops? It is not enough to see everything from one's place in the world; a combat pilot would be advised to do the same from the other person's perspective – again, doing so accurately, quickly, and repeatedly. That is a tall order.

What follows logically is that the pilot makes multiple observations, multiple orientations, multiple decisions, and multiple actions, one right after the other. Boyd took this one step further, saying that on *any given loop*, there are multiple observations, orientations, decisions, and acts (Ford, 2010, p. 23; see Osinga, 2007, figure 6.1; see generally Boyd, 1987a, p. 11). For example, the pilot looks directly through the bubble canopy at the skies, but also checks the instrumentation panel and listens to the radio. When making a decision, the pilot may have to conclude whether to fire weapons and bank left or right immediately afterward. The process is rarely so linear as the schema suggests.

By now, one would be excused for suspecting that such a complex process never ends (Ford, 2010, p. 27). In fact, it was Boyd's creed to revise one's thinking constantly – that is, to edit, finagle, and adapt unceasingly (Coram, 2002, p. 309; Robinson, 2021, p. 47). For that is what it means to be alive in a changing world. Making matters worse, though, is that at any given point in time, nobody completely masters the situation in every detail. Everybody makes mistakes. For this reason, a conceptualization that guards against likely error should be superior to one that doesn't.

When your success depends upon never being mistaken, you are setting yourself up to fail. At the heart of this realization is that reality itself is ambiguous (Ford, 2010, pp. 26 & 50). No matter how well a pilot cycles through the OODA loop, the reality a pilot is trying to navigate is never completely knowable. There will always be a mismatch between (a) the phenomenon being observed and (b) any conceptualization of it. Searching for a perfect match is a fool's errand and only makes matters worse (Boyd, 1976, pp. 4 & 6). One must account for the inevitability of a mismatch. It follows that each decision will be made on imperfect knowledge.

The origins of the OODA loop can be traced to a realization by Boyd about entropy. No system is 100% effective (Coram, 2002, p. 131). You always lose something during throughput. This can mean drag to an airplane, friction in a machine, or noise during communication. Or parasites in the bloodstream. The system requires infusions of energy, without which its processes will eventually grind to a halt. Once you close a system you condemn it to death (Boyd, 1987b, p. 28f). By implication, however, an open system entails friction (Osinga, 2007, p. 192).

It is in the system's interest to reduce entropy in the first place, to become supremely aerodynamic like a jet fighter. Yet some drag (friction, noise) is inevitable; it is the price one pays for forward momentum. Except that some drag is actually useful (Boyd, 1986, p. 4). This is not a trivial insight. Drag contributes for example to maneuverability, allowing the system to slow and shift quickly into new directions. The sleek design can overshoot. One can serve a system's interests by becoming not sleek but nimble, using drag artfully to alter the trajectory. One uses friction or noise to one's own advantage (Boyd, 1987a, p. 4). Even so, steady progress requires a balancing of thrust and drag. Drag fits into the calculations of flight. Nevertheless, some drag is regrettable, best to be diminished somehow. And since all of this talk about drag applies as well to business and interpersonal communication and life generally, this raises some interesting possibilities.

Boyd's philosophy was not entirely about acceleration, racing through one's OODA loop at breakneck speed. Some delay (or drag) in the system is wholesome, even necessary. There is always so much to do; there is frankly a lot out there for anyone to process. And the situation keeps changing, requiring you to start over. The best advice is to acknowledge drag, keeping it to a minimum in the design of the aircraft and in the angle of attack, but also using it deftly for maximum effect.

For the sake of thoroughness, we must acknowledge that Boyd's ultimate conclusions about strategy are far more complex and exceed the idea of a simple OODA loop (Osinga, 2007, p. 233). Nevertheless, the OODA loop is better known and relatively handy to use in day-to-day operations.

Elaborating on OODA loops: From dogfights to CogWar

Voices are being raised criticizing the use of OODA loops, both with regard to the military (e.g. Masakowski & Blatny, 2023; Danet, 2023; Johnson, 2023, p. 45; Robinson, 2021; Bryant, 2006) and beyond (e.g. Shawe & McAndrew, 2023; Snowden & Boone, 2007; Osinga, 2007, p. 5f). Perhaps it is more accurate to say that OODA loops may not always be preferable in complex or chaotic situations. Furthermore, in many instances, decision-making is a group activity and not the responsibility of a single human being; when that is the case, OODA loops must be adapted for group processes (Masakowski & Blatny, 2023, p. 9-5; cf. Boyd, 2007, p. 115). In addition, some degree of synchronization among units is necessary; the decision-maker cannot afford to behave autonomously (Robinson, 2021, p. 253f; cf. Osinga, 2007, p. 149; see Boyd, 1986, p. 12).[10] David Bryant, to cite one critic, mentioned the common practice of subordinate commanders disseminating plans and information to the rest of the organization, and then gathering and threshing through the reports that come back from the front lines in order to decide what to tell the boss (2006, p. 191). He mentioned this because decision-makers in nearly any complex organization belong to such a telescoping structure of decision-making – something that Boyd advised the military to avoid (e.g. Osinga, 2007). Yet the process is unlikely to be restricted to one's formal command structure. Decision-making often requires informal collaboration and ad hoc groups across boundaries, as for example, when international military forces with distinct command structures must find ways to collaborate in the field (Spoor, & de Werd, 2023, p. 10). Perhaps it goes without saying that in addition to factoring in so many participants in decision-making, the OODA loop presupposes *human* decision-making, whereas increasingly decisions depend on a role for artificial intelligence (Masakowski & Blatny, 2023, pp. 7-3 & 15-2; see Osinga, 2007, p. 245).[11] Some authors refer to this possibility as the human-machine symbiosis (Masakowski & Blatny, 2023, p. 9-5).

Stephen Robinson (2021) set out to explain the extent to which Boyd misinterpreted the historical evidence justifying his opinions, in part because he was being misled by people who had reason to lie about what

---

10 **Synchronization** among units (having them move together according to a shared plan) is not the same thing as **harmonization** (having them move independently according to a shared understanding of the overall purpose) (Brown, 2018).

11 James Johnson (2023) warned about some of the limitations of relying on artificial intelligence and machine learning in the execution of the OODA loop. He wrote that "the line between machines analyzing and synthesizing … data that informs humans who make decisions … will become increasingly blurred… (p. 44)."

had happened in the past; worse, though, Boyd ignored contrary evidence when it became available. Boyd was no historian, to be sure, and he relied on a few bad ones.[12] Ultimately, there is a place for his lessons, as Robinson admits, but only within a larger, more complex array of choices to be used pragmatically, on a case-by-case basis. The OODA loop serves a purpose, albeit a limited purpose, such that the challenge today is to figure out its strengths and weaknesses as a method, when it is appropriate and when it isn't. In a manner of speaking, Robinson adapts a metaphor that Boyd often used to describe a snowmobile as a strange hybrid of skier, motorboat, bicycle, and toy tractor (2021, p. 47; see Osinga, 2007, p. 202f; Boyd, 1987b, p. 6ff). The military is advised to incorporate such devices as the OODA loop, without making it into some kind of dogma. Boyd's ongoing zeal in puncturing dogma, which alienated so many experts at the time, requires a comparable spirit today to be turned around and used against him, as well.

Science has consistently demonstrated how truly complex it can be just to **observe** a situation and **orient** oneself accordingly. So much nuance goes into these functions that it is not enough just to tell decision-makers to go observe and orient. These are exceedingly difficult tasks to begin with (e.g. Robinson, 2021, p. 183). Bryant made the straightforward remark, for example, that decision-makers are increasingly inundated with data, probably too much data to process (2006, p. 186). Johnson (2023) called this phenomenon a "data tsunami" (p. 52). Plenty of that data is ambiguous, incomplete, or simply inaccurate. The volume of data – even good data – outstrips the human capacity to understand it. Making sense of this plethora requires increased powers of conceptualization. Thus, it can be burdensome to train every decision-maker to grasp the subtleties of their job (e.g. Masakowski & Blatny, 2023, p. 14–15). Frequently, such training is not even attempted, so decision-makers are expected to know what to do without specialized training. Now, to be fair John Boyd was aware that his model was a simplification of a far more complex process, with lots of subprocesses, but it is still a legitimate question to wonder about the extent to which decision-makers appreciate that fact. Do they instead understand the OODA loop to be a relatively simple process to be executed step-by-step? That would be a mistake. Even so, let us assume, going forward, that the decision-maker is adequately trained.

---

12 Osinga (2007) emphasized that references to historical examples were primarily for purposes of illustration. Boyd's most important insights were the product of his considerations of the natural sciences and not of history (pp. 53 & 241; see Boyd, 2018, p. 2ff, Boyd, 1987b, p. 12).

Bryant pointed out that the OODA loop model omits certain other salient functions, such as intent. The whole purpose of using the model is to select and accomplish some task. The **purpose**, however, doesn't feature in the OODA loop model (2006, p. 187). The purpose or superordinate goal is simply taken for granted, which may have been satisfactory on the battlefield where the purpose is relatively clear. Even there, however, the existence of some overarching purpose, which we might think of as the commander's vision, tends to presuppose a single point of view (2006, p. 190); what is less clear are the sub-purposes for discrete units in how to achieve that overarching vision, as well as the possibility of that vision changing *in extempore.*

Bryant also explained that **perception** is no longer regarded as merely the reception of stimuli, as though the decision-maker is a passive recipient of information. The decision-maker shapes what is being perceived (2006, p. 187f). Is he or she aware of that influence?

Bryant added that no matter what **conceptual framework** the decision-maker adopts while orienting to reality, we know that there are other, equally legitimate ways to conceptualize reality. The OODA loop model does not adequately help the decision-maker select from among these alternative conceptualizations and, as necessary, shift among them fluidly (2006, p. 188).

Finally, Bryant wanted to see a greater emphasis on disconfirming what one knows and believes, which he referred to as **critical thinking** (2006, p. 189). The conclusion of Bryant's argument is that the OODA loop model, standing alone, does not sufficiently incorporate what we know today about cognition. But there are other concerns about relying exclusively on the OODA loop model.

The point can come in the heat of battle when a decision-maker trying to use the OODA loop keeps going through the process over and over again so rapidly in response to confusing and changing circumstances, that it leaves little or no time to pause and reflect (Masakowski & Blatny, 2023, p. 8-4). Some missions, such as counterinsurgency, require patience and not so much "getting inside" an adversary's decision cycle rapidly (Robinson, 2021, p. 283). After all, the guerrillas themselves are probably not executing OODA loops (Osinga, 2007, p. 6). Later, upon further reflection and scrutiny, a commander might be held accountable for decisions that did not provide for an opportunity to reflect on the "correctness" of the decision, for example, whether the act was legally permissible (Masakowski & Blatny, 2023, p. 9-4). It might be that the commander simply takes the position that he or she had to act quickly and assumed some risk in doing so, but the institution – and here one might think of a military tribunal – might conclude otherwise.[13] They might judge that the commander made the wrong decision, in retrospect, or that the commander did not need to make a decision at all. This problem of judging the results of using an OODA loop with hindsight (*ex post facto*) introduces an element of caution that can seem to a battlefield commander unduly crippling (e.g. Boyd, 1987, pp. 20f & 31). At such times, the commander might be expected to use two different decision-making models in response to two separate adversaries, one of which is the enemy and the other of which would be the institution's agents of oversight back at headquarters. Fold in the judgment of the public, often informed by the media, and you now introduce a third "adversary" in response to which decisions are to be made: how will this decision appear to the folks at home?

The OODA loop tends to emphasize decisions in terms of a single adversary. As Robinson worded it, the OODA loop tends to presuppose a bipolar conflict (2021, p. 290ff). Often, a decision-maker must cycle through multiple loops simultaneously, in response to multiple "adversaries."[14] One could generate a list of other possible actors and stakeholders, including politicians, attorneys, business representatives, cultural influencers, and so forth, since frequently a struggle can be transferred from one domain (such as the battlefield) to other domains (such as economic trade or public relations). As Spoor and de Werd (2023) state, "UN military units are merely one of the components for a head of mission to use. Military information (or intelligence) hence ties to multiple domains [including] political, military, economic, social, information and infrastructure perspectives (p. 11)."

The emphasis on haste in decision-making would not necessarily pertain to mission planning, where the objective requires more research and reflection, which is to say that some decisions don't have to be rushed (Osinga, 2007, p. 101). At the other extreme, though, where time is of the essence,

---

13 A fascinating study of the role of tribunals in judging military commanders after the fact appears in Stockhausen, 2008. Paul Woodruff, writing specifically about ancient Athens, mentioned more than once that military commanders at the time, especially under a democracy, worried about how the folks back home would judge their decisions (2005, pp. 40, 53, 124, & 167). Robinson (2021) describes a concrete example of this sort of second-guessing during Iraqi Freedom (p. 278).

14 In the world of business, the same considerations apply. Every leader must account for multiple (and sometimes incompatible) stakeholders, including the board of directors, rival firms, customers, government regulators, insurers, juries, and the general public. To account for this element of complexity, some theorists have modified OODA into what is known as a Holistic Bowtie Model (Masakowski & Blatny, 2023, p. 9–6f), which it would be unnecessary to explain in these pages.

an OODA loop can be unnecessarily, even fatally time-consuming where intuition in conjunction with AI might suffice (Masakowski & Blatny, 2023, p. 8-5f; cf. Osinga, 2007, p. 60). In addition, the OODA loop tends to underemphasize the option to do nothing, to refrain from taking action (Masakowski & Blatny, 2023, pp. 9-3 & 9-6), which is in many instances preferable. For another thing, the OODA loop treats the decision-maker as a cognitive angel, sufficiently rational and capable of ignoring such things as physical strain, emotion, and personal values (Masakowski & Blatny, 2023, p. 9-7).[15] This expectation is probably unrealistic. Similarly, the OODA loop has been criticized for omitting tacit knowledge, which by definition is not held consciously in one's focal awareness (Bryant, 2006, p. 186f; see generally Polanyi, 2009), although Frans Osinga (2007) denies this claim categorically (p. 80; see Boyd, 1987a, p. 13). The decision-maker knows a lot without being able to specify or articulate, and this knowledge will be relevant to decision-making processes. By the same token, of course, the decision-maker knows a lot tacitly that is just not true. These errors can interfere with sound decisions, despite the decision-maker being unaware that he or she is even using tacit knowledge.

Perhaps most critically, a sophisticated adversary knowing that you rely on using OODA loops might be able to exploit that knowledge to its advantage, based in part on everything I have just said (Masakowski & Blatny, 2023, p. 9-9; Price, 2023). Begun in 2021, "the NATO HQ ACT Concept Development Branch is currently developing a NATO concept on CogWar (Masakowski & Blatny, 2023, p. 1-3)." CogWar (or cognitive warfare) is a concept that is still being defined, but in essence, it would appear to have as its goal "to exploit facets of cognition to disrupt, undermine, influence, or modify human decisions (Masakowski & Blatny, 2023, p. 1)." If one side is pursuing this goal of interfering with the adversary's OODA loops, chances are that the other side is doing so as well. And it is common knowledge now that many significant militaries around the world have formally adopted some version of the OODA loop (Bryant, 2006, p. 184f; Robinson, 2021, p. 15).

OODA loops for studying leadership: Examples from military history

A student of leadership might examine an episode using the OODA loop, tracing what occurs from step to step. As mentioned previously in another chapter, the student of leadership will have limited access to what a leader

---

15 The idea of cognitive angels can be attributed to Kwame Anthony Appiah (2017).

thinks. The steps that a decision-maker goes through occur in the mind of the leader. A lot that happens during the OODA loop is accompanied by no outward behavior. In these circumstances, the resourceful investigator might be able to locate a trustworthy record of what the leader was thinking, especially according to first-person accounts such as memoirs and personal letters. Again, this is assuming that the account can be trusted. Without such an account, however, one might be forced to draw inferences from the available evidence, such as it is. In this regard, sometimes works of literature or cinema will disclose more than an actual leader might be willing or able to share. These examples from the world of art, while not empirical in the conventional sense, since they are fictional, can reveal something of the process that a leader undergoes. In this section, I would like to offer several examples where the OODA loop might be used profitably to analyze leadership – in this case, military leadership.

Observe

On 3 June 1863, General Robert E. Lee had ordered his Army of Northern Virginia northward toward Union territory and eventually into the heart of Pennsylvania. En route, Major General J.E.B. Stuart, in command of the cavalry division, was surprised at Brandy Station, where he battled to a draw. Daniel Landsman (2023) contends that this encounter "came at a great cost to his cavalry forces and his reputation, as he had been caught off guard by two surprise attacks during the battle." The Richmond *Enquirer* (1863, June 12) even criticized Stuart in print: "If Gen. Stuart is to be the eyes and ears of the army we advise him to see more, and be seen less.... Gen. Stuart has suffered no little in public estimation by the late enterprises of the enemy."[16] Not long after his inconclusive encounter at Brandy Station, Stuart received orders to ride around the east flank of the Union army that was marching to intercept Lee. Landsman (2023) picks up the story:

> Instead of taking a direct route to Ewell's Second Corps, Stuart decided to take the brigades of Wade Hampton, Fitzhugh Lee, and John Chambliss north toward Rockville, Maryland, moving between the Union Army, who were marching north through Virginia about 50 miles east of Lee's army, and Washington, D.C. However, by the time Stuart began his ride on June 24, Union movement was underway and Stuart's desired route was blocked by columns of Union soldiers. This unexpected obstacle forced Stuart's cavalry further east than originally planned and not only

---

16 Quoted in Wert (2008, p. 251).

hindered Stuart's ability to reach Ewell's right flank, but also deprived Lee of vital intelligence that a more conventional cavalry screen would have provided.

Separated now from his chain of command and the rest of the army, Stuart would be surprised again on June 30th in Hanover, where he lost precious time and over 200 men. For several crucial days, as the two primary forces converged on the town of Gettysburg, Stuart was grievously absent. Not only was he absent, but he failed to keep delivering news of the Union's strength and position, so Lee was entering into the engagement virtually blind.[17] When an advance unit under the command of Brigadier General J. Johnston Pettigrew approached the town, looking for supplies, they encountered a substantial presence of Union soldiers already there. This surprised Lee and his staff, who had originally assumed there would be little more than some local militia. Thus, the leadership of the Confederate forces did not know what to expect.

According to one report, when Stuart finally did arrive with his beleaguered cavalry at Gettysburg, two days into a three-day battle, Lee said to him in exasperation, "General Stuart, where have you been? I have not heard a word from you for days and you are the eyes and ears of my army (Foote, 1994, p. 60)." In his official report on the battle (published in 1889 under the direction of Lieut. Col. Robert N. Scott), Lee had stated that "the absence of the cavalry rendered it impossible to obtain accurate information (p. 307)" and, in a second report, that "the movements of the army preceding the battle of Gettysburg had been much embarrassed by the absence of the cavalry (p. 321)." Unable to observe, the leader complained that he was at a disadvantage.

Orient

Marshall Michel Ney, under the command of Napoleon I at the Battle of Waterloo in 1815, witnessed movement across the battlefield at 4:00 pm, which turned out to be the evacuation of wounded soldiers. Ney interpreted the departure of so many men as the beginning of a retreat, which it was not. Having few infantry at his disposal, Ney ordered all cavalry to charge the enemy, so that he could rout them in their impending disarray

---

17 Wittenberg and Petrucci (2006) point out that Stuart did try to send messages that never got through to Lee. In addition, Lee had other cavalry at his disposal that could have been used to monitor the Union's whereabouts. After the battle, Lee confirmed that during this ill-fated ride Stuart had acted within the scope of his orders. None of these details changes the fact that Lee was operating without vital information.

(Siborne, 1895, pp. 443–449). He initially committed 4,800 horsemen, then raised the total to 9,000, straight into the center of the line.

Napoleon was appalled at this decision (Esposito & Elting, 1999, p. 354, Map 166). Ney had not only misinterpreted the enemy's movement to begin with, but he committed the cavalry without infantry support, leaving the horsemen vulnerable to precisely the response by the Duke of Wellington on the other side. It was a classic blunder. The following quotation from an eyewitness from the British side explained:

> About four p.m., the enemy's artillery in front of us ceased firing all of a sudden, and we saw large masses of cavalry advance: not a man present who survived could have forgotten in after life the awful grandeur of that charge. You discovered at a distance what appeared to be an overwhelming, long moving line, which, ever advancing, glittered like a stormy wave of the sea when it catches the sunlight. On they came until they got near enough, whilst the very earth seemed to vibrate beneath the thundering tramp of the mounted host. One might suppose that nothing could have resisted the shock of this terrible moving mass. They were the famous cuirassiers, almost all old soldiers, who had distinguished themselves on most of the battlefields of Europe. In an almost incredibly short period they were within twenty yards of us, shouting "*Vive l'Empereur!*" The word of command, "Prepare to receive cavalry", had been given, every man in the front ranks knelt, and a wall bristling with steel, held together by steady hands, presented itself to the infuriated cuirassiers.
>
> *(Gronow, 1862, p. 95)*

The French were unable to convince their horses to fling themselves against the bristling wall, so they rode around and around, frustrated, while British marksmen picked them off. Soon, the exhausted and depleted units, incapable of penetrating Wellington's squares, fled back across the open field to their own troops, having lost countless men while accomplishing very little. The leader (Ney) had observed what was happening, but misunderstood it, excitedly (and carelessly) hoping to capitalize on a situation that did not exist.

Decide

In 2012, Winston Groom published a history of the Battle of Shiloh, which had been conducted during the Civil War across two dates, April 6–7 in 1862. Brigadier General William Tecumseh Sherman had just endured ridicule in the press for requesting an extravagant number of troops to defend

Louisville against the Confederates. Stung by the publicity, he reacted soon after by refusing to overreact to alarms that a substantial rebel army was headed his way along the banks of another river. There he sat, at Pittsburg Landing on the west side of the Tennessee River, with orders to await the Army of the Ohio before proceeding further south. While stationed there, he used the time to drill his raw recruits up and down the flat farmers' fields. What he did not do, however, was entrench and build fortifications, in anticipation of an assault. Neither did he extend a line of soldiers westward to intercept incursions. A number of reports accused Sherman of overcompensating for his folly over Louisville by neglecting genuine threats. As Groom put it, he received more than a few warnings that forces were en route. So why did he while away his time in training? When the enemy suddenly came upon his camp, the Union forces were surprised and ill-prepared to engage.

Leading up to the battle, Sherman made his opinion known to his superior, Major General Ulysses S. Grant. Groom (2012) tells the story.

> "For weeks," [Sherman] scoffed, "old women reported that [the Rebel army] was coming, sometimes with 100,000, sometimes with 300,000." He brushed off these worried reports by saying that at worst the Confederates were conducting a "reconnaissance in force." On April 5, the very eve of battle, Sherman sent a note to Grant in response to an inquiry about enemy activity in the army's front: "I have no doubt that nothing will occur today other than some picket firing. The enemy is saucy, but…will not press our pickets far. I do not apprehend anything like an attack on our position."

Groom (2012) continued:

> Because he had consistently sneered at reports of an enemy attack, Sherman was forced to eat his words…. Sherman later said—in what must be one of the most profound understatements of the war—that as a Confederate battery began shelling his camps, 'I…became satisfied for the first time that the enemy designed a determined attack on our whole camp….Our infantry and artillery opened along the whole line and the battle became general.'

Almost immediately, recriminations for being caught flat-footed appeared in newspapers (Masters, 2020). On April 14th, one week after the event, the *Chicago Tribune* gave an account, followed by two papers from Cincinnati – each of which relayed that Sherman had gone into the engagement unprepared. Papers in Columbus and Cleveland, hoping to rebut accusations that Ohio boys had proved cowardly in the field, repeated the charge that the commanding officers were at fault. Ohio's Lieutenant Governor Benjamin Stanton, sticking up for native Ohioans, decided to publish his dissatisfaction with the failure to prepare, and it was in response to his allegations that Sherman decided to reply and justify his command. Apparently, Sherman went to his death insisting he had done nothing wrong. Yet he did agree that he had decided not to fortify his position and he did agree that the enemy took advantage of that fact. In the days leading up to a significant battle, this leader had reason to make a decision pertaining to reports of impending conflict, but for whatever reason chose not to do so. Whether he was justified in this course of action warrants scrutiny by leadership scholars.

Act

A leader who was blamed for costly delays was the Athenian general Nicias during the Peloponnesian War (431–404 BCE). Interpretations vary, but apparently, Nicias had a reputation for hesitating even when he knew the best course of action.

In an attempt to deprive their enemy of much-needed grain as the conflict with Sparta dragged on, Athenians decided to send an expeditionary force westward to Sicily, under the command of Alcibiades and Nicias, and there intercept supplies. At the very least, the Spartan forces would be diverted away from the front, alleviating the Athenian war effort. The people of Athens authorizing the raid worried that Alcibiades seemed young and impetuous to command such a venture, so they chose the older Nicias to command alongside him as a voice of caution. Almost immediately upon arriving on Sicilian shores, however, Alcibiades fled to Sparta in order to escape prosecution for crimes back in Athens, so Nicias was temporarily left in charge of the entire operation. Upon landing, the armed forces waited to siege Syracuse, despite the popular assumption that an invader is most fearsome when he first arrives (Kopff, 1976, p. 29, n. 15). The Athenians had just won a battle in the open field, so why not capitalize on the momentum and march directly into the city? This hesitation gave Sicilian forces time to mobilize and appeal to Sparta for help. Only after the winter did the fighting begin in earnest.

After a number of discouraging encounters, it became obvious that the Athenian enterprise was doomed. Nicias agreed that the time had come to return home, in defeat. But then in obedience to an omen, he recommended delaying the departure, which gave the Sicilians – reinforced from Sparta – the opportunity to beset the retreating forces and capture them. Lieutenant Colonel J. D. Dowdy (2001) summarized the outcome thus: "The 7,000 survivors of the nearly 50,000 soldiers and sailors that Athens had sent against Syracuse, found captivity in the Syracusan quarries (p. 26)." The expedition had been a complete failure. And Nicias, executed on foreign soil.

The historian Thucydides, who had himself commanded troops in battle, defended the hesitation to attack Syracuse right away. He regarded it as prudent to obtain supplies for a siege and await the arrival of more men. Then, before heading back to Athens, Nicias hoped that reinforcements would soon arrive. Thucydides also acknowledges the role of a second Athenian general (replacing Alcibiades) who ordered the withdrawal. Nanno Marinatos (2022b) defends Nicias and interprets Thucydides as vindicating the losing general. Thucydides did mildly complain that Nicias had deferred too much to soothsayers before sailing home (Marinatos, 2022a). Benjamin Niedzielski (2017) offers a more balanced interpretation of what Thucydides seems to have thought about Nicias.

Many years later, Plutarch (apparently informed by another historian named Philistus) more vehemently castigated Nicias, claiming that these were not only poor decisions but also evidence of character flaws. Plutarch of course had to rely on sources such as Philistus of Syracuse, inasmuch as he was writing many years after the events. Philistus had been consistently critical of Nicias (see Kopff, 1976). Several esteemed historians have since agreed more with Plutarch's interpretation (e.g. Westlake, 1968; see Stockhausen, 2008, p. 2).

Regardless of who decided on these delays, whether at the beginning of the campaign or at the end, the expedition failed miserably, and Nicias rightly or wrongly became a byword for culpable diffidence on the part of leaders.

Concluding remarks

Theorists in Leadership Studies have occasionally found an excuse to explain the idea of the OODA loop, but it is less obvious that they have penetrated beyond the surface. The idea turns out to be a handy heuristic – or worse a bromide, trite and unoriginal. The reasoning behind the idea and its implications for practice have been investigated primarily by the military, which is only natural given its provenance; but the foregoing chapter has been an attempt to bring those investigations to a wider audience. Ultimately, the OODA loop is grounded in some of the most sophisticated scientific principles of the twentieth century about uncertainty and entropy. Furthermore, its implementation by the military provides an empirical testing ground. In my opinion, those of us teaching and writing about leadership might reacquaint ourselves with John Boyd's lessons.

References

Appiah, K.A. (2017). *As if: Idealization and ideals*. Harvard University Press.

Boyd, J. (2018). "A discourse on winning and losing." *Unpublished Presentation*. Retrieved 20 February 2024 from https://www.ausairpower.net/JRB/intro.pdf.

Boyd, J. (1987a). "Organic design for command and control." *Unpublished Presentation*. Retrieved 9 March 2022 from https://www.ausairpower.net/JRB/c&c.pdf.

Boyd, J. "Strategic game of? and?" In Richards, C. & C. Spinney (eds.) (1987b). *Defense and the National Interest*. Retrieved 8 March 2022 from https://www.ausairpower.net/JRB/strategic_game.pdf.

Boyd, J. (1986). "Patterns of conflict." *Unpublished Presentation*. Retrieved 20 February 2024 from https://www.ausairpower.net/JRB/poc.pdf.

Boyd, J. (1976). "Destruction and creation." *Unpublished Presentation*. Retrieved 8 March 2022 from https://pogoarchives.org/m/dni/john_boyd_compendium/destruction_and_creation.pdf.

Brown, I. (April 29, 2018). "John Boyd, maneuver warfare, and MCDP-1 (Part 2) with Major Ian Brown." *Professional Military Education*. Webinar Retrieved 23 March 2024 from https://www.professionalmilitaryeducation.com/warfightingepisode-12-john-boyd-maneuver-warfare-and-mcdp1/.group.

Bryant, D. (2006). "Rethinking OODA: Toward a modern cognitive framework of command decision making." *Military Psychology*. 18: 183–206.

Coram, R. (2002). *Boyd: The fighter pilot who changed the art of war*. Little, Brown and Company.

Danet, D. (2023, June). "Cognitive security: Facing cognitive operations in hybrid warfare." *In European Conference on Cyber Warfare and Security*. 22(1): 161–168.

Dowdy, J.T. (2001). *The Syracuse Campaign: Failed opportunities, failed leadership*. US Army War College.

Esposito, V.J., & Elting J. (1999). *A military history and atlas of the Napoleonic Wars*. Greenhill.

Foote, S. (1994). *Stars in their courses: The Gettysburg Campaign, June-July 1963*. Modern Library.

Ford, D. (2010). *A vision so noble: John Boyd, the OODA loop, and America's war on terror*. Warbird Books.

Gronow, R.H. (1862). *Reminiscences of Captain Gronow...: Being anecdotes of the camp, the court, and the clubs, at the close of the last war with France*. Smith, Elder.

Groom, W. (2012). "Sherman's folly at Shiloh." *History Net* excerpting Groom's *Shiloh 1862*. Retrieved 9 July 2023 from https://www.historynet.com/shermans-folly-at-shiloh/.

Hammond, G. (2001). *The mind of war: John Boyd and American security*. Smithsonian Books.

Johnson, J. (2023). "Automating the OODA loop in the age of intelligent machines: Reaffirming the role of humans in command-and-control decision-making in the digital age." *Defence Studies*. 23(1): 43–67. https://doi.org/10.1080/14702436.2022.2102486.

Kopff, E.C. (1976). "Thucydides 7.42. 3: An unrecognized fragment of Philistus." *Greek, Roman, and Byzantine Studies.* 17(1): 23–30.

Landsman, D. (2023). "Lee's cumbersome cavalry: J.E.B. Stuart's troubled ride to Gettysburg." *American Battlefield Trust.* Retrieved 8 July 2023 from https://www.battlefields.org/learn/articles/lees-cumbersome-cavalry.

Levine, D. (2015). *Social theory as a vocation: Genres of theory work in sociology.* Transaction Publishers.

Marinatos, N. (2022a). "A note on the *theiasmos* of Nicias in Thucydides." *Classica et Mediaevalia.* 70: 1–16.

Marinatos, N. "Games of chess: Thucydides and Brasidas, Nicias and Gylippus." In Marinatos, N. & R. Pitt (eds.) (2022b). *Thucydides the Athenian* (pp. 143–163). Alexandria Publications.

Masakowski, Y.R., & Blatny, J.M. (2023). *Mitigating and responding to cognitive warfare.* NATO STO Technical Report RDP STO-TR-HFM-ET-356.

Masters, D. (2020). "Surprised at Shiloh? Hell no, said Sherman." *The Western Theater in the Civil War.* Retrieved 9 July 2023 from https://www.western-theatercivilwar.com/post/surprised-at-shiloh-hell-no-said-sherman.

Niedzielski, B. (2017). "The complex depiction of Nicias in Thucydides." *UCLA Historical Journal.* 28(1): 37–50.

Osinga, F. (2007). *Science, strategy and war: The strategic theory of John Boyd.* Routledge.

Palaoro, H. (2010, 4th quarter). "Information strategy: The missing link." *Joint Force Quarterly.* 59: 83–85.

Polanyi, M. (2009). *The tacit dimension.* University of Chicago Press.

Price, B.R. (2023). "Colonel John Boyd's thoughts on disruption." *Journal of Advanced Military Studies.* 14(1): 98–117.

Proctor, R.W., & Schneider, D.W. (2018). "Hick's law for choice reaction time: A review." *Quarterly Journal of Experimental Psychology.* 71(6): 1281–1299.

Richards, C. (2009). "Briefings - Colonel John R. Boyd, USAF." *Air Power Australia.* Retrieved 9 March 2022 from https://www.ausairpower.net/APA-Boyd-Papers.html.

Richards, C. (2004). *Certain to win: The strategy of John Boyd, applied to business.* Xlibris Corporation.

Robinson, S. (2021). *The blind strategist: John Boyd and the American art of war.* Exisle Publishing.

Scott, R. (1889). *The war of the rebellion: Official records of the Union and Confederate armies* (series I, vol. xxvii, part II). Government Printing Office.

Shawe, R., & McAndrew, I.R. (2023). "OODA and CECA: Analysis of decision-making frameworks." *American Journal of Industrial and Business Management.* 13: 457–464. https://doi.org/10.4236/ajibm.2023.136029.

Siborne, W. (1895). *The Waterloo campaign, 1815* (4th ed.). A. Constable.

Snowden, D.J., & Boone, M.E. (2007). "A leader's framework for decision making." *Harvard Business Review.* 85(11): 68.

Spoor, B., & de Werd, P. (2023). "Complexity in military intelligence." *International Journal of Intelligence and CounterIntelligence.* 1–21. https://doi.org/10.1080/08850607.2023.2209493.

Stockhausen, J. (2008). *The price of failure: Conceptions of Nicias' culpability in Athens' Sicilian disaster* [dissertation]. Ohio State University.

Weick, K.E. (1995). *Sensemaking in organizations.* Sage.

Wert, J.D. (2008). *Cavalryman of the Lost Cause: A biography of J.E.B. Stuart.* Simon & Schuster.

Westlake, H.D. (1968). *Individuals in Thucydides.* Cambridge University Press.

Wittenberg, E., & Petrucci, D. (2006). *Plenty of blame to go around: Jeb Stuart's controversial ride to Gettysburg.* Savas Beatie.

Woodruff, P. (2005). *First democracy: The challenges of an ancient idea.* Oxford University Press.

7

USING THE PRINCIPLES OF ANALOGISM

Nothing is identical, but resemblances abound

Introduction to the chapter

The children's television series "Sesame Street" includes a recurring lesson in which four different items are presented to the audience, accompanied by a song that goes like this:

> One of these things is not like the others,
> One of these things just doesn't belong,
> Can you tell which thing is not like the others
> By the time I finish my song?
>
> *Lyrics written by Jon Stone*

Children must develop their powers of comparison, practicing the art of classification. They must detect and then find meaning in the various distinctions they encounter, because these skills will become necessary throughout one's life. Is this food or a poison? Are you a friend or foe? Is it cold or hot outdoors? Is the bedroom upstairs or downstairs? The human mind constructs an elaborate map of reality based in large part on these operations. And that's a good thing. An educated mind possesses many complex, nuanced, and adaptable maps about the same reality, grounded in the most basic operations.

Of course, many of these maps turn out to be mistaken or of limited utility. Or the underlying reality shifts so that a map that was once accurate no longer applies. It takes quite a while for the child to recognize that he or she can overlay different maps over the same reality, in the same way

DOI: 10.4324/9781003540526-8

that a road map is not a topological map, is not a political map, and so on. Often, the problem is knowing which map to use for which purpose. Furthermore, these various "maps" are often connected to one another, as part of a larger, more comprehensive schema about reality.

> The brain maps the world around it and it maps its own properties. Those maps are experienced as images in our minds.... Thus, the entire fabric of a conscious mind is created from the same cloth – images generated by the brain's map-making abilities.
>
> *(Doerig, Schurger, & Herzog, 2021, p. 62)*

We are all in this sense mapmaking creatures. But to create, use, and occasionally revise these maps, we must constantly rely on our powers of comparison.

The following chapter introduces an ontology that Philippe Descola referred to as analogism, in which one begins with the principle that no two objects in reality are identical, even though resemblances are abundant and instructive. Several fields of study address the prospect of identity, as for example, manufacturing in the pursuit of zero defects and biology regarding the possibility of clones. Several fields of study address the attempt to *seem* identical, as for example, biology and the tactics of camouflage, as well as culture and the dynamics of fashion. Nevertheless, analogism depends on the proposition that no two items are in fact identical. Nevertheless, resemblances can be instructive, often in the unlikeliest places.

What is analogism?

Philippe Descola, chair of anthropology at the Collège de France, published his magnum opus in 2005, to be translated later into English in 2013 as *Beyond Nature and Culture.*

> In it, [Descola] classifies ontologies according to a ... structural matrix. He sets up a two-by-two table setting interiority (soul, essence, spirit, mind) against physicality (body, physical stuff) and shared against nonshared.... Analogism [is the quadrant where neither interiority nor physicality are shared, which is to say that analogism] holds that humans differ both physically and spiritually from other lives, but that there are countless interpenetrating essences, flows, or qualities that link us all into a vast web.
>
> *(Anderson, 2015, p. 209)*

As an ontology, analogism sets forth the proposition that no two things are identical, which is a principle that casts any claim of identity into question, although it also opens up a range of possible ways that two things might resemble one another. Two objects might be the same shade of red, for example. Or they might cost the same amount of money. Or they might weigh the same. Or they might remind somebody of their long-deceased grandmother. The possibilities for comparison are limitless.

Two siblings should resemble one another to a great extent because of both nature and nurture, yet they might find separate friends outside of the family with shared interests. Brothers might look alike, yet one is a poet and the other a stonemason. Two buildings might present interchangeable facades to the outside world, yet one is a school and the other is a prison. The significant question is always *in what respect* any two things are alike. Making comparisons of this kind will be fruitful, so long as one does not leap to the conclusion that because they resemble one another in one respect, then they are altogether the same. The truth is probably otherwise. To make that mistake is a classic perceptual error (e.g. Thorndike, 1920). Two puddles in the street can look the same to a motorist, yet one is shallow and safe to drive across and the other deep and dangerous. When detecting these similarities, it makes sense to guard against impermissible inferences.

Elsewhere, I have used the simple example of my grandmother's tin of discarded buttons. These buttons can be dumped onto a table and sorted by size, shape, or color or substance. Two buttons might be the same shape but of different colors. Two other buttons might be the same color, but of different shapes. This process of sorting (or classification) can go on forever, according to different criteria. Which student in the classroom is the tallest, the oldest, the fastest, or the smartest? We can categorize in a multitude of ways. Any two objects can be identical in one respect, but not in another. Thus, the conscientious investigator must make these criteria clear. What then is the basis of comparison?

"In what respect...?"

One of the more intriguing possibilities is finding two things that are very much *not* alike which do resemble one another in some unanticipated way. A cloud in the sky can look like a lion. Tea can taste like a flower smells. Two songs that sound nothing alike can each declare the lyricists' love for a woman. A stereotypical military commander and a director of hospice can each practice the same style of leadership. Just as two objects can resemble one another and tempt a person to assume they are otherwise the same, so also two objects can differ dramatically from one another and tempt a person to assume they are nothing alike. The Venus Flytrap is a carnivorous plant. Poker and rugby are both games. At a sufficient level of abstraction, one can uncover strange and insightful lessons. A resemblance between A and B does not mean identity, and differences between A and B do not mean there is nothing similar. One must look more closely. It is a matter of **discernment**.

Analogism not only permits but actually encourages making these comparisons. We have much to learn from our powers of comparison. What analogism complicates are our expectations. The persistent need to categorize can freeze things into their classification unnecessarily in the form of literalism. This is a version of the fallacy of the Black Swan, by which scientists who knew only white swans argued that swans could not be black, when in fact in other lands they most certainly are (Taleb, 2007). It adds nothing to stomp your foot and insist on being correct contrary to the known facts. Classifications are not magic. They are cognitive devices and hopefully useful devices. Analogism simply expects investigators to be the master of their own devices.

Speaking to fellow psychologists at Eranos in 1976, James Hillman once explained that the academic search for "types" has contributed to our understanding because "types help to organize a vast number of similar events into rough groupings" (1980, p. 8). It is useful to detect similarities. However, he cautioned, these groupings are not meant to be strict, like little boxes into which one tosses examples. They are at most handy devices for making sense of a range of experiences, but that is all that they are (1980, pp. 6–18). They orient us, but they do not define boundaries. In fact, using "types" to categorize any array prevents us from seeing what makes each example unique.

To be fair, Descola described three other ontologies that rely on different principles. And he acknowledged that we can use them productively as well. Each of these "ontologies" will yield useful results, if managed properly. The following pages, however, will adhere to the principles of analogism, not so much to prove them superior to all others, as it is to demonstrate their plausibility and to suggest their utility.

To what extent are things identical?

Many have heard it said that no two snowflakes are alike. Of the billions of snowflakes that fall from the sky each winter, there is purported to be no duplication whatsoever (see generally Libbrecht, 2003). Whether this is true turns out to be a matter of some dispute to this very day.[1] But

---

1 I never expected to find that scholars would still be debating whether this claim is empirically true. Chemists, statisticians, and mechanical engineers, for example, have considered

if it is true – or if in principle it can be accepted as true for purposes of investigation – then one has to wonder to what extent any two objects are identical.[2]

In several fields of study, identity is actually an important concept, if not the ultimate goal. Take manufacturing, for example.

Manufacturing

Since Gutenberg, industries have sought the interchangeability of parts. According to John Paxton, "Interchangeable parts would reduce the expense of manufacture, the expense of use and the expense of repair (2012, p. 76)." The idea of mass production presupposes replication, such that the system results in the same output every time. One Ford automobile of the same make and model should be indistinguishable from all of the others. Exact duplicates are the ideal. Toward this end, manufacturing has adopted a credo of zero defects, aiming to eliminate even the tiniest discrepancies.[3] Beyond a certain limit, variation among widgets poses a problem. At this moment in history, for instance, certain firms are adopting nano-scale surface replication that only a laser-scanning confocal microscope can detect (see Baruffi et al., 2019). Other firms rely more

---

the assertion to be true (see e.g. Pilipski & Pilipski, 2006; Bejan, 2015). As recently as 2021, one article from the Institute of Electrical and Electronics Engineers explained its methods.

> We describe a unique approach to the characterization of winter precipitation through the synergistic use of advanced optical instrumentation for in situ microphysical and geometrical measurements of ice and snow particles; image processing techniques to obtain the fall speed, size distribution, 3D shape (mesh), density, and effective dielectric constant of snowflakes; method of moments (MoM) scattering computations of precipitation particles; and state-of-the-art dual polarization radars for the measurement of polarimetric scattering observables (Notaros, 2021).

Nevertheless, it has been reported that two snowflakes were once observed to be alike, and physicists have conducted experiments showing that they can create two identical snowflakes under controlled conditions (Nichols, 2000).

2 Making analogism more plausible are the latest findings regarding complexity, chaos, and the butterfly effect, topics which exceed the scope of this chapter.

3 In 1965, the United States military distributed a handbook to explain the concept of Zero Defects or ZD (*Quality and Reliability Assurance Handbook*). Interestingly, it refers to the doctrine as a "motivational approach to the elimination of defects attributable to human error (Assistant Secretary of Defense, 1965, p. 3)." Three years later, the military retreated from this position, arguing that ZD is not only a motivational approach (Assistant Secretary of Defense, 1968, p. iv). This is significant, because private industry has also transferred the ideal to pertain to any error whatsoever. By 1980, Philip Crosby was urging ZD as a desideratum, regardless of the source. He stated unequivocally, contrary to what the military had originally said, that ZD "is not a motivation program (2005, p. 63)."

broadly on artificial intelligence to accomplish their goal (e.g. Fragapane et al., 2023; Leberruyer et al., 2023; Caiazzo et al., 2022; Cheng, 2021). The assumption is as follows: "Many systems assume homogeneity and, in its absence, will be inefficient (Krevat, Tucek, & Ganger, 2011, p. 1)."[4] Identity would seem to be the goal, even though Crosby (2005) had confessed that perfection was never the standard.

Engineers have been trained to approximate this ideal, requiring models of exacting precision. Engineers therefore aspire to create digital models that most closely match the reality they are working with. What they are seeking is what is known as a digital twin or DT. So not only should the physical output at a factory be consistent from one item to the next, but the digital version that engineers study should most closely represent reality as well (Psarommatis & May, 2023; Psarommatis et al., 2020; see Alexander, 1964, p. 8).[5] We might say that the desideratum would be identity between the physical object and its digital model, although such a quest would appear to be excruciatingly asymptotic.

In certain industries, however, the objective turns out to be the presence of discrepancies, variation, visible flaws, and uniqueness (marketed as one-of-a-kind), for example, among handmade coffee mugs, diamond rings, wedding dresses, bespoke suits, and oil paintings. The value of sports memorabilia often depends on its authenticity, for example, that this is the very baseball that Babe Ruth hit out of the park in 1929 and subsequently signed for a young fan who kept it as a souvenir (e.g. Owens, 2021).

Biology

The original version of biological identity, of course, would be twins who share the same DNA. Recently, scientists have tried cloning DNA, such that an animal gives birth to a version of itself (see Keefer, 2015; Evers, 1999; see generally Harris, 2004). The identity of DNA is very much like software clones, whereby a string of information is replicated in another location (Koschke et al., 2012). To argue that twins (and clones) are identical relies on a different meaning of the term identical (Segal, 2001). They are identical as to codes, perhaps, but not as to experience or context. No matter what "nature" says, nurture plays its part (see Fraga, et al., 2005).

---

4 It turns out, though, that this assumption is not true, such that engineers are now being advised to *expect* heterogeneity and use it to maximum advantage (Krevat, 2011).

5 In a manner similar to manufacturing, bioengineers hope to develop models that duplicate the living reality they study, so they create what are called virtual simulacra, which is akin to the idea of digital twins (Amram et al., 2023). These attempts at similarity have interesting implications for ethics that exceed the scope of this chapter.

Two organisms might share a string of DNA without being identical otherwise, as twin studies have demonstrated for many years. And this finding presupposes a shared upbringing. Cloning completely ignores that part of the process because there is little chance that a clone undergoes an identical upbringing or context. Two cell's existence might begin the same, though it is unclear how quickly the two paths diverge. As Keefer (2015) asks, not unreasonably, "When is a cell's fate set and how plastic is that fate?" This tendency for identical cells to diverge over time is known as epigenetic drift (Fraga et al., 2005, p. 10609; e.g. Bertucci-Richter, Shealy, & Parrott, 2024; Bertucci-Richter & Parrott, 2023).

The pursuit of cloning technology promises to help medical practitioners replace lost or damaged organs, for example, by using completely compatible replacement cells. But once adapted to a specific function (i.e. once differentiated), these cells will vary from one another.

"Although genomic information is uniform among the different cells of a complex organism, the epigenome varies from tissue to tissue, controlling the differential expression of genes and providing specific identity to each cell type (Fraga et al., 2005, p. 10609)."

One study hypothesized that two identical starting points would result in identical outcomes, all other things being equal (which of course is not possible in the real world), yet at the quantum level, the authors discovered that due to something called entanglement no two systems – however similar at the start – will evolve in a similar fashion (Thekkadath et al., 2017). What we encounter, even at the smallest magnitude, is a version of the so-called butterfly effect, by which the tiniest variation in the starting conditions will, over time, result in large differences, even if the external factors are the same. What we find after a cursory investigation is that the concept of identity has limited utility in the biological sciences.

No identity across time (history)

Heraclitus once remarked that you cannot step into the same river twice, because it always changes. It is no longer the same river (Diels & Kranz, 1951, B12). This conundrum refers to the problem of identity across time. Is a thing identical to itself? We know that beaches erode and organisms age. What may have been true once upon a time is no longer true. Meanwhile, the physical universe drifts toward entropy. The clockwork winds down and will eventually stop. The Paris which I refer to today is different from the medieval city. There will be certain resemblances, to be sure. One can see in a child the man he grows up to become. But the very notion of change means that identity across time is unlikely, if not impossible. A thing can be the same with regard to some feature X, many years later, but not with regard to Y, as my receding hairline cruelly reminds me.

Julius Caesar matured over the course of his political career, such that a thorough investigation of his leadership requires some sensitivity to his biography. We should want to appreciate where he came from and what happened to shape his ongoing development. It would be a mistake to presuppose that Caesar was the exact same at every stage in his life. Kahneman, Sibony, and Sunstein (2022) make the case:

> Within the same person, there is variability, too. Your heartbeat is not exactly regular. You cannot repeat the same gesture with perfect precision. And when you have your hearing examined by an audiologist, there will be some sounds so soft you never hear them, and others so loud you always do. But there will be some sounds that you will sometimes hear and sometimes miss.
>
> *(p. 40f)*

In the same fashion, the academic discipline known as history tells us there is no such thing as identity across time, whether we are talking about a city, a people, or an empire. Egypt persisted in the same basic form for millennia, for example, but even within its longevity one can detect shifts and transformations (see Breasted, 1964). Rome may be known as the Eternal City, but that is because it adapts, incorporating elements of predecessor regimes. Institutions and civilizations can endure, but nothing is forever. And upon closer examination, with fine granularity, there will be currents and cross-currents, upticks and upswings, surges and controversy, over and over.

Part of what makes history so interesting are the resemblances, the recurring patterns. Mark Twain is credited with the aphorism, "History never repeats itself, but often rhymes." In what sense are two entirely different epochs similar to one another? And why is that? Can we discern regularities or historical laws that will recur? Two periods might undergo equivalent crises, such as civic unrest or pandemics.[6] Will they respond in the same fashion? Correlation is not always indicative of causation, yet sometimes the correlation can be instructive. Does increased government spending cause inflation? Does appeasement prevent war? Can enslaved peoples not only win their freedom but also successfully become assimilated? These are the types of questions scholars (and pundits) frequently investigate. Again, just to state the obvious, nobody claims that any two epochs are completely identical. Even so, they might resemble one another in instructive ways.

---

6 On the possibility that two states of chaos resemble one another, see Harter (2023, p. 59).

To what extent do things *seem* identical?

Resemblances indicate that something similar is going on in both instances, for example, the cascade of a woman's hair falling like a waterfall or a network of veins in the human hands laid out to look like tributaries of a river flowing across a landscape. The resemblance suggests a common principle. This is not always the case, inasmuch as many resemblances are optical illusions or the product of coincidence. Interestingly, it is often the case that two things that are very much not alike can resemble one another in certain, limited respects. The function here is to *seem* similar when they are not in fact similar. Let us take a brief look at two common examples.

Camouflage, mimicry, masquerades, and disguises

In nature, Darwinism detected many examples of animals (and even plants) engaging in some version of camouflage (see generally Nokelainen & Stevens, 2016).[7] The practical effect of camouflage is to make two things that are not alike nonetheless appear to be sufficiently alike in order to mislead predators. One recent study made the following report: "Research into camouflage has exploded over the last decade or so, with interdisciplinarity proving to be a key feature for progress (Lovell et al., 2022)." Obviously, prey that camouflages itself does not become *identical* to something else. It simply must appear to be so, long enough to escape detection. "The lesson is that any system that takes shortcuts in processing information can be exploited. This is what camouflage does (Merilaita, Scott-Samuel, & Cuthill, 2017)." The predator sees or smells or hears nothing to draw its attention. It is a matter of Signal-to-Noise ratio (SNR): either the prey minimizes its own signal (e.g. standing still and keeping silent) or it increases the presence of noise e.g. blending into the background, looking like something innocuous, whether by resembling its color, shape, size, scent, etc. Or by overwhelming the predator with too many conflicting signals.[8]

---

7 According to Skelhorn, Rowland, and Ruxton, within this overarching category of camouflage, there apparently exist sub-categories in the field of biology. such as Crypsis, Batesian mimicry, and Masquerade (2010, p. 3; see also Skelhorn, 2015). This usage of the language is not to be confused with the masquerade syndrome in Ophthalmology (Read, Zamir, & Rao, 2002). The term "masquerade" has uses in psychology as well (e.g. Tseëlon, 2001).

8 A cursory online search reveals that parasites also sometimes evade detection from the host by disguising themselves (see e.g. Wanderley et al., 2020; McLaren, 1984). Chulanetra and Chaicumpa (2021), for instance, wrote: "Several infecting parasites cover themselves with the host/host-like factors, *e.g.* proteins or glycoconjugates, so that they will not be recognized as foreign substances by the host immune system."

Needless to say, nature is not without its countermeasures.

> Substantial progress has been made in the past 15 years regarding how prey use a variety of visual camouflage types to exploit both predator visual processing and cognition, including background matching, disruptive coloration, countershading and masquerade. By contrast, much less attention has been paid to how predators might overcome these defences. Such strategies include the evolution of more acute senses, the co-opting of other senses not targeted by camouflage, changes in cognition such as forming search images, and using behaviours that change the relationship between the cryptic individual and the environment or disturb prey and cause movement. Here, we evaluate the methods through which visual camouflage prevents detection and recognition, and discuss if and how predators might evolve, develop or learn counter-adaptations to overcome these.
>
> *(Galloway et al., 2020)*

In other words, an apparent identity can be misleading. One must consider strategies to check the extent to which this might be happening. Is the signature on the sonar of a whale actually an enemy submarine? Is the suspect of a crime blending into the crowd and making good his escape? Has an accountant somehow hidden the extent to which a film has earned box office revenue, thereby cheating someone who possesses a percentage share of the take? Does a clever political candidate sound sufficiently congenial to win my vote? Can a plagiarizing undergraduate evade detection? Will certain undergarments create the illusion of an hour-glass figure? Sometimes, a person must be just as clever and often quite patient to uncover the deceit.

In Chapter 10 of Mark Twain's classic *The Adventures of Huckleberry Finn* (1884), Huck disguises himself as a girl in order to persuade a woman to trust him, but the woman discovers his secret by dropping a spool toward his lap. Huck instinctively brings his knees together in order to catch the wayward item, but then the woman points out that a girl in the same situation would know to splay her legs and let the folds of her dress catch it. Busted! Detective novels also portray cat-and-mouse intrigues whereby the detective must laboriously and brilliantly undo the culprit's stratagems. The very word "detective" refers explicitly to the art of detection. Criminals prefer not to be recognized or caught. In the film version of Stephen King's *Shawshank Redemption* (Darabont, 1994), the protagonist covers the hole in his wall with a poster of Raquel Welch, so that prison guards are unaware until it is too late that behind it is a completed tunnel to the outside.

The underlying schema is simple. One participant resembles something or someone else because by doing so it increases the likelihood of misleading or otherwise frustrating another participant. Its success (whatever is meant by that term) depends on resemblances.

Fashion

Gabriel de Tarde put imitation at the center of his sociology (see Harter, 2023, ch. 6). One of the most obvious examples of imitation is fashion. By its very nature, fashion indicates at least some resemblances from one person to another. In fact, the function (if not purpose) of fashion is to encourage imitation. Again, as we have been saying in these pages, the goal is not so much identity as similarity.

Georg Simmel, also a sociologist, wrote that humankind operates between two extreme poles (1957). He identified imitation as one of these poles, whereby the imitator does not have to think as much and can more readily fit in with the crowd, transferring responsibility away from oneself. Obviously, each person lives between this pole (seeking sameness) and the other extreme of pursuing uniqueness, distinction, and adornment. Some folks as individuals are more inclined toward one end or the other as a disposition or tendency. Nevertheless, people slide in both directions at different times, and in fact it is the case that we adopt fashions in certain aspects of our lives, such as clothing, though not in other aspects of our lives, such as religion; in either case, nobody stands alone forever at either one of these poles. We live in the in-between. Furthermore, each culture varies in the extent to which it clusters at one end of the spectrum or the other, and culture itself changes in this regard, which is to say that there can be periods of widespread fashion and periods without. We could also investigate further the role of social class as a differentiator, but the primary lesson from Simmel has to do with the human tendency toward sameness within one's social group as a gesture of belonging. Simmel wrote that:

> fashion furnishes an ideal field for individuals with dependent natures, whose self-consciousness, however, requires a certain amount of prominence, attention, and singularity. Fashion raises even the unimportant individual by making him the representative of a class, the embodiment of a joint spirit.
>
> *(p. 548)*

In other words, fashion has the peculiar power to deploy sameness as a distinction.

Consider therefore what fashion implies. Fashion reflects a transient preference, here today and gone tomorrow. We all know that fashions change. This fact does not prevent us from paying attention and maybe even making decisions based on such ephemera. We might say that fashion auditions to become customary. It is an experiment, a venture, like trying on a pair of new jeans to see how they fit. The world wasn't always like it is today. And it will not be the same tomorrow. We know this. To that extent, fashion has very little to do with sameness across time. Instead, it has to do with sameness in response to the passage of time. Together, we assert ourselves, collectively inserting into the never-ending flux a shared expression of taste. We all know it cannot last, but that was never the point. Fashion meets the intrinsic need to change, to move, to participate willfully in the river course and not be stuck, staid, left behind, frumpy, passé, behind the times, out of date, i.e. old.

Fashion is an adhesion to the present, if not a little into the future that is emerging. Nobody wants to be too late or too early to the dominant trends, for to do so brings unwanted attention. Fashion establishes that the person has chosen to belong to the group, the class, or the crowd, with an eye on tomorrow. Like the starling fluttering through its murmuration, we orient ourselves by one another, banking left or wheeling right, rolling in unison across the open field in perilously close proximity without ever colliding in midair. To borrow another metaphor, fashion is like a performance on a dance floor, hundreds of gyrating bodies in sync with the same music, its patterns discernible only from the balcony. The neglect of fashion makes you stand out, isolating you. Fashion establishes and then reestablishes the peak of the bell curve, where it is safe to be within the parameters of what is the same. We seek sameness in our fashions for the same reason that the prey struggles to look like something else: to blend in and hope that nobody notices.

"Look at me!" we shout. "I am so much like the rest of you!"

The utility of resemblances when studying leadership

When describing the way that Michel Serres conducted his research, Christopher Watkin (2020) identified what he called recurring "figures of thought." Like figures of speech, a figure of thought is "an identifiable way of thinking that remains isomorphic, though not necessarily identical, across multiple instances of its deployment and across different texts (p. 36)." We might label these logical archetypes, of sufficiently broad applicability to be found in radically different investigations. One might imagine an argument, for example, as a series of steps, laid out in a linear sequence, from the simple and clear premises toward more complex inferences. This "figure of thought" can be found routinely in mathematics, logic, and various sciences. It is a common figure of thought. Another common figure of thought is the Venn diagram, depicting two overlapping sets (Venn, 1880). Yet another figure of thought is the table, such as the periodic table in chemistry, by which elements are classified in a formal taxonomy. These figures of thought can be used in many different fields of study. They are in one sense transferable abstractions, picked up from one academic discipline and then readily superimposed onto another.

Watkins explains that Serres adopted a number of less familiar figures of thought, of which I will mention two. First, Serres would set out to refute conventional wisdom not by proving it wrong, but instead by multiplying alternative explanations (Watkins, 2020, p. 72). Serres would illustrate that there is more than one way to portray, depict, or model the same reality. We are not stuck with conventional imagery. Oftentimes, a different model will reveal something that was otherwise undetected in the more accepted model. You and I can look at the same thing and see it in two entirely different ways, each of which can be accurate. Watkins calls this "opposing by generalizing" (2020, p. 89). Second, Serres searched for "a higher synthesis of apparently chaotic phenomena [in order to] find the complex relations between the seemingly unrelated (2020, p. 47)."

When utilizing these figures of thought, Serres would pick two wildly different things – things that we ordinarily would never compare to one another – and point out ways in which they do resemble one another. For instance, as I have had reason to mention elsewhere, he found a resemblance between noise and parasites (2007), offerings to Baal and the 1986 Challenger disaster (2015), bullrings and lectures halls (2019), memory and DNA (2018). Not all of these choices are poetic. He was not just dabbling in metaphor. The same underlying principles were at work in two dissimilar examples. The really interesting part, as I have already indicated, is in what respect they are alike.

Having said that, however, the broader lesson is that any two things are alike in many different ways. Like those discarded buttons, we can sort them in a variety of ways and not insist on only one. In any given community, for example, people might share ethnicity, faith, language, culture, history, or territory – what makes them a unity, in other words, is not just one trait or aspect. It will be many. And despite efforts to "sort" people into subunits in order to include only some participants and exclude others, these commonalities persist, so that people might be divided over questions of political party yet divided differently by socio-economic status, race, age group, educational attainment, and religion. Folks call it "intersectionality" today. The way Serres saw it, even when you can divide a community along one of these dimensions, there are so many other ways that folks identify with one another. They can look past their differences to cheer for the national team or to take up arms together in order to repel a common aggressor. In this way, enemies can share a bond with one another that transcends their hostilities. Serres would have us look for those commonalities and build something wholesome based on that.

One comparison that I would like to address for purposes of illustration pertains to leadership, which is a process by which one person influences others. What is leadership like? Where might we turn to see equivalent principles at work? We might say that leadership represents the introduction of novelty, the departure from routine, a kind of spark where the grasslands have become too dry. A routine requires no leadership. It will continue of its own inertia, grinding away, though gradually winding down toward entropy. Instead, then, leadership operates in the same way as early atomic physics tried to understand eccentric motion. Lucretius had famously adopted the term "clinamen" to refer to the unexpected, unpredicted, spontaneous, fortuitous swerve or deviation from the linear motion of atoms (1946, quoting *De rerum natura*, book II; lines 289–293). Without these occasional twists and turns, a body of atoms will simply co-exist in an indeterminable sameness, steady, uniform, and impossible even to detect – like a white space without shadows. That would be true even if this body of atoms is flowing at the same rate in the same direction. Indeed, there is no way to know whether such a block of atoms is flowing or standing still. One must stand outside of that compact reality in order to see it. One must become (to borrow a term from Sverre Spoelstra) extra-ordinary, which means residing outside of the prevailing order (2018).

Leadership then follows the same principles as any turbulent medium, whether water or gas. Leadership twirls and swivels from within, changing direction, zigging where everybody else zags. It disrupts the laminar flow and channels it in a new direction. Leadership is an uncaused disturbance, the introduction of chaos, struggling to interrupt the tendency of all things to stabilize and ultimately to perish. This burst of disorder compels the larger system to seek a new, more complex order, a renewal of sorts, on a higher plane of existence.

Again, I am not using the language of fluid dynamics as a colorful metaphor, namely that one thing is somehow like the other, a resemblance or similarity. I am saying that these are the same phenomenon, the selfsame figures of thought found to be applicable in vastly different domains, in the same way, that a baseball and the earth are both spheres. What we can learn from the one just might be useful in understanding the other. Analogism lends this tactic at least some plausibility.

Perhaps the most familiar example of analogism in leadership studies is systems thinking (Donaldson & Harter, 2023). Leaders are themselves systems, leadership is a system, and leadership takes place within a context of systems – organizational, economic, legal, political, and historical. The principles of systems thinking serve as a fairly elaborate "figure of thought" with extraordinarily broad applicability, from business and athletics to art and healthcare. Accordingly, scholars have been trying to explain the extent to which they detect resemblances. A military commander is not identical to a classroom teacher. Heck, a military commander is not identical *to other military commanders*. Nevertheless, leaders from all walks of life and from every epoch will look alike when considered through the lens of systems thinking.

Let's get more precise. Maybe the reason that scholars have stumbled repeatedly to define leadership indicates that the term probably has no definition. Leadership is instead a "set of phenomena that have a family resemblance but no single unifying definition (Cave, 2013, p. 82)." This way of talking comes from the philosopher Ludwig Wittgenstein (Cave, 2013, p. 86, n. 24). Instead of a single thing, leadership is a category for multiple similar things. And because none of them are entirely identical to one another, the boundaries for the category will be famously fuzzy[9] – not because of a failure on our part to discern, but inherently, given the nature of categories. Phenomena within that set are alike in certain respects (analogs), but they can be decidedly different in other respects. No category "contains" its members, as in a box; rather, it describes arrays or clusters, more like heavenly constellations of completely independent stars. It is because of this way of thinking that Max Weber had generated "ideal types" which are fabrications of the human imagination attempting to depict what an array of phenomena have in common. There wouldn't have to be a real-world example.

Something of the sort can be used to identify colors on a spectrum. Red bleeds into orange gradually at the "boundary" between these two colors. An ideal type (if we may use the term) from the visible spectrum is simply "red" or "orange," even though plenty of red things are slightly different shades, tints, and hues of red. "Red" identifies a pure type, representative of one portion of the spectrum based upon radiant energy with wavelengths of approximately 630–750 nanometers. Orange is a different ideal type, despite the fact that at the margins orange looks more and more red-like, and vice-versa. And at the other end, as we all know, it looks more and more yellow-like. Using this imagery, then, we can say that leadership

9 L.A. Zadeh (1965) explained the notion of a fuzzy set as an imprecisely defined classification with an absence of sharply defined criteria which nonetheless plays an important role in human thinking.

is like the color red on a vast and subtle gradient, situated among other phenomena such as tyranny, seduction, management, and so forth.

Resemblances indicate discernable categories of thought that permit comparison without insisting on hard boundaries. They can be useful, even when they are fuzzy. And like those buttons in a tin, there is always more than one way to categorize things, depending on your purpose. All I am insinuating in these pages is that leadership shares a "category" with the turbulence of fluid dynamics (see generally Serres, 1995).

Concluding remarks

This idea of analogism suggests that even though no two things are identical, there should be myriad ways in which various items can resemble one another. We ended up by saying that leadership can be imagined in the same way, which is to say that no two leaders, no two episodes, and no two historical examples will align perfectly, such that you could apply what worked in one situation to another, step-by-step. That's just not likely. Nevertheless, there is quite a lot of similarity among leaders and episodes to learn from, if you remain open to the evidence. Sometimes, in fact, two very different leaders or situations, with very little in common, might share at least one important aspect. Part of leadership studies, therefore, might include some unlikely pairings. How is this X over here like that Y over there? As we saw, relying primarily on Michel Serres, investigations of this kind can be instructive.

By the same token, two very similar leaders or situations might be significantly unlike one another in important respects. It can be a trick of perception to leap to conclusions when two items look alike. A leader might try to evoke the mental associations of a previous, beloved leader, for example, imitating his gestures or his cadences, hoping to appear sufficiently like him or her in order to win your support today. We have known since before Machiavelli that people judge by appearances, and thus are easily duped. Leadership scholars have a duty to root around and find fresh analogies and also to guard against analogies that are too facile and misleading. John Keegan (2011), for example, did this brilliantly in his study of military commanders, where he explained the extent to which some leaders such as Hitler were only pseudo-heroic and despite their exertions utterly false in their attempts to seem otherwise.

It has been my contention that leadership more than resembles something known as turbulence. It is instead both a cause and an effect of real turbulence in the flow of human events, such that we might consider importing into our field of study some of what turbulence has meant in the physical sciences, down to every swell and eddy in the persistent flux.

Leadership is fundamentally *anadyomene,* which is a Greek term for a surface phenomenon, like Aphrodite being thrown up from the sea (Serres, 1995, p. 121).

References

Alexander, C. (1964). *Notes on the synthesis of form.* Harvard University Press.

Amram, B., Klempner, U., Leibler, Y., & Greenbaum, D. (2023). "In their own image: Ethical implications of the rise of digital twins/clones/simulacra in healthcare." *The American Journal of Bioethics.* *23*(9): 79–81.

Anderson, E.N. (2015). "Book review: Beyond nature and culture. By Philippe Descola." *Ethnobiology Letters.* *6*(1): 208–211. https://doi.org/10.14237/ebl.6.1.2015.481.

Office of the Assistant Secretary of Defense (1968). *Zero defects: The quest for quality.* Washington, DC.

Office of the Assistant Secretary of Defense (1965). *A guide to zero defects: Quality and reliability assurance handbook 4155.12-H.* Washington, DC. extension://efaidnbmnnnibpcajpcglclefindmkaj/https://apps.dtic.mil/sti/tr/pdf/ADA950061.pdf.

Baruffi, F., Gülçür, M., Calaon, M., Romano J. Penchev, P. Dimov, S., Whiteside, B., & Tosello, G. (2019). "Correlating nano-scale surface replication accuracy and cavity temperature in micro-injection moulding using in-line process control and high-speed thermal imaging." *Journal of Manufacturing Processes.* 47: 367–381.

Bejan, A. (2015). "Every snowflake is not unique." *Mechanical Engineering.* *137*(1): 40–41.

Bertucci-Richter, E.M., & Parrott, B.B. (2023). "The rate of epigenetic drift scales with maximum lifespan across mammals." *Nature Communications.* *14*(7731). https://doi.org/10.1038/s41467-023-43417-6.

Bertucci-Richter, E.M., Shealy E.P., & Parrott B.B. (2024 January 26). "Epigenetic drift underlies epigenetic clock signals, but displays distinct responses to lifespan interventions, development, and cellular dedifferentiation." *Aging.* *16*(2): 1002–1020. https://doi.org/10.18632/aging.205503.

Breasted, J.H. (1964). *A history of Egypt: From the earliest times to the Persian conquest.* Bantam Books.

Caiazzo, B., Di Nardo, M., Murino, T., Petrillo, A., Piccirillo, G., & Santini, S. (2022). "Towards zero defect manufacturing paradigm: A review of the state-of-the-art methods and open challenges." *Computers in Industry.* 134: 103548.

Cave, T. "Unsettling thresholds: Mignon and her afterlives." In Mukherji, S. (ed.) (2013). *Thinking on thresholds: The poetics of transitive spaces* (pp. 73–85). Anthem Press.

Cheng, F.T. (ed.) (2021). Industry 4.1: *Intelligent manufacturing with zero defects.* John Wiley & Sons.

Chulanetra, M., & Chaicumpa, W. (2021). "Revisiting the mechanisms of immune evasion employed by human parasites." *Frontiers in Cellular and Infection Microbiology.* 11: 702125. https://doi.org/10.3389/fcimb.2021.702125.

Crosby, P.B. (2005). "Crosby's 14 steps to improvement." *Quality Progress.* *38*(12): 60–64.

Crosby, P.B. (1980). *Quality is free: The art of making quality certain.* Mentor.

Darabont, F. (1994). *The Shawshank redemption.* Columbia Pictures.

Descola, P. (2013). *Beyond nature and culture* (J. Lloyd, trans.). University of Chicago Press.

Diels, H., & Kranz, W. (1951). *The fragments of the pre-Socratics* (6th ed.). Weidmann.

Doerig, A., Schurger, A., & Herzog, M.H. (2021). "Hard criteria for empirical theories of consciousness." *Cognitive Neuroscience. 12*(2): 41–62.

Donaldson, W., & Harter, N. "Systems thinking." In Goethals, G., S. Allison, & G. Sorenson (eds.) (2023). *Encyclopedia of leadership studies* (pp. 911–914). Sage.

Evers, K. (1999). "The identity of clones." *The Journal of Medicine and Philosophy. 24*(1): 67–76.

Fraga, M., Ballestar, E., Paz, M., Ropero, S., Setien, F., Ballestar, M., Heine-Sun~er, D., Cigudosa, J., Urioste, M., Benitez, J., Boix-Chornet, M., Sanchez-Aguilera, A., Ling, C., Carlsson, E., Poulsen, P., Vaag, A., Stephan, Z., Spector, T., Yue-Zhong W., Plass, C., & Estelle, M. (2005). "Epigenetic differences arise during the lifetime of monozygotic twins." *Proceedings of the National Academy of Sciences. 102*(30): 10604–10609.

Fragapane, G., Eleftheriadis, R., Powell, D., & Antony, J. (2023). "A global survey on the current state of practice in Zero Defect Manufacturing and its impact on production performance." *Computers in Industry. 148:* 103879.

Galloway, J.A., Green, S.D., Stevens, M., & Kelley, L.A. (2020). "Finding a signal hidden among noise: How can predators overcome camouflage strategies?" *Philosophical Transactions of the Royal Society B. 375*(1802): 20190478.

Harris, J. (2004). *On cloning.* Psychology Press.

Harter, N. (2023). *An historical assessment of leadership in turbulent times: Lessons learned from Clovis I, King of the Franks.* Routledge.

Hillman, J. (1980). *Egalitarian typologies versus the perception of the unique.* Spring Publications.

Kahneman, D., Sibony, O., & Sunstein, C.R. (2022). *Noise: A flaw in human judgment.* Little, Brown and Company.

Keefer, C.L. (2015). "Artificial cloning of domestic animals." *Proceedings of the National Academy of Sciences. 112*(29): 8874–8878.

Keegan, J. (2011). *The mask of command: A study of generalship.* Random House.

Koschke, R., Baxter, I.D., Conradt, M., & Cordy, J.R. (2012). "Software clone management towards industrial application (seminar 12071)." *Dagstuhl Reports. 2*(2), 21–57. Schloss Dagstuhl-Leibniz-Zentrum fuer Informatik.

Krevat, E., Tucek, J., & Ganger, G.R. (2011). "Disks are like snowflakes: No two are alike." In *13th Workshop on Hot Topics in Operating Systems (HotOS XIII).*

Leberruyer, N., Bruch, J., Ahlskog, M., & Afshar, S. (2023). "Toward zero defect manufacturing with the support of Artificial Intelligence: Insights from an industrial application." *Computers in Industry. 147:* 103877.

Libbrecht, K. (2003). *The snowflake.* Voyageur Press.

Lovell, G., Sharman, B., & Scott-Samuel, N. (2022). "Round table on camouflage." *Vision (Switzerland)*. 6(4): 1–2. Article 1. https://doi.org/10.3390/vision6040057.

Lucretius, T. (1946). *On the nature of things* (C. Bennett, trans.). Walter J. Black, Inc.

McLaren, D.J. (1984). "Disguise as an evasive stratagem of parasitic organisms." *Parasitology*. 88(4): 597–611.

Merilaita, S., Scott-Samuel, N.E., & Cuthill, I.C. (2017). "How camouflage works." *Philosophical Transactions of the Royal Society B: Biological Sciences*. 372(1724): 20160341.

Nichols, P.M. (2000). "Two snowflakes are alike: Assumptions made in the debate over standing before World Trade Organization dispute settlement boards." *Fordham Int'l LJ*. 24: 427.

Nokelainen, O., & Stevens, M. (2016). "Camouflage." *Current Biology*. 26(14): R654–R656.

Notaros, B. (2021, April). "Meteorological electromagnetics: Optical and radar measurements, modeling, and characterization of snowflakes and snow." *IEEE Antennas and Propagation Magazine*. 63(2): 14–27. https://doi.org/10.1109/MAP.2021.3054298.

Owens, J. (2021, June 16). "1929 Babe Ruth ball comes with rare video of Babe signing autograph, slugging home run." *Sports Collectors Digest*. Accessed 7 January 2024 from https://sportscollectorsdigest.com/auctions/babe-ruth-baseball-autograph-video-1929-thomas-newman-collection-memory-lane-auction.

Paxton, J. (2012). "Mr. Taylor, Mr. Ford, and the advent of high-volume mass production: 1900-1912." *Economics & Business Journal*. 4(1): 74–90.

Pilipski, M., & Pilipski, J.D. (2006). "A treatise on the preponderance of designs over historic and measured snowfalls, or no two snowflakes are alike: Considerations about the formation of snowflakes and the possible numbers and shapes of snowflakes." *63rd Eastern Snow Conference*. chrome-extension://efaidnbmnnnibpcajpcglclefindmkaj/https://static1.squarespace.com/static/58b98f7bd1758e4cc271d365/t/5e692fdbc104fd669e96d0b0/1583951835250/23+Pilipski+and+Pilipski.pdf.

Psarommatis, F., & May, G. (2023). "A literature review and design methodology for digital twins in the era of zero defect manufacturing." *International Journal of Production Research*. 61(16): 5723–5743.

Psarommatis, F., May, G., Dreyfus, P.A., & Kiritsis, D. (2020). "Zero defect manufacturing: State-of-the-art review, shortcomings and future directions in research." *International Journal of Production Research*. 58(1): 1–17. https://doi.org/10.1080/00207543.2019.1605228.

Read, R.W., Zamir, E., & Rao, N.A. (2002). "Neoplastic masquerade syndromes." *Survey of Ophthalmology*. 47(2): 81–124.

Segal, N.L. (2001). "Human cloning: Insights from twins and twin research." *Hastings Law Journal*. 53: 1073.

Serres, M. (2019). *Hominescence* (R. Burks, trans.). Bloomsbury Academic.

Serres, M. (2018). *The incandescent* (R. Burks, trans.). Bloomsbury Academic.

Serres, M. (2015). *Statues: The second book of foundations* (R. Burks, trans.). Bloomsbury Academic.

Serres, M. (2007). *The parasite* (L. Schehr, trans.). University of Minnesota Press.

Serres, M. (1995). *Genesis* (G. James & J. Nielson, trans.). University of Michigan Press.

Simmel, G. (1957). "Fashion." *American Journal of Sociology. 62*(6): 541–558.

Skelhorn, J. (2015). "Masquerade." *Current Biology. 25*(15): R643–R644.

Skelhorn, J., Rowland, H.M., & Ruxton, G.D. (2010). "The evolution and ecology of masquerade." *Biological Journal of the Linnean Society. 99*(1): 1–8.

Spoelstra, S. (2018). *Leadership and organization: A philosophical introduction.* Routledge.

Taleb, N.N. (2007). "Black swans and the domains of statistics." *The American Statistician. 61*(3): 198–200.

Thekkadath, G.S., Saaltink, R.Y., Giner, L., & Lundeen, J.S. (2017). "Determining complementary properties with quantum clones." *Physical Review Letters. 119*(5): 050405.

Thorndike, E.L. (1920). "A constant error in psychological ratings." *Journal of Applied Psychology. 4*(1): 25–29. https://doi.org/10.1037/h0071663.

Tseëlon, E. (ed.) (2001). *Masquerade and identities: Essays on gender, sexuality, and marginality.* Psychology Press.

Twain, M. (1884). *The adventures of Huckleberry Finn.* Chatto & Windus.

Venn, J. (1880). "On the diagrammatic and mechanical representation of propositions and reasonings." *The London, Edinburgh, and Dublin Philosophical Magazine and Journal of Science. 10*(59): 1–18.

Wanderley, J.L.M., Damatta, R.A., Barcinski, M.A. *et al.* (2020, 29 October). "Apoptotic mimicry as a strategy for the establishment of parasitic infections." *Research Square.* https://doi.org/10.21203/rs.3.rs-100311/v1. Retrieved 17 March 2024 from https://www.researchsquare.com/article/rs-100311/v1.

Watkin, C. (2020). *Michel Serres: Figures of thought.* Edinburgh University Press.

Zadeh, L.A. (1965). "Fuzzy sets." *Information and Control. 8*: 338–353.

APPENDIX

Confessions of a Pollyanna, in sonata form:
A literary experiment inspired by Michel Serres

Introduction to the appendix

Along the coast of Portugal, the massive waves fling themselves against impervious cliffs, exploding into towers of exuberant spray before falling together again and rolling back out to the sea from which the next gargantuan assault has already begun. Which of these, O Muse – the relentless surge or the monumental rock – portrays my mind? Perhaps there, in an isolated crag halfway up the verge (do you see it?), my mind clings to the inhospitable stone like a pretty weed, with nowhere else to go. Perhaps with the next violent inundation, it will finally be loosed and then tumble into that insistent surf and perish under the crushing depths, reclaimed forever by the rhythm of the planetary tides.

Exposition A: Three intersecting multiplicities

O, hear then my confession.

I am a point of intersection – intersecting multiplicities. In every direction, look! – the apeiron, noise, confusion. I am the overlap in a Venn diagram of three circles, each circle of which is a chaos. (Can there be more than one chaos?) In no particular order, therefore, there is first the multiplicity that is **paramount reality**, the brouhaha and hubbub of a million exchanges, across the globe and down through the ages. Every bolt of lightning, every disemboweled carcass, every pact with a wayfaring peddler, spit on your hand and shake it. The world is too much with us. Second, there is the multiplicity of thoughts and ideas in the various literatures – in novels, textbooks, and scientific journals – clamoring for attention, claiming to be true. Even in the so-called university, which is unified in name only, self-righteous scholars win tenure by defending their version of reality against one another. Not only do they quarrel laterally, against other disciplines, but they also quarrel vertically, challenging their predecessors in a shared field of inquiry, hoping to displace their elders. Call this the multiplicity of **human knowledge**. Then there is in third place the chaos of **my own mind,** the many facts and hopes and memories and associations that populate my brain, begun in 1959, adding more every day and making mischief of my nights. Three multiplicities, each of them beyond comprehending.

The noise at this busy intersection can be overwhelming. Just watch the evening news. So many crimes and creeds and colors. Paramount reality in the first circle is by definition encompassing. In the second circle, a library where you can be shushed for making too much noise is a symbol of the noise of published works – read me, read me! So many voices committed to print. I cannot read them all. I have neither the time nor the inclination to do so. And even if I could, my brain could not integrate them into any meaningful message. The signal gets lost in the noise. And the noise itself is not a signal. Libraries are full of shouting. Shall I go read Euclid, Emily Dickinson, or Lenin today?

What I happen to think, in the third circle, bears a personal stamp. I do not ponder the painter's palette, for example. I do not perform calculations for fun. I have no acquaintance with most of the cultures around the globe. I could die tomorrow without ever reading the *Aeneid*. And that's okay. I'm even reluctant to say howdy in the checkout line at the grocery because I just don't care who you are. A guy has to acknowledge his limits.

Anxiety manifests in part as the proverbial monkey mind, chattering, coming at my attention from every angle, dredging up old laments, imposing fresh worries, reminding me about tomorrow's chores. One of my ways of coping with the incessant Din-Within is to concentrate on anything, maybe an article I promised to edit by the weekend; but notice that by concentrating on one thing I am not contemplating the rest. Not consciously. In my quiet moments, though, I am aware that this tangle of synapses is firing rapidly, at all times, like Rapid Eye Movement for the entire brain. Flickering, swerving, often into forbidden zones, i.e. stuff I would rather not think about. Welcome to what Augustine called the Unquiet.

For too long, I aspired to make sense of everything. I had hoped to unlock the secrets of the universe, obtaining wisdom, as though the spangled heavens would ultimately constellate. Then, O Reader, I could write such books. Then, I could teach students. Then, I could rest myself in the knowledge.

Maybe one day, my peers would invite me to deliver a keynote address, where they could give me a lifetime achievement award, and at the conclusion of my remarks, they would carry me around the ballroom on their shoulders shouting huzzah. Well, well, if my late night studies en route to that destiny should lag, as they invariably do, I have trusted in divine providence to reveal what I might need to understand, to enlighten me. Little by little, corners wrapped in shadows would find themselves illuminated. I have understood something! It makes sense now (whatever "it" is). The excitement at my discoveries also promises relief, if only for a season. This minor thing over here, this shard, some aspect of the Great Kaleidoscope, it now *means* something to me. Yippee! At which point, the happy chemicals flush through my brain, addicting me for, lo, these sixty-plus years.

Michael Polanyi had insisted more than once that concentration of one's attention on the parts of something/anything dissolves any worthwhile comprehension of the whole. You'll miss the forest for the trees. Still, I had to take my victories where I could find them. My curriculum vita is an enumeration of such little shards.

Not too many years ago, I experienced a relapse, Saturn Returns, the resurrection of old anxieties, in part (I now realize) because it has finally dawned on me (again, the imagery of light) that nobody really cares what I think. Nobody will bear me on their shoulders. They will sooner bear my casket, and then only six of them. Because they have to. I am not a big deal in my profession. Because (I note with considerable sadness) I have not figured out what is true, I have failed. I am a failure. In which case, what is all of the noise out there but a burden, a headache? Let's think about this for a moment. Polanyi (who was no Pollyanna) had written that when you believe that your discovery reveals a hidden reality, you will expect it to be recognized equally by others. So is it also the case that when others recognize *nothing* in what you say, then you should infer that your so-called discovery reveals nothing worthwhile? Maybe it wasn't a discovery at all.

I actually sit here brooding over the dark thoughts of self-deprecation, intoxicated by a mood.

First circle: The universe/reality/nature

The universe makes a tremendous noise. Some of it we humans can hear. We pass through a cacophony, at every magnitude – high and low, soft and loud. Two spinning objects generate a whistling whirl. Why would that not be true in outer space, where giant bodies orbit one another, too slowly for us to detect; but maybe there is in fact a music of the spheres beneath the threshold of human perceiving. The scientist objects, saying, look, noise presupposes an atmosphere. There is no atmosphere in outer space.[1] Or go in the opposite direction: with all of those orbiting electrons in every atom, how could that not perpetrate a subatomic noise?

The thing is, noise is more than sound. It is information. Noise includes visual stimuli, for example. And if Michel Serres is to be believed, then everything everywhere transmits information of one kind or another. It registers. Otherwise, we would conclude that it does not exist. And this includes black holes, where information cannot escape! – which is itself a fascinating bit of news.

My brain is tuned to only so many frequencies anyway. Yet it is tuned to many frequencies at the same time. Like radio stations all playing simultaneously, the very definition of static. An interview, a jingle, a golden oldie, a sermon, a partisan rant, an exposé on NPR. Bits of information interfere with one another, sometimes cancelling each other out, sometimes increasing the volume, but ordinarily garbling any discrete signal – William James' buzzing, blooming confusion, yeah? In the uproar, how on earth am I to discern the message? With noise as a background, the signal is easily overlooked or misunderstood. Or is there even a message at all? I cannot tell. This tumult is oppressively real even before we get to the question of interpretation, i.e. what does the message mean? No, we have difficulty isolating the signal to begin with.

As Serres points out, it could be that we fail to realize there are many signals being sent by the universe – odors and colors and signs of distress. How hard it must be to single out the one signal from among so many, like trying to hear a conversation at a crowded cocktail party where the acoustics are lousy. All of them signals, to be sure, bouncing around the room. Which one is the one I need to hear? Even if I were to recognize the Master's voice, would I hear it clearly, unimpeded? For all I know, I've been attuned to the wrong signal all along, missing other needful messages.

Elijah expected to hear YHWH in the whirlwind and in the quake. He was really listening, too. But as the Good Book says, God was not in these dramatic overtures, the *Sturm und drang*. He spoke in a still, soft voice, on little cat feet. He came to the prophet as a whisper.

What am I to notice then? From where I sit, my eyes scan the backyard, with green textures of every tint fluttering against a field of sky blue. I do not even notice the rusty chain link fence; I look right past it, as though it isn't there. But what am I looking *for*? I am at the same moment playing

---

1 "As matter streams onto the proto-neutron star, turbulence around the core sets it oscillating at around 300 hertz — musically, about F above middle C (Reddy, 2019)."

a selection from Beethoven, despite the grievous fact that it plays "in the background." (What an uncultured clod I am, a low brow.) I wouldn't understand its nuance anyway. It's lovely, to the extent that I actually listen, but I'm not trained to hear the specific instruments or chords. Was that a helicopter I just heard overhead? All this time, the computer screen wants to alert me about some crisis in politics, in the economy, in severe weather reports, as though I should care about each calamity, each tiff. My skin knows that it has become warm indoors. Maybe I should reset the AC. I do not even notice the irregular clacking of the keyboard all this time that punctuates my thinking. My elbow will feel the pounding later. Can you get tennis elbow from relentless one-finger typing? Apparently so.

Did I mention I have monkey mind?

The world is a multiplicity filled with noise. Information radiating, broadcasting, crisscrossing, contradicting itself. Some of it is wrong, fake news. Much of it is subliminal. Most of it is useless. Yet I live as though it is imperative that I detect the one true message, that I receive what the universe wants me to know. I scan the horizon for clues, intimations, prodigies, portents, omens, idiot lights, warnings, alerts, and invitations. Like any citizen, I should be well informed. And let's be fair, much of the world promises to delight the senses. Who knows which odd glance today, which scent will burn a memory that accompanies me years from now in my dreaming?

For some reason, I daydream about discrete moments, reveries

- such as jogging home through Anderson College during their annual camp meetings in June when the black tar on the street was fresh,
- such as lying under a tree by the White River on a specific autumn day, the high clouds scuttling past,
- such as walking alone uptown at night as a twelve-year-old to attend chess lessons at the Y.

Why this moment or that moment and not another? And if I cannot predict why any given input will sear itself into my brain long term, the next epiphany could be poised to happen right this afternoon! I should be on the lookout. But for what, exactly?

A big part of anxiety as a condition (and not as a mood) is the hyperawareness induced by the limbic system. One becomes conditioned over time to notice subtle cues as signals and then of course exaggerate their importance, or at least fret over their significance. Polanyi had cautioned against defects and error. Anxiety is both. I often suspect that being raised in the church has magnified my sensitivity, because literally anything can bear meaning. Anything could be the voice of God. Or of Satan. Every twist and turn represents some theological truth, if you but look. The bread on the paten signifies Jesus. The numeral 666 signifies evil. The color white in the paraments signifies purity. Or it could be a meaning that is quite profane. I mistype a word: damn, does that indicate that my subconscious knows it would be the wrong word in this situation? Maybe I should stop and reconsider. I stub my toe: will this suggest that I'm having a bad day? (Talk about profane.) On the way home from a party, I must de-brief: what did that woman mean by that remark? Did you pick up on that one gesture? And was that guy at the bar hitting on you, my sweet?

Differentiating the signal from the noise is tough. But then human beings are pattern-seeking creatures. We combine data looking for coherence. How does it all hang together? Does it? We take the stimuli and put it all together, often mistakenly, inferring a whole that will be assuredly incomplete. Leonardo da Vinci laughingly advised students to examine coffee stains for inspiration. You can see animals in clouds in the sky and faces in the gnarly undergrowth, gnomes in the carpet, and conspiracies on the internet. The brain will insert facts that do not exist in order to complete partial impressions, to flesh out the apparent. Geometry teachers count on our ability to do so, converting approximations in chalk into pristine images in our minds. "Now, class, here is a circle...."

The world is too much with us. Too much. Umberto Eco opened up the question for us whether our suspicions prove only the inventiveness of our perceiving minds. It takes a creative imagination to see plots and witchcraft and sinister forces just beyond the evidence. Garry Wills called them "random ingenuities." Were the Chinese really trying to undermine America by exporting a virus two years ago? How plausible is the plot? Were Satanists masking secrets by hiding them in vinyl record albums spun backward? There just *has to be* a narrative to explain what's going on. Somebody is behind this. And Fox News will happily spill the beans. "Alert! The people-we-all-hate are at it again!"

I am a conservative in the twenty-first century. Plenty of pundits try to persuade me that the folks on the far end of the spectrum, the wacko, sicko, pinko leftists – you know who I mean – they hate me, want to take my guns and destroy me, turning my kids into dope-smoking terrorists with sexual identity issues. Up to a certain point, I believe them. My confirmation bias in a sea of 300 million people (and their bots) crawling all over social media will convince me. What we need right now is a hero. What we need right now is a champion.

Oh, but not that red-headed clown. Wrong hero.

"If you were waiting for God to call on your sorry ass, dude, look no further. The Woke are your vocation. Rise up and do battle." As I contemplate the clarion call, to gird my loins for holy war, I gaze out the window and notice the patch of mint (which I am told is a hardy plant) surprisingly thin this year. I wonder why. Did I neglect it? Will I need to go outside and do something remedial this afternoon? … and just like that, the roiling conviction to bend my life toward crusades against implacable foes in a genuine holy war gets sidetracked, distracted by an herb.

Monkey mind.

Nobody has experienced the entire cosmos. Nobody could. Even if a person could be exposed to it all, the human brain could not make sense of it as a whole. But even if the brain could make sense of it all, it can do so only from a point of view, and there is (or are) an infinite number of points of view. But even if *per impossible* the brain could swing among every conceivable point of view and amass the entire array of perspectives out there, from left and right, top and bottom, front and back, inside and out, this does not mean it could derive the same exact knowledge somebody else with different interests and training could derive. Where I see apples to eat, you might see a crop to sell.

An inventory of all the little metallic parts lying on a black velvet cloth does not tell you that, once assembled, they tell time. It behooves me to pass through the universe as a single point, a singularity, one among an infinite number of loci, albeit my own foci. My umwelt. My context. My world.

The first circle in that Venn diagram is massive beyond comprehending, complex and ambiguous. Extensive, exhaustive, busy, and full. And it is only one of three such circles! Did I happen to mention that it also constantly *changes*?

Second circle: Human knowledge, aka the library

The second circle represents human thoughts and ideas, beliefs, research, the accumulated knowledge bound up in part by books, at the library. I am unaware of most of them. I could not even suspect what they are all about. Many of those which I do encounter, I have no interest in reading. This assumes they are published in English; otherwise, I am doomed. But among those that might interest me, in English, plenty are simply too hard to understand, for any one of a number of reasons. I lack the requisite background knowledge about the subject. Or I do not appreciate the jargon. Some are just too hard to follow. Maybe they are poorly written. Or I've decided that I don't have time to sink into the lacunae – even in my fields of interest. Plus, we all know not to read *that book* over there, right?

I remember one summer I made a project of reading John Milton's *Paradise Lost*. Another summer, Alexander Solzhenitsyn's *Gulag Archipelago*. I have only so many summers.…

Narrow the range to a single academic discipline, such as philosophy. (Throw aside chemistry, physics, mathematics, sociology, anthropology, numerology, gossip, biography, horticulture, the fine arts, engineering, joke books.) *Which* philosophy? Existentialism? Phenomenology? Pragmatism? Ethics, epistemology, ontology, metaphysics? I've found merit in each. Instead, we can narrow the number of *authors* in philosophy. In my journey, I have been attracted to some and not others. A few such as Immanuel Kant frankly intimidate me. Somehow, I've traced an arc from Heraclitus through Plato and Augustine toward William James, Georg Simmel, Eric Voegelin, José Ortega y Gasset, Jan Patočka, and lately Michel Serres. I've had fruitful conversations with Hans-Georg Gadamer, Maurice Merleau-Ponty, Hannah Arendt, and Alfred Lord North Whitehead. One semester many years ago, I set about to study what I called the bad boys, and by that, I meant Nicolo Machiavelli, Karl Marx, and Friedrich Nietzsche. To this day, I am an expert in none of these. Each of them surpasses me. Add to this list Isaiah Berlin, Michael Polanyi, Michel Foucault, Margaret Archer, Margaret Wheatley, Mary Douglas, Ruth Benedict, and Leo Strauss. Every so often, a new figure swims into my ken.

Add layer upon layer of secondary sources, lesser lights hoping to comment on the luminaries. On my personal bookshelf, I have four feet of the collected works of Eric Voegelin, with another four feet of commentary just about him.

This particular line of self-reflection is limited to the scholars in the field of philosophy and does not include the other writers who make substantive contributions to human thought, such as Albert Camus, Carl Jung, Fyodor Dostoevsky, and Martin Luther. Maybe it would be useful to conduct an inventory of books that made a deep impression on me – aside from the Bible, which fills an entirely separate category. Here are only some of the titles, in no particular order:

- James Carse. *Finite and Infinite Games*.
- Kenneth Boulding. *The Image*.
- Jonathan Rauch. *The Constitution of Knowledge*.
- Kwame Anthony Appiah. *As If*.
- Martin Heidegger. *Aristotle's* <u>*Metaphysics*</u> *Θ 1-3*.
- Sigmund Freud. *Civilization and its Discontents*.
- Robert Pirsig. *Zen and the Art of Motorcycle Maintenance*.
- Ken Wilber. *The Marriage of Sense and Soul*.
- James Hillman. *The Soul's Code*.

Make of that what you will. I have been profoundly negligent in failing to integrate these influences, to the extent they even *can* be integrated. The

French pejorative "dilettante" was meant to describe me. Now, lest you, my faithful reader, wave your hand and waive my objections as an elaborate Imposter Syndrome, a Socratic expostulation that the only thing that I know is that I know nothing, you underestimate my ignorance and the accompanying sense of self-reproach. What good is reading all these pages if there has been no corresponding effort to remember everything, let alone integrate everything into some master system, like a cathedral? The only thing that omnivores leave behind is their dung.

(Is this document ... dung?)

In short, the second circle in my master Venn diagram is capacious, overwhelming, contradictory, and scattered. Pluck one apple but leave the rest? My reading habits are far more haphazard than my eating habits. Yet I hasten to add, this portion of my confession is less about me as a student and more about the vast, bewildering literature that exists out there, a multiplicity, and dare I say it? A chaos, a glut, a noise. Made worse each year as more and more titles tumble forth, let alone the latest translations I might wish to access at long last. The minds of other men become manifest. I defy *anyone* to master it all, even within one tiny alcove. The old joke about Ph.D. students knowing more and more about less and less until they know everything there is to know about nothing at all, a generation's expert on Portuguese irregular verbs! God bless his heart.

I am tempted to begin a scholarly article with only a title and then a massive 8,000 word footnote, explaining.

Maybe Rousseau had this much right: we are born free, albeit in only the most peculiar sense of the word since at birth literally we can do nothing and have no autonomy. Parents feed us and tote us around for months. After that, we have sixteen years of doing chores. But the Apostle Paul is at least as right when he wrote that we are born *broken*. Original sin goes all the way down, through and through, the clinamen that curls in upon itself and warps the entire fabric of existence, enfolded, so that each of us is broken in relation to God, to nature, to society, and even within our own minds. Shattered, fragmented, veined with irregular cracks. I am plural, I am multiple, I am complex, I am dis-integrated. Psychiatrists, therapists, and counselors seek to help us as clients individuate and integrate and render us whole, even though James Hillman asked (not unreasonably) why that happens to be the desideratum. To some extent, the unity of each identity is an illusion. And in the process of trying to glue it all together and make peace for or among the inner self/selves, something will be left out, banished to the closet, stigmatized, disavowed, disallowed, cut off and repudiated, confessed – only to return under cover of darkness as pathology. The unpropitiated gods come back to haunt us.

Those French philosophers can be awfully *clever*. I'm just not persuaded anymore that's a compliment. Serres insists that everything is unified and interconnected. The more remote: the more fascinating the linkages. A rooster and a clock, the clump of dirt and star stuff, thoughts and machines and slimy fish and the Mona Lisa. One universe manifests in myriad ways, intriguingly interwoven, beyond our powers to appreciate. Where, oh where, is the accommodation of the single most irrefutable doctrine of the Christian faith, i.e. that we are in fact broken? Fascination – drawn to that which has been drawn together as fasces, in fascism – fascination does not offset the evidence. Unless, that is, one finds the kaleidoscope of little colorful beads tumbling around in a cylinder fascinating. Maybe disorder and violence and heartbreak and shame are indeed fascinating, not unlike car wrecks and tragedies, but are they anything to celebrate?

I'm convinced that those in Plato's allegory of the cave found the dancing shadows on the far wall utterly engrossing. They spurned the guy who interrupted them with tales of life outside of the cave, for he seemed quite incapable of interpreting the reality shimmering right in front of their faces. "Look, I know that's a goat, and that's a crescent moon, and that over there is a steam engine. If you don't see that, dude, then what good was your little 'excursion' into this alleged sunlight?" Plato's allegation in the cave.

Third circle: My mind

This third circle in the Venn diagram – the part that is me – is at least as bewildering as the other two and maddening. Augustine had accepted the fact that the mind cannot understand itself. Billions of synapses clustered in unique patterns, stretching back into the interior of the brain from Hebbean learning, firing, and wiring in endless knots of condensed signification – a plastic constellation slowly hardening with age, and wrong, wrong, wrong about so many things. How many thoughts can you think during a 400-meter dash? Not a single one of any lasting value. But I've spent literally decades trying to make sense of certain things. I've read lots of books, and I've catalogued my experiences (which are paltry, I admit) and I've sat there pondering the truth of things. None of it clear, consistent, or coherent, except perhaps little islands of knowledge in a massive ocean of ignorance and confusion. Perhaps I am an exception, paralyzed like Augustine by a lack of an ordinating principle.

"Jesus loves me. This I know. For the Bible tells me so." Do I? Do I know it? If I did, there would be an end to the anxiety.

One might ask (though I certainly wouldn't, because I admire him too much), but one might ask whether Serres would critique my Venn diagram altogether from the start. I am making a distinction that he would have found pernicious. There aren't three separate circles, separate multiplicities. They all participate in the same multiplicity. Human knowledge, wherever it is located, belongs to paramount reality. So also the distresses in my private brain case – still altogether real and interknit with everything else. One multiplicity, one chaos. Beware the making of distinctions.

On the other hand (because philosophers always need at least two hands), Serres could argue that each multiplicity is an example of a larger array of multiplicities. It is multiplicities (like turtles) all the way down. My brain is only a single instance of the imprint of chaos. There is an uncountable number of other instances, ranging from Lake Erie to that grasshopper over there to a thirteenth-century text written in Latin. Each a manifestation, an example, of the same basic confusion. Inscope toward quarks, outscope to the galaxies. Everything is broken. As Michel Serres once mentioned, scan the globe and you will find the human race fragmented, Babel-like, by languages/dialects, currencies, scientific disciplines, and religions (sects).

Water – Air – Fire – Earth – Life. The pre-Socratics may have picked different elements to emphasize, but they weren't mistaken about the basic range of possibilities. Parmenides was correct: it's all one. It just is. Heraclitus was correct: it's all dynamic and perspectival. Have we really made much progress since? The mind with which we presume to understand the universe is stricken with the same defects as the universe itself. Maybe Socrates was not playing dumb. Maybe he was wise because he knew, given the situation, that he knew nothing. Believing that you know something just might be the most basic error.

Close of Exposition A

The world, aka paramount reality. Human knowledge, aka the library. My brain, aka Nathan. Three impossible fields of disjointed pieces, too vast to master and changing all the time. How on earth was I supposed to domesticate any of these wild beasts, let alone all three in some harmonious whole? My confession begins therefore with the only truth apparent to me, which is that I never had a chance. I should be grateful for what little lucidity I do enjoy. Only by the grace of God.

Let me close this section in the following manner. The phenomenologist Edmund Husserl, early in his career, wrote about the philosophy of mathematics, and he began with the idea of a multiplicity. This idea, central to the opening section of my manuscript, depends on more than one "thing" or entity being in some kind of relationship with one another simultaneously. Etymologically, the term "multiplicity" derives from the imagery of many folds – a manifold. He then contemplated the functional difference between the idea of "multiplicity" and a unity. Offhand, we might assume they are somehow opposing ideas. Husserl pointed out that a multiplicity can be comprised of many unities (such as atoms or musical notes), but a multiplicity can itself be regarded as a unity (such as a molecule or a melody). One can conceive of a multiplicity of multiplicities. That is succinctly the situation I find myself in this summer, as a multiplicity among multiplicities.

Exposition B: Leadership studies

My field of professional interest is Leadership Studies.

The emergence of this field of study

The phenomenon of leadership has existed in one form or another since the dawn of recorded time. The oldest evidence recounts the exploits of kings and commanders, prophets and bishops, a never-ending saga of interpersonal influence, sometimes succeeding and sometimes failing, but always drawing the attention of those who record history. Today, scholars have reason to believe that leadership of some kind contributed to success on the savannah, long before the first pages were ever written. We may not possess their names, but it stands to reason that leaders ensured the survival of their tribe into the Neolithic Age. In between pre-history, on the one hand, and contemporary accounts, on the other, oral traditions were passed down through the generations, primarily to memorialize extraordinary feats of heroism and wisdom. These names, such as Gilgamesh and Moses and Ulysses and Arthur, we do have.

Historians today might lament the long tradition in their discipline of paying almost exclusive attention to the outsized characters thought to be responsible for the course of humanity, but it was a commonplace among scholars to tell the story of preeminent figures and ignore the rest. And so, one will encounter on the bookshelves great studies into the significance of a Charlemagne or Cleopatra or Simón Bolívar. The extraordinary origins of the United States of America, for example, can be recounted as the work of the Founding Fathers. The great American upheaval known as the Civil War is often portrayed as the contestation between rival generals, such as Jackson and Stuart and Lee versus Meade and Sherman and Grant.

Journalists and voters continue to lavish attention and sometimes affection on the celebrity of those who would influence the polity, blurring the line too often between steely analysis and abject worship. Not a few academics have succumbed to the temptation to see in flesh-and-blood authoritarians the magic, the seductive aura to which they gladly subordinated their powers. Nobody purchases the autobiography of another nobody. Most of us still scan the horizon for a savior, the man on the white horse, the paragon delivered to us in our hour of dismay. It is not something we in the modern age have outgrown. Psychologists have tried to explain our infantile dependence on such a cult, the authority, the primal father of the horde, what Freud referred to as our prosthetic God.

Scholars have since argued that this obsession with leaders has blinded us to the deep engines of our past, whether that engine be economic or subconscious or racial. Or systems thinking. History is now thought to be more than the cascading interplay of biographies. To a great extent, they now suggest, a fixation on leaders serves as an illusion, albeit a comforting illusion. No doubt, leaders themselves cultivate this illusion for their own ends, issuing in propaganda and not a small dose of intentional mystification. "If what the people crave is an anointed leader, then by god let's give it to them." Maybe it is the case that leadership originates in divine unction. Or we choose to call it fate or destiny. Or from our limited perspective, we interpret nature to have provided us with superior specimens, smarter and better looking and energetic and visionary.

The study of leadership formalized around World War II. Not only were we captivated (then and now) by the personalities of FDR, Churchill, Stalin, Hitler, and Mussolini, at the macro or wholesale level; but also at the micro or retail level, face-to-face, the military needed to find out quickly who should be promoted to positions of command. They had learned after years of strenuous combat that unit leadership made a difference. You couldn't install just anybody into higher ranks. Some guys were objectively better at it. Let's find out who they are, and quickly. That insight then carried over into the post-war period, when resources could be dedicated to documenting the impact that leadership might have on groups, teams, and organizations. Psychologists, political scientists, sociologists, management theorists, anthropologists, and still historians turned their disciplined gazes onto this phenomenon, deploying systematic methods to define and measure leadership. The literature grew like topsy. Gradually, these scholars started bumping into one another. They read one another's papers. They haunted the same breakout sessions at conferences. They came to realize the overlap that was there and found merit in crossing various boundaries to learn from one another. James MacGregor walked across campus to interrogate a psychologist. In this one incident, I see the contours of a way forward for Leadership Studies.

By the 1980s, these various scholars had formed an association, launched academic journals, held conferences, wrote textbooks, and convinced universities to offer coursework on leadership. Not a few of these early adopters found the field lucrative, to-boot, selling their expertise to ravenous corporations and publishing how-to manuals for easy consumption. (Sound familiar, Barbara?) Programs in Leadership Studies started popping up like mushrooms in unlikely places, without any central coordination. As these things evolve, egos get in the way. Little subgroups contended with one another as to what leadership even means, let alone which theories to use or which research methods to adopt. Everybody began from a different intellectual point, with their own local emphasis. Many persisted in talking past one another. Along the way, imperious individuals would come among us proclaiming that they had finally solved the eternal puzzle. They had the complete answer to our queries. If they had been empowered to do so, they might banish the rest of us, conducting what are known as pissing contests, readily adopting the role of gatekeeper. Except there never was a consensus. There still is none.

Efforts to unify around a grand theory, conducted by the most celebrated scholars with seed money and the best of intentions, failed spectacularly. One fellow out in San Diego documented the unnerving fact that we cannot even agree on what the word "leadership" means; he tallied hundreds of definitions, many of them incompatible with one another. To date, we seem to have adopted an attitude of considerable tolerance for the various ways that our peers talk about leadership, yet occasionally some recent university graduate sallies forth with what he or she insists is the one true, holy, and apostolic definition. The rest of us are wrong. How could we have been so stupid? And so the sounds of irritated grumbling over terminology resumes, with no end in sight.

In the intervening years, the associations, conferences, journals, textbooks, and curricular programs have proliferated, without any expectation that what drew people together in the twentieth century would continue to do so. Today, thousands of scholars, authors, consultants, teachers, trainers, and outright quacks go their separate ways, barely acknowledging one another. Try as I might (and I don't try any longer), there is no possibility of staying on top of the literature. What we call by a single name, i.e. Leadership Studies, has become a fragmented and uneven mélange.

Into this unkempt garden has crept a further challenge to what we are calling Leadership Studies, and that is the increasing call for the leadership-we-prefer – whatever that happens to look like. Fewer and fewer careers are being built on objective assessments of what occurs out in paramount reality; the literature has become swamped by prescriptions, what I call happy talk, faux research into models the authors would like to see enacted in the world. Normative dimensions crowd to the fore. Writers infuse their agenda with variations on a theme, on leadership that isn't leadership, on being nice, on affirming this or that disadvantaged identity, on anybody, really, who epitomizes the opposite of a familiar stereotype.

[Here I deleted two lengthy paragraphs illustrating my animus, because they would be the only portion of my entire work that would draw any attention – all of it negative. Let's call my discretion at this juncture an example of self-censorship. For I am that stereotype.]

I digress.

What then is leadership? What do we study?

Despite the lack of any consensus, I would hazard to adopt one *tentative* definition of leadership, at least to get things started. It runs as follows: leadership is a process by which one person influences others toward desired goals and objectives. I am explicitly ignoring the many attempts to include things such as self-leadership, or groups of people leading other people, or the purpose itself (whatever it happens to be) being that which leads, or a leaderful group (whatever that means), or algorithms and AI determining our choices, or fakes or fools or phantasms. There is time enough for such variations on a theme. Let me concentrate here on human agency, on the possibility that individual human beings, working together, can bring about change in the world. Whatever else gets factored into the equation, whether the means of production, culture, systems, or subconscious drives, the field of Leadership Studies has to insist that individual exertions matter. Otherwise, what's the point?

In what way do these exertions matter? Well, there isn't just one way that this is true. Leadership can look like many different things. It overlaps with a plethora of other activities, many of which resemble leadership – activities such as management, seduction, manipulation, marketing, command, education, administration, plotting, scheming, loving, loosening, and even letting go. The need to draw bright boundaries around these activities just goes to show how complicated the practice of leadership will in fact be. Good leaders sometimes do bad things, they sometimes fail, they do things other than leading, and they often follow! Trying to disentangle the many activities intrinsic to interpersonal striving, so that you can erect a conceptual fence and say, no, that is not leadership? Well, that's naïve and less than helpful in a reality that mixes everything together.

This is not to say that leadership is comprised of everything and anything. I am not opposed to making distinctions. Making distinctions is ordinarily the beginning of critical thought. We cannot go through life refusing to make distinctions. Poison is not food. As a friend of mine has catalogued, however, Leadership Studies is lacerated by the making of distinctions. Frequently, submissions to journals exist exclusively to make yet another distinction. They proliferate beyond reckoning. And the obvious thing should not go unsaid, which is that the making of a distinction is only the first step. And here, I believe, the works of Michel Serres are especially valuable.

a Serres frequently complained about the excluded middle, the gradient between two poles that we so often overlook. Just because you split something into two, have you considered the extent to which you bypassed everything in between? You lose so much if you see only Red and Violet on the visible spectrum. In geometry, you indicate a line AB, labeling it by the endpoints known as A and B, even though as a line it is necessarily an infinite series of adjoining points lying in between. Don't ignore all of that stuff. When judging leadership, if you insist on finding victory or defeat, you neglect the possibility of compromise. Distinctions are sometimes just the two extreme poles along a dimension.

Lest we forget, the two extremes might just be toxic, the excess and deficiency that bring harm. See Aristotle.

b At a deeper level of sophistication, we experience other dimensions of color such as hue and tint. Just because you make one distinction (between north and south) does not mean you couldn't also differentiate east from west, let alone altitude. Any distinction you can make will be complemented by others. There is never just one distinction. Transactional/Transformational leadership (one distinction) is not the only possibility; you can also assess a leader as hands-on or laissez-faire, solitary or communal, theory X or theory Y, and so on. One yardstick is never enough. One distinction, standing alone, doesn't explain very much.

c Not only that, but so much in reality is both/and. A bifurcation at the conceptual level might obscure a blending at the empirical level. A good leader might also be a bad man. It happens. So in the literature on leadership, you classify between people-oriented and task-oriented when the ideal supposedly is both! In the same spirit, Luther had insisted that Jesus was both God and Man, and I am both Saint and Sinner, and at the Lord's Table we eat both the Bread and the Body of Christ. A conceptual distinction in the sky, so to speak, might overlook an empirical mixture on the ground.

d Another version of both/and is abstraction, backing up from two different things to an encompassing reality. The tomato, lettuce, carrot, onion, and cilantro – distinct ingredients – together constitute a salad, a composite both/and. Ask the physician: the organism is a delicate integration of multiple tissues. Tending one of them might injure another. You have to see it whole. The multiplicity can be regarded as a unity. In the same fashion, leadership is never just about the leader. One must account for the followers and the encompassing situation. Two species can belong to a shared genus.

e Serres frequently indicated the many ways that seemingly separate items are truly the same. This over here and that over there– both represent the exact same referent. The bread and the Body of Christ. The flag and the anthem. The hero's myth and developmental psychology. We have a hard time seeing the linkages across categories. A large part of his work draws attention to the surprising both/and, e.g. the parasite, noise, turbulence, multiplicity, chaos, and the character of the Harlequin. Often, we call it a simile or metaphor: "That leader is the straw that stirs the drink." But Serres insists that disparate things often obey the same basic patterns. They are not simply metaphorically alike. They are behaving in the same way, like cascading waters and a woman's curly hair. They obey the same principles. So, for example, we can examine the dynamics of leadership using fluid mechanics. Seen from a point of view, they follow identical laws. Leadership is the expenditure of energy to overcome entropy (physics). Investigators in leadership could do more of this kind of work. Two totally unrelated items can be more alike than we might expect.

f No distinction persists without considering the time dimension. Black becomes white. Up becomes down. Leaders rise and fall. Friends become enemies. Viable and supple organizations harden into bureaucracies. Dominant industries lose market share. Romance withers. The son supplants the father. The cute kitten becomes a daily burden to feed and comfort and scoop out her poop. The garage band morphs into a traveling glam show, relying on its single hit song to sell merch. No snapshot of reality survives intact with the passage of time. Distinctions can transmogrify or evaporate completely.

g Even if two things are clearly differentiated, split into X and Y, there remains the work to explain in what ways X and Y are related to one another. Are they contraries? Do they quarrel? Did one of them create or cause the other? Are they complementary to one another? Do they alternate back and forth? Are they allied somehow against a third position Z? For example, leadership contributes to the development of culture, while culture determines what sort of leadership occurs. The two are mutually influencing in a never-ending reciprocity. In short, once you have differentiated X from Y, be prepared to answer the next question, which is "So what?"

h Finally, a variation on a theme: two things, two polar opposites might be held in a tension, maybe in equipoise, neither one able to win completely or lose, but clasped forever in a Manichean struggle. For a time, maybe one side has the upper hand, but soon the other will gain the advantage. Tensions exist throughout the physical universe, pulling, and they serve at the pumping heart of living things, of life. In my own mind, I swing back and forth constantly between competing possibilities. Every sailor knows that in order to reach the pier, you might have to tack this way and then that way, depending on the conditions. Leadership is no less of a practical undertaking. Freedom and order, persistence and novelty, continuity and change, accelerating or decelerating – no leader is required to choose one and abandon the other. In fact, that would be a mistake. Each has its place in the toolkit. The trick is knowing when to pick one over the other.

Close of Exposition B

One of the lenses through which I analyze leadership as a social phenomenon is called systems thinking, an approach with its own history going back to cybernetics. Systems is one way to describe the context within which leadership occurs. Leadership is a mode of participating in systems, such as creating social systems (entrepreneurs), operating social systems (managers), revising social systems (reformers), renewing social systems, and even on occasion diverting social systems. Under closer scrutiny, given the fractal nature of systems thinking in which one system can be found to have been nested within another, leadership itself – the actual exercise of interpersonal influence – can be plotted as a system with stock-and-flow diagrams, feedback loops, and so forth. And if we were to magnify our lenses even further, the leader standing alone in isolation is a system. Systems working on systems. Systems responding to systems.

The model of a system accounts for the hierarchies of social life, wherein some multiplicity (such as a business, university, or squadron) orders itself for a shared purpose. That system in turn then passes through an environment consisting of other systems, bumping up against one another or seamlessly overlapping, while at the same time united conceptually in an even larger, encompassing system, outward to the stars. My three Venn diagrams from the first exposition can be construed as distinct yet interlocking systems, except I'm not convinced they are each systems. I do *hypothesize* that they are.

I have found this tool of systems thinking useful when trying to make sense of so many things, especially leadership. As with any tool, it cannot prescribe how it will be used. A klutz might try to use a hammer as a screwdriver or as a doorstop or as a weapon, with varying degrees of success. Still, systems thinking comes in handy surprisingly often, mostly because it exemplifies one of the principles enunciated by Serres, which is that two unlike things can resemble one another because they adhere to the same basic patterns. A fox in the henhouse is surprisingly like an acid, if you know what to look for. If you grasp what is happening in the flower garden, you can use that lesson to fight a war. A large part of genius is to recognize these similarities, transporting familiar knowledge into unanticipated situations. I think the management gurus call this lateral thinking.

Three cinematic examples.

In the fortified "Masada," the Roman legion was pounding at the formidable gate in order to gain entry and kill the occupants. "Shall we reinforce the gate?" No. Instead, let us build another gate a foot behind the one under assault. "What good will that do, except postpone the inevitable? The engineers will only resume beating our hastily built barrier." Ah, said the leader, you would be correct. Before they do break through the first gate, then, let us pour sand between them. This will change the nature of our resistance. Let the Romans pound sand. The battering ram suddenly became useless in the assault.

In the film "Master and Commander," the captain of a smaller vessel disguises itself as an immobile merchant ship, seemingly stranded, billowing smoke, in the hopes of attracting the sleek pursuer closer and closer, letting down its guard, relying on the greed of the adversary to bring it within range. The advantage of the smaller vessel lies in close quarters. The smaller ship appears to be a vulnerable prize for the menacing French privateers. Only then, when it is too late, strike the colors, fling open the portals, and blast away at the mast, in order to disable the enemy, while launching the marines across the gap and onto the deck for hand-to-hand combat. It is a trap.

In another feature-length film titled "The Founder," Ray Kroc exploits what he learned about McDonalds as a fast food restaurant/slash/hamburger joint to fling the franchise far and wide, much to the dismay of those who first developed the idea on which McDonalds had been founded. At a critical point in the story, a clever advisor reminded Kroc that the firm isn't in the hamburger business. It is in the *real estate business*. They sell millions of hamburgers out of so many prime locations. Hamburgers are what they advertise. Let the franchise owners make those hamburgers. The entire time, McDonalds controls prime real estate in every city. It was a moment in the movie when the proverbial light bulb goes off, above Kroc and above the audience.

Systems thinking makes such breakthroughs easier to see. And I would contend that often what we ascribe to leadership is in reality a breakthrough of this kind.

Be careful, though. Systems thinking brings with it a number of problems. Systems begin only after an initial assembly of the parts. It is built on a premise of some sort. And it must, therefore, exclude things that do not fit the mission. I will mention only one problem, however. Once you see the world through the lens of systems, you recognize (at least to some degree) the extent to which every node in the network implicates every other node. When I buy a product at the grocery, I reward one merchant at the expense of another. When I dispose of rubbish, it ends up accumulating somewhere. Each breath distributes CO_2. Any unkind remark can resound like the crack of a whip through gossip and social media. Little gestures can have gigantic consequences. Anything I know to be wrong, anywhere, is in part my fault, assuming I don't use my powers to fix it. And if I try to fix one thing, millions of other things are going wrong simultaneously. In a world of scarcity, neglect, suffering, and crime, we have nobody to blame but – well, not me, per se, but the system.

We are witness to a strange alchemical transformation, from (a) thinking that I am responsible for all the ills of the world because of my complicity in systems to (b) thinking that nobody is responsible and instead displacing responsibility onto an impersonal force. It is the system's fault. So of course young people who have been cosseted their whole lives blame the system constantly. It stands to reason they would urge one another to burn it down, dismantle the whole structure, topple the statues, fling the Molotov cocktails, disrupt the ceremony, deride the authorities, cancel the comedian, show up at the justice's home address bearing insults and coat hangers, because somebody somewhere had their feelings hurt. The mighty system of systems that plays the role of God did not prevent that harm. Theodicy. Therefore, the system is culpable. Therefore, eradicate the system. It is a brilliant and brilliantly stupid politics that results from such reasoning.

I would ask the following question: when in prior generations did children learn to avoid such nonsense? (Or did we? My siblings raised a ruckus back in the 1960s.) Nevertheless, here is my answer. They once read the Great Books. They underwent the rigors of a catechism. They bent over hard physical labor. They saw up close the concrete reality of polio, dementia, and caskets. They never got the chance to hear that some human system would sanitize life for them. Serres said that lately we cycle too quickly from what is **possible** to what is **actual** to what is **desirable** to what is **necessary** and a legal right, funded by taxpayers. In my book, that means we have become spoiled. We seem to believe nowadays that we should be able to stop all madness, war, crime, racism, and failure itself. No more school shooters. No more saying the word "retarded." No more headache. No more teacher's dirty looks. In a population of 330 million people?

Expect much?

The idea of a system implies the idea of an environment for that system. And the idea of an environment implies a multiplicity. I have Whitehead to thank for that insight. Leadership in systems presupposes an encompassing multiplicity. But the idea of a system presupposes a multiplicity that took some kind of coordinated form. So leadership is part of a multiplicity engaged in a broader multiplicity. It helps to explain *in what way* that multiplicity engages in the broader multiplicity.

Codetta

The beautiful clover, bountiful to bees, manifests for but a season, to be mown down at man's convenience as a weed and forgotten once the locusts raise their insistent noises in the summer's final days. I, who live three score and who mow these blossoms weekly every summer, I am far less beautiful, far less bountiful, far less hopeful reaching upward toward the sun (as they do now), a sun from which I hide of late, troubling over my vocation.

Development

In 1989, the hiring committee at Purdue University asked the following question at my job interview: State two reasons we should *not* hire you for this faculty position. Good question. I answered, "I have not ever taught before. And I've never studied leadership." They hired me to teach leadership anyway.

It is not completely true that I had never studied leadership. Leadership was implicit in much of my curriculum, especially in Political Science. Going further back, though, I had been learning about leadership since infancy. I grew up in a parsonage, the sixth of eight children, so the family gave my parents and older siblings opportunities to lead. And as I matured, I could try leading now and then in the family context. My father was the Lutheran pastor of a good-sized congregation, where he practiced leadership professionally. Leadership was weekly on display. In school, of course, I witnessed leadership in the classroom and on the playground.

Athletics provides plenty of opportunities to witness and practice leadership. In the fourth grade, I made the school's basketball team which proceeded to lose every single game that season. The next year, a new coach came in with basically the same talent, and we *won* every game, including the city championship. I saw up close the difference that Leo K. Witt made on us boys. He did the same thing in football, reversing the won-lost record completely. Maybe I hadn't studied leadership per se. I had *experienced* it, nonetheless.

The specific moment that illustrates his impact, however, came in track and field. Our team trained on a cinder track that ran twice as long as most because it followed just inside a horse track, hard by the White River with a dandy view of the city skyline. I was assigned to run 440 yards, also known as the quarter mile. To an elementary kid, that was a long race. But Coach Witt, exasperated at our attempts to pace ourselves, told us in no uncertain terms that the 440 is a sprint, a dash. We had been too lackadaisical in our approach. Here, let me show you, he said. Let's run the next one together. He proceeded to lay down his clipboard and tuck his whistle into his short pocket. He flipped his clip-on necktie over his shoulder, and there in his dress shirt, dress pants, and black leather dress shoes, he crouched for the start and took off abruptly, almost violently, leaving the rest of us gob-smacked, giggling at the ferocity of his departure. Nevertheless, we followed as best we could. He ran the entire distance and staggered after the finish, breathing hard and sweating profusely. (We saw this all from a distance, because we had not even reached the finish line yet.) But that exhibition made an impression on a kid who loved to run. It's no coincidence that the 400 became my event in high school. He led us that day in more ways than one.

Children experience leadership in many ways, being told what to do, being invited to try things, being barked at, warned off, directed, judged, forbidden, inveigled, induced, rewarded, inspired, alienated, intimidated, seduced, manipulated, taught, exhorted, and shot a look that says, Don't even try it. Children also lead one another.

In the eighth grade, our civics teacher introduced a little simulation in which different groups of students formed businesses. One other group was the state government. And one was the labor union. I had just finished a Readers Digest Condensed novel about corporate intrigue, so I hatched a plot. I offered to each classmate my services as their "attorney" in exchange for a number of shares in their firm. I did this in such a way that I could accumulate over 50% of each one. (Several just handed me all of their shares because they didn't care about the class.) Then, I made a deal with the state government, run by my closest friend, to employ only prisoners, ostensibly to reduce the costs of incarceration and help to rehabilitate them. Meaning that the labor union would have no members employed anywhere. Then, a few days into the little game, I asked the instructor if I could address the class. I stood up, came to the front, and said, as of this moment I own the entire classroom. Mayhem ensued. And the teacher quietly quit the game. Was that an example of leadership? It was an example of something.

Children are exposed to leadership as well in the literature, with heroes and kings and little neighborhood misfit baseball clubs that win the big game. Watch TV or most children's movies. In my home, I immersed myself in a lovely series called *Living Biographies*. So enthralled was I by these narratives (with an accompanying sketch of each face), that I recall being curled up in a corner getting lost in the feats of scientists, explorers, politicians, and painters. When my folks passed away many years later, I made a point of retrieving that particular set of books as a part of my inheritance, because they (the books) had meant so much to me.

In high school, I hatched a plan to win the office of president of the senior class, and it worked – much to my chagrin for the decades to come, since I have no interest whatsoever in reunions. In college, I became more aggressive, in part because I had been radicalized reading the works of William F. Buckley, Jr., who made it cool to be a conservative. This was when Ronald Reagan rose to the presidency and the Religious Right emerged as a political force. My activism had alienated many on that small campus, but I had been paying attention to the power dynamics so that by my junior year I recruited a guy to run for Student Assembly president. We gathered a merry band of misfits to run the campaign, while I stayed in the shadows. Slowly, we attracted the unlikeliest allies, but such was our vision and discipline that when the time came nobody of any stature dared to run against our man. Only one obscure little guy in a no-account fraternity tossed his hat into the ring. The outcome was the greatest margin of victory in the history of campus politics. And our little band had solidified into being close friends, a proverbial hot group.

Consequently, I had learned lessons as an undergraduate, some of them cautionary tales. I didn't like myself as a conniving agitator. My victories were shallow, indeed hollow. So, when I left for law school, I kept my head down and my mouth shut. I became a grind. There was no other way to survive. But I was surrounded for the first time by a slew of intelligent, ambitious, and sophisticated peers, each of whom was going places. And they did, many of them taking leadership roles in life.

I continued to be interested in politics, power dynamics, elite formation, exhibitionism, institutions, elections, and political thought. My orientation was Christian, Conservative, Capitalist/Anti-Communist, American, Republican, with a streak of Libertarian attitude. Where I might end up, God only knew, and I pestered Him often to reveal to me where to go next. I wrote poems about my latent ambitions, portraying myself as a coiled snake, just waiting (impatiently) for permission to strike. But the word never came. Life happened. Setbacks ensued. Little did I know that during an era when there was no such thing as Leadership Studies, I had been circling the topic my entire life. Being hired to teach it gave me an excuse to crystallize my understanding, so I began at Purdue staying a chapter ahead but slowly sunk my mind into the literature (such as it was at the time), occasionally writing up little articles to help me formalize my position.

All the time, while growing up, the evening news exemplified leadership. I sat there in my living room as a nine-year-old watching protests in Chicago. I came to maturation during Watergate. I witnessed the providential convergence of Reagan, Thatcher, Gorbachev, and John Paul II. By 1989, therefore, I did have a lot of material about leadership to draw from.

Needless to say, I've spent every year since that job interview trying to make sense of leadership. Only thenceforward, I had to inspect the literature on leadership (that confounding second circle) as it was booming outward.

The problem, so far as I can tell, is that I have no way of discerning order amidst the chaos. I require an ordinating principle, an acceptable framework properly applied to my situation. As Polanyi was to put it, I have been trying in my haphazard way to grasp disjointed parts into a comprehensive whole. Maybe everything begins with a gesture of sorting. Marsilio Ficino urged his reader to resolve, define, and demonstrate – in that order. *Resolvit primo, secondo definit, postremo demonstrat.* To "resolve" is to sort among the specimens. To "define" is to enclose the specimens within their appropriate categories (e.g. species, genus). To "demonstrate" is to show what a difference these categories make. Dogs do this thing over here, but cats do that over there. I have had over thirty years to do the resolving, defining, and demonstrating of this thing we call leadership.

What should interest you as a reader, by the way, is the equivalence of what I have been trying to do as a *student* of leadership and what leaders themselves are so often credited with doing, which is bringing about a sense of order, sometimes referred to as sense-making. I am confronted with a similar task. Is this an example of what the mathematicians call homothety, a dilation of the same basic form? Do not be deceived: as Serres reminded us, fighting a battle (leadership) is harder than writing about it (leadership studies). "[P]ast battles don't kill their historians." What we are doing is similar, in one sense, but totally different in another sense.

Consider the history of geometry. (This will be useful, if you give it a chance. Trust me.) Serres noted that as opposed to some linear progression from point A to point B and then on to point C, the history of geometry took a different path. It progressed from point A to point B, then returned again to *a new point A* (call it A_1) which progressed to a new point B (call it B_2). Very intelligent people have kept revisiting its foundation, reimagining geometry. The result of course is that instead of possessing just one history, we possess multiple histories, each one of which was begun from a different place, from a different point of origin. Only by taking a giant step back can we speak of a history of histories, in which $A_1 \rightarrow B_1 \rightarrow C_1$ is replaced by $A_2 \rightarrow B_2 \rightarrow C_2$, and so on.

Was Clovis I, King of the Franks in Late Antiquity, a representative of (a) Germanic migration (as the war chief of the Franks), (b) Roman collapse (as the barbarian consul tasked with presiding over a sclerotic bureaucracy), or (c) the rise and solidification of the Catholic Church (as the solitary believer of royal status in the West baptized into the orthodox faith)? Which version should we pick?

In each history, we will unearth the same basic sequence of A → B → C, which is as follows: purify the origins by ejecting the detritus (i.e. get a start fresh), set boundaries to defend (i.e. draw bright lines around what is and what is not to be included), and then go to work cultivating the territory. Clear the land, enclose it with a fence line, then put it to use. I should be doing the same thing here, intellectually. One of the troubles we face is that one history did not exactly *replace* another, but instead, they all continue to exist out there, mingled together. Today, you or I can return to A_1 or A_2 – or A_n, for that matter.

As a consequence, one can locate books describing leadership as a function of communication or a function of power or a function of societal health. Each chooses a different point A, a different premise. One group splits away in order to examine Critical Theory, while another steeps like a teabag in the literature of management and organizational behavior, while that group over there prefers to spend all day on gender issues. They each claim to begin at some beginning, then they define what they are trying to do, so that there is no mistaking. If everything turns out fine, then each group can start doing normal research in order to describe reality and prescribe the leadership which their particular approach necessitates. Multiple histories, existing side-by-side, each of which traces its origins to a different precept. Clean, defend, and cultivate *the same exact tract of land.* You might ask, how on earth do they coexist? As Serres concluded, let justice redress these overlapping imperializations and rectify the confusion. By doing what? By making way for yet another ordinating principle? Was that his advice? Are we to go in search of a superior origin point A and generate yet another history? I was often tempted to attempt it.

Each new god must brand its predecessors as devils. One must slay the old king before taking the vacant throne. If we look with an unprejudiced eye at the literature regarding leadership, we see all of these competing, incompatible points of origin, ranging from A_1 to A_n. Our field of study resembles polytheism, a cacophony of voices rising up. What have we as a community of scholars been doing about that fact? To some degree, we ignore the fragmentation, accepting it. You go your way; I'll go mine. I will go to my breakout sessions; you attend yours. I'll publish in this little journal; you publish in yours. And never the twain shall meet. Every so often, though, one of these groups tries to subjugate the rest, dominating the field, insisting that their god is the one true God, the creator and supreme authority. Academic monotheism. That's one possibility.

Tactically, a few will ally themselves against a common adversary, which is precisely what has happened to something called the Great Man Theory. Everybody ganged up on it, agreeing that whatever the differences among us, on our side, we all despise the Great Man Theory. Right? In the spirit of René Girard, we found unity in scapegoating what had been a relatively weak victim to begin with. Unify under one flag. (Whose?) Unify against a common enemy. (Whom?) So I ask myself: is there another way to unify such disparate voices?

Recall that after Zeus overthrew his father, he immediately feared his own children, and rightly so. What goes around comes around. The solution, he thought, was to eat his offspring, to consume them. Thereafter, they would pose no threat. As all of us remember, from his forehead there emerged the goddess Athena – a daughter not to displace him, but to manifest as wisdom. So here is another way to unify: to consume one's children. To take within oneself that which you fear. Could this be a homothetic version of dialogue with one's acquaintances? The analogy is not that far-fetched. Let me explain.

Serres showed that dialogue is a contest between the participants, on the one side, and the intrusion of meaningless noise, on the other. You and I must draw aside to a quiet place and limit the cacophony of the world's distractions in order to make any progress when we talk together. We must voluntarily and with good intentions engage one another against a common enemy. And that takes commitment to one another, across the boundaries, even when we have no real image of what we might obtain as a result. Phrased indelicately, we must *consume* one another so that Athena might be born.

Almost immediately during any genuine dialogue, we will encounter barriers, you and I. And the image of a barrier is a recurring theme in these pages, so hear me out. We speak different languages. We bring different experiences. There is a practical reason we have kept ourselves apart till now. Is it even possible for us to understand one another? (Is it even possible to understand oneself?) Here I am in my labyrinth. There you are in yours. And we discover that somehow we occupy the same labyrinth! As Serres pointed out, there were always two different ways to escape the labyrinth. One was to retrace one's steps by following Ariadne's thread (which exemplifies algebra). The other was to put on the wings of Daedalus and fly up and away (which exemplifies geometry). Each of them worked. But could Ariadne and Daedalus understand one another? My experience of the labyrinth is different from yours. My strategy for escape is different.

All of that theorizing is well-and-good. Except the problem is that in reality here I sit, languishing in the twisting corridors of my own labyrinth, afraid, uncertain what rude beast stalks the maze. I am sitting here using neither method. I am simply a victim, trapped in the confusion. If you spurn both the thread and the wings, as I am tempted to do, you just might deserve to perish. What now?

I began these meditations asking where I am, in the midst of chaotic multiplicities and unrelenting noise. I asked where I might be going. I've used terms such as understanding, meaning, order. Then I risked answering the awkward question about where I began this journey. Seems my origins are autochthonic: I began in the very dirt I am trying to cultivate. The great God scooped up a handful of clay and fashioned me in His image. Nathan the Clay-Baby. I am going nowhere new. I belong to the very soil. I was an anxious kid from birth, easily overwhelmed, yet fascinated with leadership all of my days. Which raises a fourth question posed by Serres, a variation on the first: through what field therefore am I now passing? What is this place in particular, in June of this year?

Initially, my ambition was to clear, defend, and cultivate one small patch, the land to which I belong. That ambition soon involved me in untoward contestations, struggles with those who would purge the same little acre and grow their own crops. We are each seeking to enclose and possess the same corner of the vineyard, when perhaps the solution is to open up, share, without fixating on whether it is any longer "mine." **Openness** turns out to be a key concept.

Serres repeatedly cited Rousseau's explanation that the concept of property began when one fellow enclosed a space and persuaded other people it was his. Whether Rousseau is correct as to real estate and property law, he is doubly correct that intellectuals often like to think the same way, despite the fact that they are not permitted this possessory interest in their thoughts and ideas, unless (that is) they share it. You and I have an easement across anyone's tract. (I was about to say one's holdings, but we don't "hold" onto our insights.)

Speaking poetically, we are all riding on one of the glassy bits of a primordial explosion that dwarfs the biggest thing we know.

When you and I huddle over cups of coffee, in order to engage in dialogue, what are we hoping for? Is there a single master map, a grand exposition of the reality we hope to understand? Do we believe that everything ultimately fits together? Perhaps in some metaphysical sense, like one of Plato's Forms. I am humble enough to acknowledge that I will never know the answer. To possess the answer is to know the mind of God. Such an ambition exceeds my powers. Even with all the time in the world and infinite computing capability, I cannot literally comprehend the entirety, to seize the whole. Neither can you. Working together across the ages, it is still impossible. To some degree, of course, any truth-seeker believes that there is such a thing as truth. Every scientist believes that knowledge is possible. Columbus did not know what he would find beyond the sea, but he expected to run into *something*, yes? Otherwise, our labors on the ship of academe would be futile, ridiculous. In a crude sense, therefore, we are fideists, resting our position on faith. (Can we all admit this much?) Nevertheless, to believe in such a thing when you doubt you can ever achieve it yourself is not – repeat *not* – to reject the possibility that you can know *something*. The part might be accessible even when the whole exceeds yourgrasp.

The danger, as Serres well knew, was insisting that the shard is enough. He wrote, "The pieces of the gods, broken, become deified…. Any fragment can substitute for the [whole]." That would be a mistake. It always has been.

In dialogue, therefore, we pool all of our little shards, dumping them onto the table. I'll show you mine if you show me yours.

To some extent, the ideal of a master map serves as a regulative principle, a destination we might never reach, even if an individual human being can get nearer and nearer, in an asymptotic fashion. Asymptotes, if you recall, are lines. I complained earlier that instead of one line getting nearer and nearer, we are all casting separate lines toward the same inaccessible end – scientists, poets, philosophers, theologians, and children. Whatever the abstract reality at the furthest reaches of human understanding, we seem to be working on unrelated versions of it. Are there many roads to Truth? I am committed to this possibility. And lest you balk at my contention: these uncoordinated efforts are more substantive than a matter of taste: you say to-may-to, I say to-mah-to. I can believe in a master map and yet surrender the hope that we can ever reach it; we are scrounging around in the dirt, doing the best we can. That isn't nothing. In my opinion, it is a far sight smarter to proceed in this way, pursuing our separate answers and then coming together to talk, than to organize everybody from the outset to adopt the exact same methods and work cheek-by-jowl on the same projects simultaneously. One point of origin, one method, one journey? I disagree. Order will emerge without anybody telling us what to do. Polanyi was fundamentally correct that those who share a pursuit and take it seriously will regulate one another, while at the same time remaining open in principle to novelty, to course corrections. We don't need a superintendent.

Let a thousand flowers bloom?

Management gurus have taught me that all models are wrong, yet some of them can be useful. Some models can be altogether wrong, to be sure, even nonsense, but many of them might be partly correct and worth using. At the same moment in time, therefore, we might find ourselves in possession of multiple *different* models for the same phenomenon, each of which has something to contribute, like different maps for the same territory. This I learned from management gurus. I should not feel threatened by that possibility. Neither should you.

I would go a step further in saying that the one unforgiveable fallacy is insisting there is only one model, yours – all the rest are wrong. Such a posture of blinkered arrogance will do positive harm to the cause we all claim to share. It is still the case, happily, that some of us are closer than others. Some models are more useful than others. I won't deny it. By saying this, draped in metaphor, I seem to occupy a pragmatic space between insistence on a single, mono-authority, at one extreme, and complete and utter nihilism, on the other. From one end of the spectrum, I might appear to be guilty of the worst excesses of yonder pole, but my attitude has evolved into something akin to Shakespeare's "plague on both your houses!" Both answers, whether "One" or "None," presuppose we can ever know. I'll cast my lot with those who say, "Some ... maybe." To paraphrase Ficino, you have to pass from one extreme to another through intermediate points. Another indictment of mere distinctions, by the way. Maybe dialogue is an intermediate point where we meet.

In the inevitable situation when two alternative models bubble up, clamoring for attention, in contention, the management gurus have taught me further that it might be prudent for them to compete. May the better model win. Ancient Greek philosophy is often presented to us as a clash, an agonistic brawl, a dialectical struggle. My training at law school certainly reinforced this method of conflict resolution. Yet there will be occasions – and I think Plato was shrewd enough to demonstrate this – when we might be able to integrate the two models, to unify. Perhaps these two proposed models are not opposed but complementary. One of them might supplement the other. No need for things to break out in a fight. In either case, whether competition to name a single winner under a single banner (unification) or dialogue and coexistence, we assume that the result of our exercises is a single something, an outcome. And in practical terms, that is probably the proper goal. In response to the very real question, What shall we do? – we will require an answer.

The strange thing, though, is that in academe we can walk away with completely different outcomes. Maybe I win. Maybe you do. Maybe we both win. Or maybe after some investigation, we both *lose*; maybe neither of us is on the right track. But I can also conceive of the possibility that nobody had to "win." Maybe winning consists of coming to understand one another. Maybe that's enough. A pale, puny brew, perhaps, especially for those craving stronger stuff, but mutual understanding just might constitute victory. It might even turn out to be the best we can do in the moment.

"What mischief," cries the fundamentalist.

What an unholy menace! We have protocols in place precisely to avoid such a permissive clown show. Please, from this point going forward, just (pick one): consult Scripture, obey the rules, follow the algorithms, mimic your professor, do penance, define your terms, begin with a literature search in an annotated bibliography, cite the seminal works, cite chapter and verse, quote from the Holy Fathers, make your submission look like all the others, make your position plain.

Have I indeed tipped over into POMO mode, playful about seeking the truth to the point of becoming irresponsible? Everybody plays, everybody wins, everybody gets a trophy?

Let me ask you a question first: how's Modernity working for ya?

You know, we talk about bringing order out of chaos, as though order is only one thing – discernible, complete. When I was mowing yesterday in order to impose some kind of order on the lawn, a solitary honeybee clinging to the clover in my path got sucked into the whirling roar of the metal blades that devastated his bucolic labor like a mechanical tornado. In my zeal to impose order, I subjected him to wild chaos, ruining his errand and possibly killing him amid the mayhem. My order was his turmoil. Can anyone say that mine was the superior purpose? I do.

Dialogue is not the signature operation of the post-modern critic. Dialogue entails real work, a process of kneading and enfolding, literally implicating over and over, in the way that a fetus develops, layer-upon-layer, being turned in upon itself, turbulent. Done properly, dialogue is not a celebration of ourselves, an easy affirmation of all things. Dialogue is hard, and it presupposes that each of us subordinate our beliefs to some shared mission. Dialogue has its own kind of rigor. Not for me the endless chain of an argument, step-by-step, the elaborate construct from base to pinnacle, a monument to my own inventiveness. Remember that the pyramids were tombs! Instead, my mind goes round and round, more like a melody – no less an art for its ephemeral nature. But I'm not so open as to be completely empty. So no, I am not like the stereotypical postmodernist. I don't even smoke cigarettes!

One evening many years ago, I joined colleagues at a seminar in Portland for dinner. The restaurant was noisy, so much so that I could hear nobody at the table trying to talk to one another. It was all a garbled noise. This was the first time I recognized my own hearing loss, not as the diminution of what was coming into my ear, as though it were suppressed or muted, but instead as a limited capacity to discern voices from out of the commotion. The room was no less loud, you see. It was just that I could make out nothing but the din itself – the clamoring on all sides of which I was not a part. I sat there moodily alone eating my salmon, wishing I were someplace else. I can think of no better allegory for my experience in Leadership Studies.

A confession is not only an account of one's faults or sins and a plea for mercy. It is also a testimony, an acknowledgment, a rendering of one's beliefs. Much of what I believe is tacit. I do not even realize. Furthermore, it could very easily happen that I've contradicted myself. Have I really reasoned through the implications of all these various claims and allegations? Or am I just being cute, indifferent to inconsistencies?

This seems to be the moment to address the elephant in the room. What I have been exhibiting in these pages might go a long way toward explaining my mental illness, clinical anxiety. Instead of a credo, maybe my confession is more like evidence of maladapted intelligence. Have I been inadvertently offering an etiology of my condition? "No wonder he's crazy...."

You know, we use certain terms to pertain to common experiences that are appropriate and even healthy. One *should be* depressed at a funeral and anxious before a competition. Reasonable people cycle through emotions in response to life's eventualities. Mental illness is something else. It might be an excessive response or a response that doesn't fit the situation. Great minds have devoted their careers to diagnosis and classification and treatment. One can consult the literature by Freud, Jaspers, Jung, Foucault, Lacan, and so forth – another intricate multiplicity I could spend a lifetime researching.

Is anxiety a physiological condition, exemplified by chemical imbalances or damaged circuitry? Is it a psychological condition, rooted in how one talks to oneself? Is it possession by demons? Or just one of the many ways that this gorgeous mosaic we call humanity introduces variation, a failed mutation perhaps. The mental patient as outlier on a simple bell curve. Is it instead a warning from the canaries in the coal mine, evidence from among the vulnerable that something outside of ourselves is going wrong. We are all under threat, it says; only some of us are too sensitive not to succumb. Heed the warning!

Foucault speculated that instead of a maladapted response to ordinary stresses, maybe some illnesses are mirrors of the environment. Some people internalize or express a contradiction that is out there in paramount reality, the *koinòn kòsmon*. The patient embodies what society as a whole suffers. This is a completely different way of talking, and it thrusts the medical concern outward, to consider the extent to which the milieu is dysfunctional. We see this often in social work, where the analysis posits that individuals in dysfunctional families will have trouble coping. They are not as individuals failing to cope with reality; instead, they are mirroring the reality within which they were raised. Therein lies the problem. Foucault asked, can a person's condition be emblematic of the situation?

Here I have been writing about these elaborate, bewildering multiplicities, too complex to understand – a situation nobody can master. Is it the case that the multiplicity in my mind is but a mirror of my experience of the world? If I possessed a more coherent worldview, would my mental troubles cease? Or would I only be fooling myself? (Or both?)

Monkey mind, as I understand it, has its correlation in what psychiatrists call the flight of ideas, a manic state in which the brain spins on an axis, going nowhere. Binswanger had apparently called it *über ideenflucht*. But what would you expect of a pigeon caught in the whirlwind? During a calm minute, I can examine these passages you have been reading as a testimony to my tendencies to mania, feathers and all. Jumping erratically around, getting nowhere – more of a flurry than an *argument* per se. What about that possibility? Well, the existentialist in me finds this diagnosis a little quaint. Why is it not rather heroic to launch oneself into the storm and not cower, as most folks do? If indeed I am the hero of my own story, then I would be tempted to valorize my condition as the understandable struggle of one who has been loosed into the tumult. Am I seeking admiration?

The very fact that I have sat down every day for weeks to tell this story should prove that I am not celebrating my vigor and the strenuousness of my *Dasein* (or whatever). These are not the words of delusion. I am trying to set forth as accurately as I can a predicament I would like to resolve. The very disruptions in the flow of my text – jumping around among technical terms, poetry, off-hand allusions, amid abrupt shifts – these disruptions are intended to convey something about the nature of this predicament. I can think of no better way to illustrate the situation where I find myself. And I suspect that my interpretation of reality is not a fiction, a fantasy. Instead, it aligns all-too-closely with your predicament and the predicament your children will face.

Which is why (hear me out) I insist on the importance of understanding the phenomenon of leadership, for leadership takes place in a bewildering context, a vast and uncertain environment. It is at the **social** magnitude what I seek at the **individual** magnitude, i.e. a governing influence, an ordering principle, a sense-making engine. Not for me the reassuring ideology, simple to say out loud, reassuring because it is false. I have been betrayed by dicta my whole life. The platitudes no longer placate. Reality requires something more mature, with more nuance. The same is true in politics, where my allies have flung themselves heedlessly into the graces of a self-aggrandizing simpleton, in part because of the business model of a television network that needs you to feel perpetually outraged. Look, we all need grace. And it would help if our leaders found a way to live in grace, definite as to principles and pragmatic as to methods. I want for myself what we should all want for the civitas.

Plato had it right all along, both psyche and polis. And what, dear reader, did he recommend, if not dialogue? Perhaps anxiety is the expression of a conscientious mind in thrall to the plenum. Do you not feel it, also? Come, let us reason together.

Recapitulation A

A career dedicated to a series of little explosions, cast outward from my mind to the page, and from the page to a publisher, and from the publisher to posterity. Explosions? Maybe call them burps. All the while in my private moments, I have investigated myself, looking inward (excessively, no doubt), occasionally rendering myself as poetry, but mostly just unhelpful brooding. Consider this project that you hold in your hands therefore an *implosion*. What is an implosion? A violence? The word sometimes can be used for a collapse of an apparent form, like the implosion of an outdated building. A structure falls in upon itself, becoming a pile of rubble and debris. Sometimes, though, the term can be used for a concentration of material into a condensed or compressed space, like an imploding star. The same basic (homothetic) form condenses, compresses, and thereby intensifies.

This summer, for personal reasons, my intellect imploded. Familiar forms are collapsing. What should I find there at the compact, impenetrable center? Debris?

Paramount reality, human knowledge, and my own mind – each has always been a bewildering multiplicity, except for the occasional breakthrough, something it would be criminal to domesticate. It occurs to me that Leadership Studies as a field of inquiry, formalized and set apart, is a game being played between the Blue team and the Green team, a distraction to amuse the Sabine men, while the Romans had ducked away from the stadium in order to go abduct their untended women. Do you know the story? While your team was winning X, I was winning Y. We were playing completely different games. Not to sound too vulgar, but I played your game in order to win tenure, promotion, and self-esteem. You were doing the same exact thing. And while you and I were preoccupied, who was championing this thing called truth? What exactly has my team won once the women are gone?

In abstract terms, leadership is a phase transition, from non-standard multiplicity, the fuzzy set or cloud, into some kind of unity – a unity that is admittedly temporary, encompassing still a multiplicity within its boundaries, yet a multiplicity that moves in the same basic direction, together. Its course across time may be understood by means of fluid dynamics, one flow among many, easily diverted by stronger currents perhaps or dissipating completely like the morning fog. Multiplicity restored to its amorphous state. The more durable of these unities creates its own channel, like a river carving its watercourse, which in turn determines where it will subsequently flow. It shapes the contours of the land and then in turn is determined by its own riverbed. Think of these riverbeds as institutions. Take a giant step back to consider the territory. From these various uncoordinated channels, cut by myriad leaders of myriad groups doing myriad things, through time, the territory becomes a landscape, even a home.

Time for a new metaphor. Specific moments in the unification of the group will require specific tactics. It might be a speech that a leader delivers, a specific decision, or some extraordinary feat. The leadership has to fit the moment like a key that conforms to the lock. Yet the ongoing success of the group requires many such keys, each one requiring a different configuration of teeth on the key; so that for one leader to succeed over time, he or she must become more of a passkey. If the contours of the key are too strict and intricate, the key will work on only so many locks, on only just the right lock. Otherwise, it will not even fit. If, on the other hand, they are so flat and smooth that they fit a multitude of locks, the key can become featureless and turn nothing at all. A leader must open many different kinds of locks without becoming so plain and vapid as to accomplish nothing at all. Yet here's the thing –

The key/lock analogy overlooks the extent to which *the lock wants to be turned* and will turn on its own once the key inserts itself. See Freud, see Foucault. The analogy works when we recognize that a key worn smooth and inserted into every lock will in many instances influence the lock to turn *on its own*. After a point, all the key needs to do is insert itself. The lock will do the rest. At the highest reaches of the hierarchy, sometimes what we require is a vapid presence, a benign and innocuous Big Brother, because we all know what to do next. We pledge ourselves to Big Brother, even when Big Brother is a video projection of nobody real, a featureless presence. Sometimes, leadership consists of merely showing up and being there.

Often in my walks across campus, I wonder if the university president is at the window, gazing down upon us, expecting us to do our best. Don't cut across the lawn. Stop to assist the visiting guest. Hold doors for one another. In the panopticon I had constructed in my own private imagining, he stands up there judging me, judging how I walk and talk and gesture. I am that very lock that wants to turn and will do so on my own, with the president's possible presence at the window. He doesn't really have to be there for his leadership to work now. Call it a residual influence.

The massive ice shelf recedes from the plain while trailing crystal waters to the sea.

Why, exactly, do the followers follow? Can we ascribe such obedience to habit, to conditioning? Or is it "in our nature" to obey? Or is it something more publicly defensible, namely that we prefer to wage war rather than endure anarchy? It's better to cooperate and comply than to experience the void? Leadership is what stands between us and disintegration? Better the devil you know? The argument has been made viz. Hitler, for instance. Is it always such a conscious choice?

My role as an academic has been to step outside of this temptation, to rise above it, to squelch any tendency to defer, to set forth a critique of the phenomenon. Serres once wrote,

> The philosopher is not a judge; if he is a judge, a critic, he never produces anything, he only kills. No. Trying to think, trying to produce, presupposes the taking of risks, the living of one's life, precisely, in the surge outside of the classings of the encyclopedias.

I have found myself outside again and again. These pages represent my effort to produce something worthwhile, for all my time in the wilderness. And for that, I must reenter the multiplicities repeatedly. I must venture back into the torrent. As Serres once said, "A crisis is a return to the multiplicities."

In an unconventional treatise, Deleuze and Guattari called this practice **nomadology**. Maybe I am a nomad, outside the authority of the state. They alleged that leadership is most decidedly NOT the construction and preservation of power structures; instead, it strikes quickly, ruthlessly, and moves on before the sun rises. It is not really about building anything. It is about the circulation of the tribe rejecting the adverse possession of the sedentary. Nomads despise borders. They belong to something bigger. And at the same time, they belong to something smaller, more immediate, in migrating little bands of blood brothers who camp out under the stars telling stories. The state would like to tame these nomads, domesticate them, put them to use – to keep them from disrupting the peace, to be sure, appeasing them, but also at the same time inciting them to go disrupt the peace of some other state across the valley. The nomads will take this tribute, sure, but their loyalty will be dubious. They belong to the open spaces, as their birthright. By morning, they will have slipped back into the landscape.

In this conceit of nomadology, the state is one space absolutized, a sacred grove or temple, surrounded by walls that just keep stretching outward opportunistically. Their mission is to regulate the various flows that constitute life. The flow of water, the flow of migrants, the flow of merchandise, the flow of money, the flow of knowledge. The nomad makes every space he travels sacred. He sets up his idols in his tent before going to sleep. Deleuze and Guattari call it the local absolute. Wherever I am is eucharistic, blessed. Small wonder therefore that I have become obsessed with the concept of the liminal! It is my home. Abraham walked with God. He owned no real property except his tomb. He worshipped a God who flows alongside.

Mark the date. June 2022 – this then constitutes my summer of crisis. Serres described it as bathing in a fractal sea of commotion. He continued: "Our thought, our understanding, our life, our masteries would just be foolish and simple if they maintained ties only to an orderly world. And the world would be stupid if it were so." A disordered mind for a disordered age.

Am I making a virtue of necessity? Since I cannot understand something, I declare that the person in the wrong is he or she who claims to understand? I am vulnerable to such an accusation. But I'm not saying that. I admire my forebearers, my colleagues, and the gigantic enterprise called Leadership Studies. I suspect that these well-educated folks know better than most the veracity of what I am trying in my haphazard way to express. Life is lived on the shoreline, between the boundless depths and the impervious rock. Life is thrown up on the turbulent beach, to glisten for an hour. Up and down the sandy stretch, what beauty, surging and receding, tossed by the waves, in a perpetual process of becoming. I want to be a part of that tremulous violence. Together with the water and the wind, we sing the Genesis song of recurring creation – not a singular moment, neither a Big Bang nor a first principle, but a rhythm. *Creation is always happening right now.* My philosophy is to join in that rhythm, to participate, and to be contented to play a part in the dance. My search for bedrock has been a mistake. I must learn how to flow.

Maybe theorists have the easier job. Maybe being a theorist when the world needs intervention is irresponsible. Karl Marx explicitly thought so.

Serres used the imagery of a handkerchief with a pattern of dots. Fold, crease, crumple, wad that handkerchief up to stuff it into your pocket, and those little dots find themselves in strange relationships with one another. What had been maybe five inches apart is now less than half an inch, turned in upon itself in three dimensions. Economists have used similar imagery to predict markets. It is no accident that the brain appears equally implicated.

Who can know what another person, such as you, associates in his memory? While convalescing with my first ankle sprain at twelve years of age, I had to sleep downstairs, where those who were older than I could stay up to watch television. One night, they watched "The Jazz Singer" with Al Jolson on network TV. Fast forward to today. In 2022, when I hear his version of "Toot, Toot, Tootsie, Good-bye" I am transported to that room roughly fifty years ago, with people who have long since died. The couch on which I lay was green. I also recall the incident that put me on my back, a playground mishap that kept me out of the big game against Meadowbrook Elementary. So tell me, who else would link these specific things together in just this configuration? Yet my brain is cluttered with haphazard associations of this kind, a seemingly endless network of otherwise unrelated nodes.

My idiosyncratic, wadded-up handkerchief is unlike yours. Thus, I should have no reason to expect that my allusion to one association based on who-knows-what-experience from my unique personal history will in any way resonate with you, given the idiosyncratic, wadded-up handkerchief that sits in your pocket. Why should I expect us to do anything more than sit here blinking at one another?

Perhaps, said Serres, paramount reality is likewise implicated. Often, the associations otherwise make no sense, yet there they are in the strangest places. He comes close to adopting the hypotheses of archetypal psychologists, who investigated the images or personifications that participated in what we might call subterranean networks of association. Hermes, the winged god who transmits messages, but only cryptically, accompanying the traveler, but also stealing cattle. First here, now gone. Untethered, always shuttling between humanity and the gods, counterbalanced by the immobile Hestia who tends the simple hearth. Each god has its unique color, its own gemstone, its own chemical element, and its own weather. These archetypal psychologists clustered poetry, mythology, alchemy, polytheism, the zodiac, Platonism, in an array of totally different and ostensibly unrelated topics, as though their constellation explains how we experience and express life to one another. My associations will often resonate with you because we possess many of the same associations. At some level, we share the same allusions. Scholars in comparative mythology team up with psychotherapists and art scholars to catalogue these shared allusions. Green is soothing, snakes are evil, and we dread the limping man....

A few years back, a friend with impeccable credentials asked me why I bothered with that Jungian junk. It was a fair question. Yet there has been some tentative vindication in neuroscience regarding some of the claims, popularized by Jordan Peterson who speaks of superhighways in the brain that bundle certain images together without our even being aware, so that the cartoon film "Pinocchio" speaks to the wayward youth in search of a vocation. I am even more impressed with archetypal psychology's promise as therapy, especially for certain types of patients, like me.

But think of it, the audacity! Not only is the brain this dense, complex, imbricated powerhouse, an energy hog, a wonder to behold, but it operates at least in part according to these hidden wormholes. Comedians are counting on this possibility. Artists (mostly painters and poets) routinely exploit them. Salvador Dali apparently lived in these wormholes. Dreams testify to this bizarre circuitry. Madness traps some poor souls in labyrinths, like Don Quixote, who came to be cured only by a man who found a way to enter into his fantasy as a villain. The entire saga of the Knight of the Woeful Countenance is a dip into the surreality of the subconscious, where the Man of La Mancha himself becomes an archetype in Western literature. An archetype is a wormhole, and literature is full of them. But so is leadership in practice, a wormhole, including such *dramatis personae* as the bully, the sacrificial lamb, the patriarch, the busybody, the hatchet man, the whiner or squeaky wheel, the coward. The nice guy.

So perhaps it is not so crazy (without the use of illicit drugs, I might add) to duck into these fantastic associations, at the very least as generative suggestions. To what extent were the Egyptian pyramids stationary points of reference for land surveyors who had to restore boundaries for farmland every year after the Nile flooded, wiping away every other evidence of who owns what? Serres raised the possibility. To what extent is the maneuverability of a fighter jet indicative of the success of blitzkrieg as a battle tactic? John Boyd saw the parallels. To what extent is the Benzene Ring like a snake biting its own tail? August Kekulé saw that image in a dream.

Maybe a sober intellectual such as yourself hoping to preserve his stature at the university will abstain from such island-hopping insanity. "No wormholes, not if you want tenure!" I am not that guy. I owe no more to the professors who parse, who confuse being unimaginative with being careful. We certainly need such intellectuals, like busboys scrambling around behind the stellar chef, even though we all know who brings in the clientele night after night.... Kuhn had called what they do "normal science," hoping not to make that sound too pejorative. Polanyi was more candid. He intuited things in chemistry, then let his staff work out the details. He had moved on to other conundrums.

One of the most successful writers about leadership was Margaret Wheatley. Having writ, the writing finger moved on. Back in 1992, everybody understood that what she had said about the utility of the new sciences for understanding leadership was important, provocative. She had intuited something profound, about chaos theory, fractal geometry, and quantum mechanics. It was all colorful and maddeningly elusive. Then, she turned her attention to other things. The rest of us in Leadership Studies are still playing catch-up, doing basic research. Maybe that is how the second circle, the second multiplicity, constellates itself, in fits and starts, punctuated by happenstance and genius. It may not be given to me to prompt that multiplicity in any particular direction, a fabulous impetus, a great man in Carlyle's sense (or a great woman). I am certainly not called to do the basic research, like a drone. I am some third thing, watching this happen.

Recapitulation B

One of the most useful lessons for me professionally from Michel Serres is his introduction to the idea of **suffrage**, which is not precisely what you might think. Suffrage is participation in a civic rhythm – in the organization, team, group, club, business, corporation, institution, community, it doesn't matter. Any social collectivity.

If:

> one begins with the idea of a multiplicity, which comes from the root for "many folds", as the base condition – not a social contract, but more of a state of nature in which everybody swirls independently, selfishly, detached from all but the most intimate relationships, though not necessarily a war of all against war, but a churning, formless, amorphous cloud of individuals, families, romantic partners, neighbors, coming together and splitting apart in an uncoordinated fashion,

then:

> you will eventually see a loose pattern or federation (emergent order), not unlike the ideal of a free market where people come and go for their own private purposes to conduct business. A unity can be discerned, even if only briefly, like the murmuration of starlings or an eddy in a stream. Nobody governs. Nobody polices. Violence breaks out sporadically, though when that happens it is a spotty affair, flaring up and dying out – totally unlike the strict militarization of the modern nation-state. At most, it will resemble hillbilly feuds, taking pot shots across the gully.

Suffrage entitles the bearer to participate in the solemn process of organizing, pledging allegiance to a shared purpose, and converting the multiplicity into a unity of one kind or another. Suffrage is the right to join others in the forming of a pact. Nobody does it for you, as though you were a dependent. You are not left out, as though you were an alien. You get to do it. In fact, you are expected to. But then, as Serres explained, suffrage also means you are then free to resume your private affairs. You are not so tethered as to be permanently political. You can return to your own farm. You can join a choir. You can play with your children in the back-yard while the lightning bugs float in the dusk. Suffrage does not have to mean complete subordination to the whole. It is a periodic session, like the Frankish warriors who gathered each spring at the *warfeld* in order to vote on that season's campaigns. Unifying and then separating, over and over. Suffrage is the rhythm itself. Being permitted to vote in elections, as we do in democracies, is only part of that process.

In August, the faculty and staff at my university assemble in a large hall just before the undergraduates arrive. We take stock. We reaffirm our values. We remind everyone what to expect. Mostly, we look around and identify with one another, as members of a shared community. We pledge ourselves to the institution, again. But then we scatter to go do our discrete jobs. One person goes to prepare the meals. Another cuts the checks. I teach my classes. We converge and then diverge, according to the calendar.

As a child, I belonged to a large family. Every evening, we cleared the dining room table and sat down to eat a meal as a family. All ten of us shared our news. We told jokes. We unified around our supper. After-ward, of course, we cleared the table again, put the food away, washed the dishes, and returned to our various pursuits – some to study for school, some to complete chores, some to play with little plastic animals until bedtime. Very much like the rite of Holy Communion. In fact, *precisely* like the Eucharist.

Each of us will have been given distinctive roles. Among those roles will be leadership, of one kind or another. Somebody summoned us by ringing a little bell. Somebody fixed the food. (Thank you, Mom.) Somebody led us in prayer. Somebody stayed behind afterward to clean up; we even had a schedule for that. The children took turns. Much of what scholars in Leadership Studies will investigate pertains to these roles, e.g. gathering, presiding, executing, and so forth. They are often separable tasks, even if in many settings the same individual such as the university president, the parent, or the priest does several of them. I hasten to add, however, that each of us enjoys considerable autonomy between such ceremonies (some of us more than others), such that there is also a kind of leadership that preserves the space wherein individuals can govern themselves or just go amuse themselves.

It can be leadership to utter the benediction, the sending forth, adjourning the assembly. "Lord, now let thy servant go in peace."

With so many expressions of the rhythms of suffrage, many of which exhibit what we ordinarily think of as leadership, are leadership scholars really all studying the same thing? On election day, the political candidate, the news reporter, the clerk at the polling station, the volunteer handing out leaflets – is it all leadership? Obviously, a person would have to step back and abstract from the peculiar little moments that might conceivably qualify as leadership. And yet, when doing so, when abstracting from the concrete instances, looking for that which encompasses them all, a person is likely to settle on something so broad and vague as to seem ethereal, detached from the hurly-burly of sharp elbows and trolling bots and smoke-filled rooms. Yet that is precisely the task set forth by Ficino, if you recall: i.e. sort, categorize, then put to work.

I no longer wish to focus on the roles themselves. As a scholar, I am not impressed that someone was identified as president, priest, or parent. Obviously, people win those roles for a reason, probably having to do in part with leadership. So it is likely that the one with the title does in fact lead. In ordinary usage, we often speak of leaders, but we know full well in actuality that leaders are not the only ones who lead. And for long stretches of time, they aren't leading anyone; they are doing something else. In a complex organization, many individuals lead. In politics, we damn well *expect* leadership to be distributed – in the American system we assert a system of checks and balances, plus federalism, let alone the periodic replacement of our leaders with somebody else. Alleging that Leadership Studies studies leaders, well, that's just lazy. We do that, yes; yet after only the briefest encounter with the evidence, we recognize that we must study something dynamic, the process-by-which, the interactions that contribute to these patterns of suffrage.

Aristotle drew a bright line between investigations into objects or things, on the one hand, and investigations into movement or activities, on the other. You can look at cars or you can look at traffic, and these will be completely different ways to analyze the same reality. You can dissect the dead specimen or contemplate life. You can engineer a product or advance an industry. You can welcome the pupil into your classroom, but at some point, you have to propel him or her toward an education. I can go online to learn about the specifications of a tennis racquet, assessing its materials and the size of its grip, checking the ratings from previous customers. I still prefer an old Stan Smith in the garage, a wooden racquet in a wooden press, with a 4¾ grip. Ultimately, though, I have to take it out onto the court and swing it. Things and activities.

Leadership is an activity. It is something that happens. *Who* does this activity and *how well* they do it will interest me, of course, but only once I'm satisfied that the activity is indeed taking place. What then is that activity? My own conclusion, which is tentative or provisional, uttered apologetically, accepts that whenever a person participates in a social process attempting to improve on the shared present, that is leadership. Here is my version of the definition I offered earlier. My colleagues will immediately howl in protest (assuming that any of them will have read this far into my confession). It doesn't matter what they think. I am getting older. I no longer harbor ambitions to impress them. I am liberated. I care what anybody has to say that will help us both come to a mutual understanding. I am open to dialogue. But there comes a stage in life when you no longer bear being corrected. You disagree? Fine. Let's chat.

As an aside, I always overlooked those moments in Platonic dialogues when Socrates had to interrupt his interlocutors to insist that they cooperate and play by the rules. (What exactly were those rules, anyway? That would interest me to know. Has anybody gone through the corpus to catalogue such moments?) In most of these dialogues, Socrates was old by antiquity's standards, a proven soldier, married, sufficiently independent to spend his days walking about accosting people, and apparently a pretty funny guy who would drink you under the table. Nevertheless, once he got the bit between his teeth, once the dialogue had begun in earnest, he could become quite abrupt whenever the other person started wasting his time. "Look," he would say, "if you insist on behaving in this fashion, we might as well quit now. I am looking for somebody to join me in good faith. Otherwise, good day to you, sir." Or words to that effect.

Anyway, leadership is a participation in suffrage, as Serres used the term. It occurs in large, complex settings, as well as in small, intimate groups. It involves both the coming together and the issuing forth. What brings the cloud together in the first place? What holds it together in its fuzzy form, or churns it into other shapes? What blows it as a cloud across the sky toward some distant horizon? By this definition, even a poet who invites one reader to stand aside for a moment in order to reflect on the fragility of life can be said to *lead*. I am biting the bullet, as they say. And I go even further to say that the reader standing aside to read the poem and reflect on its meaning is participating in leadership. That, my friend, is a bold claim.

Notice what this explanation entails. One must step outside the familiar circle, the gate, to look at one's situation in a new light. One must move, transition, even if only for an evanescent second, beyond the horizon of the present moment, before resolving with others to sink back into the enclosure and do something different. One must step back, decide with other people what to do, then step back in. (Is there a better summary of dialogue?) It's the hokey-pokey!

I now see my role in my chosen field of study as the guy who walks the periphery, checking the fence line and mending the gate, urging my neighbors to step outside now and then and bring back something for the rest of us – a rabbit to eat, a bouquet of flowers, or news from the other side of the glen. If we need to alter the border, then I'll jump in to help plot the line, dig the post holes, string the wire, and put my hand on the top rail to give it a firm shake before we go home for supper. Somebody's gotta do it. But Gatekeeper? Never.

One's style ought to reinforce the content of one's message. These paragraphs have been disclosive, scattered, almost whimsical, often cutting. Fables pop up in unlikely places. Allusions to philosophers are off-hand. The prose seems to be stream-of-consciousness. By now, you realize that the text doesn't flow in a linear fashion. It is turbulent. What you are encountering here is a multiplicity, yeah? Often, noise. Chaos. Though not without reward, I'll be bound.

Where then would a man find repose at the intersection of such interwoven, labyrinthine multiplicities? Are they all the same, following some version of the Identity of Indiscernibles (to borrow from Leibnitz)? Or are we adrift between two infinities (to borrow from Pascal)? To be blunt, how am I to orient myself? How does any nomad find his way?

Let us here employ the notion of a ratio. Something A is to B as C is to D. **Purpose** is to me as **truth** is to human knowledge. And **truth** is to human knowledge as **God** is to the universe. By transitive properties, that means that purpose is to me as God is to the universe.

Purpose:Me::Truth:Human Knowledge::God:Universe.

We have returned, as you can see, to my Venn diagram and the three multiplicities, the three circles. When my purpose is aligned with the search for truth in a universe governed by God, then I am in a good place. I have no reason to expect that I will know the truth in full, any more than I can ever know the mind of God. God is to nature the ordering principle, not a territory to be conquered, a buffet to consume. Truth is to the pursuit of human knowledge the ordering principle. My purpose in life is my unique ordering principle. And my purpose is to pursue the truth about God's universe. In my little way, I have done this with regard to a very narrow question about one phenomenon that, upon closer inspection, is far more complex than any of us ever suspected.

I could go back at my age to do further research. On what? Well, on any number of topics, and that's the problem. I could sink myself into Gestalt Psychology or once again into the works of Nietzsche or into the underlying mathematics of Chaos Theory or into the Rousseauian origins of James MacGregor Burns' attitude toward transforming leadership as an expression of the General Will or into one of several languages in order to read the original works in their native language or into, well, just about anything, since it is all purportedly connected. Or I can simply stand here moping that I haven't done these things with my life. It would take me several lifetimes just to reach the threshold level of credibility. My hat's off to the brilliant thinkers who accomplished so much more with their time on earth. I am not the guy you should hoist upon your shoulders and carry around the ballroom. I confess it, hard though it was of late to accept that fact. You should applaud Plato, Augustine, Voegelin, and Serres. The best I can do is point in their general direction.

By my definition, if I influence you to join me in this project about leadership and if I help you along your own path toward truth and God, then in my own small way I've been a leader. And the mechanism for all this, as I've been persuaded to acknowledge, is **dialogue**...not sermons, speeches, lectures, jeremiads, tirades, pleas, closing arguments, skits, or storytelling. So the decisive question you are likely to ask is this: what am I (Nathan Harter) doing in these pages, if not some one-sided, roundabout soliloquy? Here I go doing something *other than* dialogue. Even, yea, the opposite of dialogue. I've laid down dogma. Is this entire enterprise not an example of that which I am straining to reject?

Well, I'll tell you. I'm confessing. I'm confessing that I am a Pollyanna, hopelessly full of hope. I will even go so far as to allege that scholars are Pollyannas, leaders are Pollyannas, and, well, most followers are, as well. I wake up each day with purpose. That is because I believe in Truth, such that I can know some of what is true. The Truth is accessible. One doesn't *possess* the Truth, like personal property; one participates in it. That is a very different thing.[2] Furthermore, I trust in a beneficent God who superintends the universe. He is the author and jurist of what is true. He is Truth. He is the key that fits the lock in my own heart, and since puberty I am a lock that has wanted so desperately to be opened, like that bashful deity Priapus. It doesn't take much for me to turn. That old African sex

---

2 If you re-read nothing else, please re-read that sentence. One doesn't *possess* the Truth, like personal property; one participates in it.

addict, Augustine of Hippo, put it best over 1,500 years ago. Our hearts are restless till they rest in Thee.

I wanted you to know my mind, warts and all, the whiff of multiplicity, attuned imperfectly to a divine signal. Here I stand, with Martin Luther, on this busy intersection. I can do no other.

Howdy-do.

Coda

Hail to the plenum, the summer solstice and longest day of the year! When I was a child, the month of June symbolized many good things, such as vacation from school, my mother's birthday, joyful weather, free time, tennis, and travel. Hail to the plenum, the imagery of fullness, exuberance. Kids play all day, even after the evening meal, darting around until dark. Youth strip down to bask in the sunshine and frolic (do we use that term anymore?). Tanned faces, ice cream trucks, visits to a beach, long bike rides, peonies, naps in the hammock – more of life – even the lazy visions of memorable hillsides crossed by the merry shadows of unthreatening clouds, as you gaze into the river and become a part of that scene.

Is it the climate or my condition that turned summer into an ordeal? Dangerous temperatures for days on end. A crippling lassitude, that gives way to boredom. Too much time indoors. Too many screens. What felt like freedom turns out to be purposelessness, ennui. After the solstice, a period of unrelenting cruelty, perhaps like retirement itself, when the liberation devoutly to be wished was in fact a release from the demands of ambition. And therefore ... nothing? The locusts signal the dog days. I had originally hoped to get in shape, write a book, catch up on sleep, becoming a better version of myself.

As the sun went down on the twenty-first each year, I'd dash outdoors, jump onto the concrete bench in my backyard facing the west, throw up my arms in a kind of triumph, becoming taller, larger, victorious. At the winter solstice, by way of contrast, I'd curl in upon myself indoors and stay warm.

Perhaps in all those years I had overlooked the wholesome turn of the equinox, the balance, the equanimity. At neither extreme, and decidedly more colorful! – the flowers in spring and the leaves in autumn. Chilly at first, but warm in the sunlight. And things to do. Maybe it is not too late to take a pagan turn at the equinox, the world restored to an invigorating tension, where a creature such I can abide – neither full nor empty, neither hot nor cold, neither light nor dark, neither large nor small, but transitioning, en route to somewhere, and happily distracted by work among friends.

Reference

Reddy, F. (October 14, 2019). What makes stars explode? Sound waves in collapsing stars may produce supernova explosions. *Astronomy*. Retrieved 13 June 2022 from https://astronomy.com/magazine/2019/10/what-makes-stars-explode#:~:text=Such%20stars%20explode%20when%20they%20use%20up%20their,low%20on%20one%20fuel%2C%20it%20taps%20into%20another.

INDEX

Note: Page numbers followed by "n" refer to footnotes.

Printed in the United States
by Baker & Taylor Publisher Services